T0301514

BREATHLESS

BREATHLESS

Tuberculosis, Inequality, and Care in Rural India

ANDREW MCDOWELL

STANFORD UNIVERSITY PRESS

STANFORD, CALIFORNIA

Stanford University Press
Stanford, California

Printed and bound by CPI Group (UK) Ltd, Croydon, CR0 4YY

Epigraph in Chapter 4 derives from page 67 of Trawick, Margaret. 2017. *Death, Beauty, Struggle: Untouchable Women Create the World*. Reprinted with permission of the University of Pennsylvania Press.

Library of Congress Cataloging-in-Publication Data

Names: McDowell, Andrew (Andrew James), author.
Title: Breathless : tuberculosis, inequality, and care in rural India / Andrew McDowell.
Other titles: South Asia in motion.
Description: Stanford, California : Stanford University Press, 2024. | Series: South Asia in motion | Includes bibliographical references and index.
Identifiers: LCCN 2023030165 (print) | LCCN 2023030166 (ebook) | ISBN 9781503637955 (cloth) | ISBN 9781503638778 (paperback) | ISBN 9781503638785 (ebook)
Subjects: LCSH: Tuberculosis—Social aspects—India—Rajasthan. | Tuberculosis—Patients—India—Rajasthan. | Public health—Social aspects—India—Rajasthan. | Dalits—Health and hygiene—India— Rajasthan. | Equality—Health aspects—India—Rajasthan. | Rajasthan (India)—Rural conditions.
Classification: LCC RA644.T7 M282 2024 (print) | LCC RA644.T7 (ebook) | DDC 614.5/4209544—dc23/eng/20230921
LC record available at https://lccn.loc.gov/2023030165
LC ebook record available at https://lccn.loc.gov/2023030166

Cover design: Lindy Kasler
Cover photograph: Shutterstock
Typeset by Newgen in Adobe Caslon Pro 10.5/15

Awarded the Joseph W. Elder Prize in the Indian Social Sciences by the American Institute of Indian Studies and published with the Institute's generous support.
AIIS Publication Committee: Sarah Lamb, Co-Chair; Anand A. Yang, Co-Chair; Chanchal Dadlani; Sonal Khullar; Preetha Mani; Tulasi Srinivas; Tariq Thachil

CONTENTS

ACKNOWLEDGMENTS

THIS BOOK COULD NOT have been written without an immense amount of help. It is the outcome of conversations and ideas that span space and time. Any account of the debts accrued along the way will be partial, but it must begin with those accumulated in the community I call Ambawati. Everything would have been impossible but for the intellectual and practical contributions of the people there. So many opened their world to me in ways that I could never have expected and cannot repay. I hope they see themselves in the story I tell here. I also hope that this story resonates with the care and compassion that they have shown me for all these years. I have tried my best to let these same values guide my representation of the parts of themselves that they shared with me. Moreover, I hope that my efforts toward improving care for people afflicted by tuberculosis might begin to be a fitting tribute to their immense contribution.

I also thank those who gave me the language that made this work possible. Philip Lutgendorf is foremost among them. I cannot overstate the effect of Philipji's gentle and abiding encouragement to learn Hindi and intellectually engage with the subcontinent he loves. It has indelibly marked both this book and my life. Similarly, Richard Delacy, Upma Dixit, Rekha Mann, Rakesh Rajan, and Rashmi Sharma patiently nurtured my language skills and encouraged me to begin the research necessary for this book. Finally, I was a frequent guest in Srimati Nidhi Sharma's home in Jaipur for over six years. During that time, she insisted that I speak with her in Hindi, and this made all the difference. I am also grateful for all she taught me about what it means to live and practice kinship in Rajasthan.

I thank the many people who made immense contributions to my fluency in anthropological languages. Nanette Barkey's early intervention allowed me to imagine that a life of anthropology could be possible. Both

viii   *Acknowledgments*

Nanette and Philipji helped open doors for an Iowa farm boy to pursue graduate education. At Harvard inspiring mentors helped me situate and grow my shaky ethnographic voice. They include Arthur Kleinman and Byron Good, along with Asad A. Ahmed, Steve Caton, Mary-Jo DelVecchio Good, Paul Farmer, Duana Fullwiley, Salmaan Keshavjee, Smita Lahiri, and Mary Steedly. I will never forget the meeting with Smita that began my exploration of breath. Marianne Fritz, Marilyn Goodrich, and Linda Thomas were immense intuitional helps at Harvard. Others in Boston were kind enough to mentor me when I showed up looking haggard and confused. They include Mike Fischer at MIT, Sarah Pinto at Tufts University, and Tulasi Srinivas at Emerson College. Rukmini Srinivas, though long retired, has been an abiding mentor, active supporter, and inspiration.

At McGill University, Madhukar Pai and Tobias Rees helped me to think about TB as an epidemiological and technical phenomenon within global health. As part of that collaboration, Veena Das read a very early draft of this work and encouraged me to "think less architecturally." It is somehow to her credit that atmospheres have appeared. At the École des hautes études en sciences sociales and the Centre national de la recherche scientifique in Paris, Claire Beaudevin, Catherine Bourgain, Robert Desjarlais, Blandine Destremau, Sylvie Fainzang, Jean-Paul Gaudilliére, Christoph Gradmann, Christophe Guilmoto, Anne Lovell, Ilana Löwy, Laurent Pordié, Miriam Winance, and Ines Zupanov encouraged me to keep thinking about this book even as other avenues seemed more tempting. They also reminded me that "Americans write short sentences." I have tried to keep the sentences small and the ideas big.

At Tulane I have found colleagues who are generous beyond measure. Encouragement and reassurance from Marcello Canuto, Claudia Chavez Argüelles, Nathalie Dajko, Martin Dimitrov, Mariana Craciun, Trent Holiday, Laura-Zoe Humphreys, Katharine Jack, Nicole Katin, Katharine Lee, Camillo Lesley, Adeline Masquelier, Judie Maxwell, Felicia McCarren, Sabia McCoy-Torres, Jonny Morton, Tatsuya Murakami, Jason Nesbitt, Chris Rodning, Allison Truitt, John Verano, Mark Zender, Bill Balée, and the late Olanike Orie helped me finally finish this book. I am especially thankful to Mariana Craciun, Adeline Masquelier, and Allison

Truitt for reading a full draft of this book and sharing helpful insights on the art of writing while teaching.

Though the list of mentors who contributed to my intellectual growth while writing this book as teachers and colleagues is long, the list of friends who influenced my thinking is even longer. Lizzie Cooper-Davis, Namita Dharia, Nancy Khalil, Anh Thu Ngo, Chiaki Nishijima, Sa'ed Atshan, Nicholas Sterndorff Cisterna, and Julia Yezbick were supporters from the first day of graduate school until the last. Fellow students from across Harvard University—Felicity Aulino, Mou Banerjee, Naor Ben-Yehoyada, Elise Burton, Tara Dankel, Bridget Hanna, Emily Harrison, Abbas Jaffer, Farrah Jarral, Zahra Kanji, Neelam Khoja, Daniel Majchrowicz, Joe and Rosie Martel-Foley, Tej Nuthulaganti, April Opoliner, Arafat Razzaque, Mircea Raianu, Benjamin Siegel, Claudio Sopranzetti, Maria Stalford, Kimberly Sue, Anand Vaidya, Aliya Vajid, and Dilan Yildrim—helped me survive and even thrive. Joe and Rosie have shared their family with me for fifteen years and have given me a home in Boston. Finally, long-standing conversations about TB with Amrita Daftary, Emilio Dirlikov, Nora Engel, Jen Furin, Janina Kehr, Ruvandhi Nathavitharana, Vaibhav Saria, Karen Steingardt, Bharat Venkat, and Garrett Wilkinson still shape how I think about TB.

In India, M. Afshan Chishti, Rishabh Chopra, Rima Hooja, Rakesh Jain, Gaurav Sharma, Dhara and Karthikeya Sharma, Jalpa Thakker, and their families gave much advice, safe harbor, and friendship. Similarly, Susan Johnson-Roehr and Claire Snell-Rood were abiding support during my early days in Jaipur. The Gyanji Mogra family in Sadri has always looked out for me, as has Udailalji Meghwal and many others in this book. They have all made India as welcoming as a kitchen table and made sure I was never without a place to stay. I thank them.

In Paris, intellectual friendships with Marie Al Dahdah, Alila Brossard Antonelli, Fanny Chabrol, Florence Galmiche, Koichi Kameda, Claudia Lang, Lynda Lotte, Caroline Meier zu Biesen, Roland Nkoa Ngongo, Mathieu Quet, Pierre Robicquet, Vincent Schlegel, and Tyler Zoanni have all helped advance this project, each in their own way. What they taught me on terraces and in parks finds purchase here, Roland and Florence's lessons particularly. Zoom writing time with James Jones, now at Rutgers University–Newark, has long inspired me to keep going. I am so pleased that our books have emerged together. In New Orleans a great number of friends put up with me when writing got the best of my good cheer. They include Gordon Black, Ruthie Carlitz, Lance Daggs, Dewey Fleszar, Jason Gaines, Barley Halton, Chas Holliday, Laura-Zoe Humphreys, Brady Johnson, Cardozie Jones, Daniel Lee, Jonny Morton, Andrew Roberson, Derrick Rogers, Mindy Schoen, and Alexander Sorapuru. In New Orleans, I am also grateful to the Choctaw, Houma, Chitimacha, Biloxi, and other Native peoples on whose homeland I now live and wrote this book.

I have received generous financial support for this project. The Harvard South Asia Initiative financed many summers of preliminary fieldwork. An American Institute of Indian Studies Junior Fellowship made fourteen months of continuous fieldwork financially and logistically possible. In particular, I am grateful to institute affiliates Purnima Mehta, Elise Auerbach, Swamiji, and Kumarji for their help throughout the fellowship. I have also been generously supported during phases of writing by the Cora Dubois Memorial Trust, Kate Hamberger Kolleg at Ruhr Universität, the Max Planck Institute for Ethnology in Halle, Germany, and a School of Liberal Arts Dean's Office retreat to A Studio in the Woods of Tulane University, whence a first draft of a chapter about forests emerged. The Tulane University Office of Academic Affairs supported a manuscript workshop, which greatly influenced this book. I am also grateful for the academic affiliations and collaborations with the Institute of Development Studies, the Maharana Pratap Shodh Sansthan, and the Foundation for Medical Research, Mumbai, as well as for guidance by their respective directors Surjit Singh, Mohabbat Singh Rathore, and Nerges Mistry.

Too many have been subjected to early iterations of the ideas I present in this book. I must both apologize to and thank them. I am grateful to Aiden Seale-Feldman and Serena Bindi whose invitation to share my work in their seminar spurred me to think more about death. The chapter "Afterlife" is the product of a generative conversation there. I am also grateful to Northwestern University's South Asia Research Forum for an opportunity to receive early feedback on ideas about air and caste. An Association for Asian Studies conference panel with Naisargi Dave, Hayden Kantor, and Kate Zyskowski helped me to think more about futures, and another organized by Sarah Pinto in Madison, Wisconsin, with Brighupati Singh, Harris Solomon, and others inspired me to articulate a relationship between breath and atmospheres.

Others made the grave error of agreeing to read drafts of this text simply because I asked them to. Celine Eschenbrenner, Regina Kuzmanich, Claudia Lang, Caroline Meier zu Biesen, and Ursula Rao all read and helped me improve individual chapters. Mariana Craciun, Tara Dankel, Daniel Majchrowicz, Adeline Masquelier, Sarah Pinto, Tulasi Srinivas, Kaushik Sunder Rajan, and Allison Truitt read the entire text and helped me think through each part. Mariana Craciun, Daniel Majchrowicz, Sarah Pinto, and Tulasi Srinivas generously, and heroically, read multiple drafts. Tulasi has been a constant in hard times and frequent catalyst of successes. For a decade Sarah has been an email away with encouragement and a keen intellect. I worry that more ideas in this book come from Tulasi and Sarah than I could have possibly accounted for. Daniel has consistently alerted me to my attempts to take the easy way out of writing and thinking. Weekly writing exchanges with Mariana have perhaps single-handedly made this book arrive on time and made it better. I cannot repay my debt to any of them. Any faults in this text are likely the result of my failing to heed their advice. I am also grateful to Thomas Blom Hansen and Dylan Kyung-lim White at Stanford University Press who identified two excellent anonymous reviewers for this book. With their help I was able to improve this text exponentially. Dylan's steady and gentle guidance has been beyond what I could have hoped for.

Finally, I am grateful to my family and neighbors in Iowa's "four-county area," homeland of the Sauk and Meskwahki, Báxoke, and Oceti Sakowin. They made sure I knew I had a home and a history while supporting my desire to do something different. Who would have ever imagined that the child and grandchild of ditch diggers and farmers could have written a book? I am grateful to my grandparents, Larry and Nancy McDowell and Larry and Arlene Froning, for ceaselessly nurturing a desire to learn and grow, and for always knowing what to do. My aunts and uncles—Steve and Patsy McDowell, Jill McDowell and Art Thompson, Jim and Deb McDowell, Julie McDowell, Dixie Kuper, and Allen Froning—are the guideposts of my life. I thank my cousins and their children who gather me in a world of kinship and fun. My sister and brother-in-law, Molly McDowell Schipper and Brett Schipper, are always there when I need them. Finally, I am grateful to my parents, Rick and Sue McDowell. Though they may not have always known why this book was so important to me, they knew that it would be something that mattered.

This book is for the ditch digger and the farmer who taught me to work and to love unceasingly.

A NOTE ON LANGUAGE

AMBAWATIANS OFTEN CALL THEIR language a casserole (*kh-ichari*), a hill language [*mangri boli*], or a lying down language [*aardhu bhasha*]. Their point is that in this place between hills and plains mixing three languages—Hindi, Mewari, and Wagri—in the same sentence is an everyday occurrence that feels as easy and natural as lying down. These names particularly mark the difference from the Gangetic Plain's standard Hindi, which sometimes calls itself standing speech (*khari boli*). Hindi is one of India's national languages, and hundreds of millions of people speak it across the northern half of the country. Mewari is a Rajasthani language used by about four million people with a literary corpus and ties to the erstwhile princely court in Udaipur. Wagri is a largely spoken Bhili language used by over three million Bhil, Meena, Gameti, Damor, and Rawat indigenous community members in Rajasthan's Banswara, Dungarpur, and Pratapgarh districts. Most people in Ambawati mix languages when speaking, but how they do so indexes their social affinities and aspirations. This diversity and the power differentials, histories of writing, and situated language identity that come with it have made decisions about translation and transcription in this book particularly difficult.

I have tried to make the reader aware of this linguistic diversity by marking shifts in linguistic usage in the book. I use parentheses and italics to indicate that a word comes from Hindi and brackets and italics to indicate that it comes from Mewari or Wagri. If a word occurs in Hindi and Mewari or Wagri, I indicate it as Hindi because most Hindi-speaking readers will know it as such. For example, in the sentence that opens this note, the term *khichari*, which I translate, if ineffectively, as "casserole," occurs in Hindi and Mewari. Writing it as "casserole (*khichari*)" indicates it is a word that occurs in Hindi. In the same sentence "hill language" is a Wagri phrase, so it is rendered as [*mangri boli*], and "lying down language" is Mewari and rendered as [*aardhu bhasha*]. This primarily distinguishes Hindi words from Mewari and Wagri words. Because no firm demarcating line exists between Mewari and Wagri, I have been obliged to indicate their difference from Hindi without indicating their difference from one another.

In representing words in these languages, I have employed a simplified system of transliteration aimed at consistently rendering speech in these languages in a way that someone familiar with the language would easily recognize the word while someone familiar with English orthography might get a sense of its sound. To that end, I have eschewed the use of the diacritics commonly used to represent Indian languages (thus, I render *ṇ* as *n*, *ś* and *ṣ* as *sh*, *ṛ* as *r*, and *ā* as *a* or *aa* throughout).

BREATHLESS

BREATHLESS

ONE

ATMOSPHERIC ENTANGLEMENTS

And not one of these things nor one of these persons is ever quite to be duplicated, nor replaced, nor has it ever quite had precedent: but each is a new and communicably tender life, wounded in every breath, and almost as hardly killed as easily wounded: sustaining for a while, without defense, the enormous assaults of the universe.

—James Agee, *Let Us Now Praise Famous Men*

GAJANANDIBAI RAWAT[1] OPERATES ONE of rural India's ubiquitous tea stands. A homemade terracotta shingle roof supported by six roughhewn posts, it squats between a pond and a road at the edge of a village called Ambawati. On a cloudless February day in 2012, five or six men and I were gathered there. We were drinking tea and avoiding the midday heat. All was peaceful, almost languid, until Gajanandibai turned a mechanical bellows to kindle the flame under her aluminum kettle. Just then the hot Rajasthani wind blew from the west, engulfing the tea drinkers in sparks and smoke. The sudden atmospheric assault sprang us into action. We coughed and sputtered and searched our clothes for sparks. Most of the men had only one or two sets of clothes, and sparks could burn small holes in cotton or polyester garments. One man instructed Gajanandibai to be more careful as we all fanned the smoky air. Soon things settled back to normal, but Kalyan Singh Rawat kept coughing. He had recently been diagnosed with tuberculosis after finding specks of blood in his phlegm.

Years later, our intense reaction to this everyday occurrence still surprises me. We had responded, collectively and each in our own way, to

1

air and the connections it created to people and the world. Our actions—coughing, patting, fanning, admonishing—worked on bodies and atmospheres to return the sleepy tea stand to its peaceful state. Yet they were temporary. The wind would blow again. Gajanandibai's fire would occasionally send out smoke and embers. Kalyan Singh would cough more bacteria into the air. Rain would even fall, turning the slip of land to mud. Atmospheres are both the context in which life is lived and the effect of that living. They are the center of this book.

Ambawati is a community of about 1,500 Dalit and Adivasi farmers in Rajasthan's southeastern corner. It sits nearly midway between New Delhi and Mumbai, is about a four-hour bus ride from Udaipur, and has historically been associated with the nearby small town and erstwhile feudal lordship of Sagwai. For most residents, Ambawati is simply home, but it is also a place where social inequality and public health intersect with TB treatment in rural India. As Adivasis or indigenous people, Gajanandibai and her customer Kalyan Singh were among some of this relatively poor state's most socially and economically marginalized residents.[2] So were their Dalit neighbors, who caste discrimination has historically excluded from participation in many aspects of public life. As people in Ambawati shared their lives and experiences with me, I began to see TB and inequality as diffuse yet intertwined parts of everyday life there. The paired phenomena moved through Ambawati's social worlds and bodies as atmospheric entanglements, much as the sparked-filled gusts did that day in the tea stall. Furthermore, the entanglement of TB and inequality in Ambawati is as buffeted by health and development policy decisions made in New Delhi or Geneva as it is by lung-irritating dust kicked up by the western wind.[3]

This book engages the lives of people like Kalyan Singh and his neighbors to consider how people in an out-of-the-way place live with inequality and infectious disease. It shows that TB is inseparably entangled with social and climatic atmospheres. To do so, it reframes how public health and anthropology understand life with TB. Most dominant narratives of TB in public health and anthropology consider TB from the perspective of a pharmaceutically driven disease-control program or as an abject form of suffering connected to social marginalization and poverty.[4] TB, however, is far more entangled with life and its effects are more diffuse than these narratives can imagine.[5] People in Ambawati know this well.

Indeed, practices of living with TB in Ambawati subsume and evade these frames. Everyday actions at Ambawati's tea stall, its clinic, and its bedsides and in its fields and forest suggest that life with TB is a complex and moral entanglement with the world of others. Though public health systems tend to reduce TB to a deadly rod-shaped microbe seen under a microscope, Ambawatian action insists on the irreducibility of life with TB to a microbe. TB is a deeply social experience that draws meaning from existing ways of living as it shapes and is shaped by them. It does not override all other aspects of the human experience or reduce human bodies to hosts for microbes. Instead, TB reveals the lifelines and fault lines in social worlds and pharmaceutically organized interventions that attempt to kill bacteria without addressing disease.

The stories of suffering in this book often emerge from a mismatch between health system and Ambawatian ways of imagining TB care and social life. In Ambawati, TB is deeply enmeshed in forms of social living like kinship, lineage, neighborliness, caste, and ritual, as well as broader themes of Indian political life like development, affirmative action, and the fickle pastoral state. It cannot be understood outside these frames. Indeed, powerful accounts of TB-related death or financial devastation often come from public health's powerful insistence on treating TB through pharmaceuticals alone without concern for the social, economic, affective, and climatic atmosphere in which it occurs.[6] By arguing, alongside Ambawatians, that TB is an atmospheric illness, I contend that both social inequality and biological reality matter.

At the same time, TB infuses but does not wholly capture life. When someone is exposed to TB, or sick with TB, or a TB caregiver, or a TB orphan, that is life with TB, but life with TB is not about continually attending to bacilli or constantly being trapped in the mire of inequality. Joyous stories of life snatched from the mouth of death describe neighbors and family members moving through spaces and networks to provide care and achieve healing. These are moments in which care for TB is a multidirectional atmospheric care for bodies in space that attends to suffering and the world in which it exists. As an atmospheric illness, TB infuses life in ways that both are constrained by and exceed social and biological explanations. TB is simply a part of the atmosphere, be that atmosphere desperate, jovial, or mundane.

Atmospheric entanglements are complex ecologies. They enmesh human and nonhuman actors, affects, meanings, and places in sometimes fleeting and sometimes persistent webs of connection.[7] They are a constant condition of life, but they only sometimes elicit a response. As they did in the moment at the tea stand, atmospheric entanglements can snap together and fall apart, bringing worlds and lives into being and shattering them. TB, with its capacity to trouble breath, as well as individual and social lives, gathers together a knot of meanings and material things in Ambawati that invoke atmospheric responses from those afflicted by TB bacteria, their community, and occasionally the public health system. Tuberculosis's combination of lungs, microbes, fear, air, breath, care, pharmaceuticals, ideas about contagion, public health policy, and social relations connects people and things in a living atmosphere of disease, but it also shapes atmospheres of living. Thus, TB's atmospheric entanglements are useful lenses on the dynamically iterative relationship between biological and social life that influences the distribution and experience of disease. They create what medical anthropologists have called situated biologies.[8] A situated biology might foreground how breath, so necessary as a part of life, is made particular to times, places, and people through its entanglement with subjectivity, the body, politics, practice, and even climate. Atmospheric entanglements also help us think about situated biologies across scales that include microbial genetics, muddy roads, lungs, and state- and global-population health initiatives.

Though located in Rajasthan, Ambawati is rather different from the images of deserts, palaces, and land-owning warrior kings that the name might bring to mind.[9] The village spreads across a stretch of flat fertile land at the edge of a large forest and ridge of hills. Most people are small-scale farmers with between a quarter and five hectares of arable land and little money in the bank. Their crops of wheat, corn, soybeans, lentils, and occasionally medicinal plants depend on rain and water pumped from deep stone wells. If yields are good, most families can grow enough food to eat for the year and manage their annual expenses, but money is always tight. The Rajasthan government considers about half the families in the village to be below the poverty line and provides subsidized grain and kerosene when it is available.[10] When crops and rains fail, many families send a member or two off to work in the city as street hawkers of snacks or as construction workers. Bigger families nearly always have one person working outside the community.[11]

Ambawati also deviates from the Gandhian and typical anthropological image of an interdependent cluster of homes belonging to groups of people who, as interconnected occupational castes, constitute a fully enclosed economy.[12] Though poverty limits residents' purchasing power, Ambawati is connected to global grain markets and local markets of goods and services. Moreover, it is not spatially unified. Ambawati is one of south Rajasthan's scattered villages.[13] Extending over more than three square kilometers, the village comprises six named hamlets, clusters of between fifteen and thirty mud and stone houses. All but two of these clusters are home to a single extended family each. Categories of neighbor and cousin often overlap.

Ambawatians identify themselves as members of only three castes—Rawat, Meghwal, and Salvi. Members of the Rawat collective, who figure prominently in this book, make up a two-thirds majority in Ambawati. As descendants of people once known to rulers and census takers as Meenas or Bhil-Meenas, and associated with less rigidly Hindu forms of social organization and the forest, Ambawati's Rawats could take this identity and assert the political status of officially categorized indigenous people. For most of the time that I have known members of this collective, however, nearly all abjured any reference to indigeneity.[14] Instead, they worked hard to assert a status as the dominant caste, which they were in numbers, by forging historical and practical connections to Rajasthan's famous kingly Rajputs.[15] These practices were not always accepted by others, and contestations around caste status were pervasive.[16] This is particularly important because TB was often entangled with the poverty and marginality that their collective identity politics aimed to eschew. Their Meghwal and Salvi neighbors number a few hundred and also carry a collective history of marginalization due to caste.[17] Most own very little land, but some have been relatively successful in accessing low-level public employment through India's reservation system.[18] In Ambawati, the majority of Megh-wal and Salvi residents prefer to identify with the political category of scheduled caste, but scholars of caste in India would term them Dalit, a Marathi-origin word meaning "crushed" that describes those crushed or oppressed by practices of caste.[19]

Regardless of caste affiliation, residents of Ambawati are uniformly marginalized by caste and poverty. Nonetheless, people get by until a catastrophe like TB pushes them to the brink of destruction. In that sense, Ambawati serves as an example of how political and social inequality initiatives in contemporary India have left rural communities, and those marginalized by caste, out of the national story of growth and progress. It is also an ideal place from which to identify what falls outside public health's vision of TB.

TUBERCULOSIS

The burden of a global TB epidemic weighs heavily on Ambawati. Though Kalyan Singh was the only person sick with TB at the tea stall that day, seven of his neighbors were also in treatment. Several more were sick but had not yet been diagnosed, and others never would be—dying without a diagnosis. These Ambawatians made up only a small portion of the estimated two million Indians sick with TB that year, but in 2012 rates of TB in Ambawati were about two and a half times as high as India's national average.[20] TB is a social fact of life here. It also shapes life: bodily, social, and atmospheric.

Tuberculosis in Ambawati is a statistical, experiential, and biomedical phenomenon, but these aspects of the disease cannot be separated. In biomedicine, TB is an airborne infectious disease caused by mycobacteria that can afflict most parts of the body. Sometimes the body can suppress them, but sometimes they multiply and spread.[21] TB is particularly dangerous and contagious when it lodges in the lungs. There, it can metabolize tissue, reproduce, make breathing difficult, and be expectorated back into the world on coughs and breath. Epidemiologists suggest that, if untreated, a person with active pulmonary TB can infect between ten and fifteen others with whom they have close contact in a year. These are often family members, neighbors, and coworkers who inhale bacteria coughed or breathed out by people experiencing the disease's symptoms. Tuberculosis makes shared air and shared atmosphere a problem.[22]

People afflicted by TB lose weight, experience morning and evening fevers and night sweats, cough, have difficulty breathing, and sometimes even cough up blood. Many in Ambawati experience pulmonary forms of TB in this way. They report struggling to breathe, difficulty adapting to changes in weather, weight loss, chest pain, fever, and sadness. It is a slow, debilitating disease that, if left untreated, is deadly. When lodged in other parts of the body, TB can cause infertility, joint pain, and even neurological changes. However, TB's affliction moves beyond the bodies of people who harbor active bacilli. For those affected by TB through its presence in the body of another, TB is experienced as leaving school, seeking medical and other interventions, spending hard-earned savings, taking on extra work to recuperate lost income, providing care at home, mourning, and collecting medicines from Ambawati's clinic. Biomedicine consolidates this diversity of experiences as "TB" when the rod-shaped bacilli are present in slides or bacterial cultures and manages them with six months of pharmaceuticals.

Robert Koch, a Nobel Prize–winning German bacteriologist, identified the mycobacterium that causes the disease in 1882 and paved the way for its treatment by antibiotics in 1947. He famously called TB a social disease.[23] Indeed, social relations pattern how people interact, whose breath one breathes, who one might go to for help in times of sickness, and how care might be organized or financed. In that sense, a social disease is a kind of anthropological truism. All diseases are social. That this one should be deemed social by the very person who established its biological cause, however, is telling. The anthropologist Erin Koch argues that TB in particular is a threshold from which one might proceed into social and biological worlds and ways of knowing. As a threshold, Koch writes, TB "is the arena in which material, relational, and historical aspects are intertwined, framing the biosocial aspects of this classic 'social disease' as ultimately unstable and reconfigurable."[24] In this view, TB is a tangled knot in which technological, biological, cultural, and historical factors surface or submerge, but within most accounts of TB "the social" is never specified. What "the social" might indicate in narratives of TB as a "social disease" is central to interpreting its atmospheric entanglements.

Public health often views the social aspect of TB as related to care-seeking patterns, health beliefs and practices, adherence to drug regimens, and intersubjective stigma.[25] In these literatures, the social is social inequality that interacts with biological processes to shape illness outcomes by limiting available information or access to prompt and effective treatment. For anthropologists, however, the social is larger and further reaching. Paul Farmer, one of the first medical anthropologists to insist that TB is an indicator of a dysfunctional twentieth-century political and economic order, argues that TB is a pathology of unequal access to economic and epistemic power.[26] Critical medical anthropologists often follow Farmer to point out that tuberculosis is ubiquitous at global scale, afflicting about 10.5 million people each year, but not uniformly distributed.[27] Eighty-six percent of people sickened by TB in 2022 lived in South and East Asia (45 percent), Africa (23 percent), and the western Pacific (18 percent).[28] Only 5 percent of people afflicted by the disease lived in Europe and the Americas. Such a staggeringly unequal distribution, anthropologists suggest, highlights TB's connection to racism, colonialism, and neoliberal projects of economic adjustment. For them, TB is not merely a biological phenomenon influenced by inequality. Instead, inequality is TB's condition of biological possibility.

The social for TB can also describe ways of organizing people and knowledge. Randall Packard's analysis of the interaction between TB and twentieth-century-apartheid South Africa's racialized political economy shows how processes of capital accumulation proliferated the disease among laboring Black South Africans and structured what white clinicians and public health workers thought they knew about TB.[29] TB's relationship to societies and ways of knowing organized around inequality becomes even more startling when we remember that TB is, in all but the rarest cases, a treatable disease and has been for more than seventy years. Indeed, anthropologists and historians have shown that infrastructural development combined with pharmaceutical treatment for TB led to the disease's near eradication in Europe and its settler colonies but left it a major cause of death, despite available pharmaceutical treatments, in countries deemed less developed or in development.[30]

Finally, TB and the social is of interest to anthropologists because for the last century it has been a locus (and problem) of liberal governance. In settings as diverse as Nepal, Zambia, and Canada, anthropologists have shown that the state positions TB treatment as part of a social contract, both to shore up its power and to train modern productive citizens.[31] This impulse to standardize and train citizens through biomedical interventions for TB has grown since global health embraced TB control in the late 1990s, but it has a long history.[32] In his masterful ethnography of TB in colonial and postcolonial South Asia, Bharat Venkat has suggested that TB as a social disease authorized techniques of governance that manage access to cure and mobility on the grounds of social identity and social network.[33] Thus, Venkat shows that TB governance reinforces social and political differences.

Determinations of what the social might be and why it might matter for TB frame what TB is. They also guide representations of those dealing with it. In all three views of "the social," the individual and collective aspects of TB create a multi-scalar entanglement. The social can abide in global processes, like capitalism, that drive class inequality. For instance, the social is the many blind spots created by presumptions about patients in TB science.[34] It is also the political work that the liberal state does through TB treatment provided to citizens. As a threshold to multiple forms of the social and political, TB becomes a lens on subjectivity. Anthropologists use the concept subjectivity to describe complex, iterative, and simultaneous experiences both of being an embodied actor—with desires and choices that feel as if they originate from one's self and that orient action in a world of meaning and power—and of being shaped by power so that one's desires, perspectives, tastes, and even bodily attunements might be the consolidation of a series of circumstances and positions in relation to others and to power.[35]

In that sense, subjectivity in Ambawati is deeply connected to these multiple social manifestations of TB. First, Ambawatian selves and subjectivities are entangled with global economies that marginalize the rural poor in Asia and orient habits, possibilities, and desires there. Second, they are shaped by public health policies that imagine people as culture-bearing subjects whose "cultures" or "beliefs" guide a reflexive self to make choices that allow it to resist or submit to TB treatment.[36] Third, they exist and act in webs of kinship, caste, and governance that categorize individuals in relation to others and to politics. For example, Kalyan Singh shaped his subjectivity in relation to TB and the TB bacteria in his body through actions related to accessing care, taking medicine, sharing narratives of suffering, and submitting samples to diagnostic assemblages. He is an actor and his choices affect the world and sometimes even the material reality of TB bacteria. Similarly, his life and actions are shaped by the TB bacteria that make him cough, require intervention, evade simplistic diagnostic technology, and bring him into contact with uncomfortable regimes of power. Kalyan Singh's choices, ideas, experiences, and individual meanings are not wholly subsumed by the bacilli and the bacilli and relational webs they create are not wholly determined by his action. As in Kalyan Singh's experience, the subject (and subjectivity) of TB in this book is a dynamic, iterative one that operates in and is the effect of atmospheres. People make choices within atmospheres, but they must do so within an entanglement of circumstances and meanings that extend far past what any one person or even social assemblage might know.

By approaching TB as an atmospheric illness, we can account for the ways that TB substantiates the larger planetary systems of inequality that engulf Ambawati, while leaving space for the deeply situated contours of that experience in particular entanglements of meanings and bodies. It also allows us to see how meaning and everyday practices of being together move TB between people who have something in common, even if it is simply having been in the same place and time. Ultimately, this book argues that a high-TB-incidence site in rural India is an ideal location to study the embodiment of social and economic inequality through disease and to engage new ways of thinking about TB and the social as atmospheric.

ATMOSPHERES

Around the same time that I was searching my clothes for ashes and coughing out smoke at the Ambawati tea stand, anthropology had begun what is now called the atmospheric turn.[37] This attention to social and climatic atmospheres, egged on by pollution, anthropogenic climate changes, and a concern for the more than human, has been incredibly generative.[38] It helps to parse the actions that morning in the tea stall by highlighting how the human (in this case Gajanandibai's turning of the bellows), the climatic (here the wind), and the more than human (Kalyan Singh's coughed-out bacteria) come together. These forces align, for a brief instant, as an atmosphere or aerial world of action that is embodied, affective, and powerful. These moments, when atmosphere comes to matter, are more than simply the context in which life happens. Indeed, atmospheres extend life beyond themselves and beyond the living.

Atmospheres, to follow the anthropologist Kathleen Stewart, are the "force field[s] in which people find themselves."[39] They have a power to shape human and bacterial life in a kaleidoscopic set of choreographies and entanglements. These atmospheric force fields weld together climatic, semiotic, and affective ecologies to chart a course in which meanings and materials create a sense of how disparate things might be connected. As Timothy Choy and Jerry Zee suggest, atmospheres are a brief suspension of action that allow ethnography to think with scale and history in order to understand what it means to live here and now.[40]

For many anthropologists, atmospheres are also important entry points into materiality. Anthropologists like Zee and Choy have examined the ways that atmospheres become substantial through particulate matter and their effects on bodies, sciences, and a politics of air.[41] Marina Peterson examines waves rather than particles to understand how sound, such as the atmospheric noise created by airplanes overhead, remakes configurations of space and the possibility of life in a flyover zone.[42] Similarly, Cymene Howe examines the ways that affective and political atmospheres transform climatic phenomena like wind into a resource through infrastructural aspiration and capture.[43] In each case, atmospheres are the accumulated effects of human and nonhuman action.[44] They are anything but purely natural.

To think about atmospheres requires ethnographic frames on embodiment and subjectivity that can represent the ways humans, as bodies and selves, are permeated by climatic others. Atmospheres raise questions about what kinds of active and vital embodiment might emerge from attention to breath as index of bodies within atmospheres and as atmospheres in the body. They require an anthropology that is no longer breathless. Ambawatians present answers in their shaking off sparks, coughing out smoke, and admonishing Gajanandibai to be more careful. They recognize, in this instance and throughout this book, that the separation between body and world is anything but stable.

The breathing body that emerges from this book's attention to atmospheric entanglements replies to Donna Haraway's question "Why should our bodies end at the skin?" with a categorical "They do not."[45] Stories about TB and acts of care portray the body, both suffering and well, as intimately connected to the world. They grasp over and over again for new boundary markers between self and world. Indeed, these boundaries are often found in the atmosphere itself, in the limits of wind, the stickiness of mud, or the unevenly distributed effects of clouds.

Questions of the subject, like questions of suffering, come to be entangled with atmospheres. A breathing, atmospheric, and entangled subject might allow anthropology to think past the sentimentalist need to know the mind of another or to assert all action as the outcome of a reflexive self. Sometimes people do things, like breathing, without thinking, and often they do things without necessarily knowing what they are seeking or the outcome of that search. Thinking ethnographically about atmospheres allows us to theorize this kind of indeterminate not wholly self-aware subject. Doing so is essential because the subject of TB treatment rarely makes an agentive choice to access care or resist it, to live or die. Conscious choices to submit or resist almost never happened in Ambawati.[46] Instead, resistance and access were the accumulated effects of small, situated decisions in which people did their best at the time on the basis of the information at hand, cues in the atmosphere, and what felt right.

Stewart, in her own atmospheric turn, argues that people experience atmospheric connection as "a force field" that "is not an effect of other forces but a lived affect—a capacity to affect and to be affected."[47] I concur with Stewart's assessment that atmospheres are worlds of possibility in which subjectivity comes to the fore through "an intimate, compositional process of dwelling in spaces that bears, gestures, gestates, and worlds. Here, things matter not because of how they are represented but because they have qualities, rhythms, forces, relations, and movements."[48] Atmospheres in Ambawati matter because they have qualities that can and do create the rhythms and relationships that shape TB and inequality. For example, a nurse's instinct to cover her mouth and nose as my friend Daulat Singh and I waited in a TB hospital vestibule was enough to convince us that we risked expulsion if we did not lie about his past TB treatments. In that sense, atmospheres are more than ephemeral spaces constituted by air. They move things and ideas between people and bodies. They can be entanglements that come together around solidities like mud and immaterialities like the afterlife. It would do a disservice to atmospheres as a conceptual tool to limit them to the gaseous and its inhabitants.

In fact, atmospheres are biomoral. They are intertwinings of the biological/living, and the moral/meaningful. The social study of South Asia has been recaptivated recently by the idea of biomoral substances and the ways that powerful, often cosmological, meanings adhere to substances such as blood, semen, food, and placenta, to name a few.[49] In this book, I examine the ways that atmospheres, from clouds to dust to forests, take on biomoral qualities as they entangle substances and meaning.[50]

I first understood the biomoral aspects of atmospheres through the connections between TB and caste. I was fascinated by people who spoke of TB as a deeply meaningful experience of the world. TB's presence in the lives of Ambawatians was somehow a claim on the moral quality of a sufferer's relationships to others and to social worlds, and yet it created meaning without recourse to discussion of contagion. Given the long history of concern for caste as a biomoral contagion in Ambawati—its Meghwal and Salvi families were considered untouchable in living memory and sometimes still avoided by Rawats—a communicable disease might have seemed a biomoral substance par excellence.[51] However, people outside the biomedical system rarely described TB as an effect of contagious substances. Instead, whole atmospheres; villages, neighborhoods, and towns; airs and clouds; and muddy patches and dusty clinics were swept up into biomoral atmospherics of TB. Atmospheres were imbued with that found in them, but they overlapped with the spatial and atmospheric organization of caste.

Joel Lee has argued that Dalit studies needs an affective and atmospheric theorization of caste if the field is to understand how caste discrimination persists despite its disavowal on a liberal intellectual level.[52] By considering the ways atmospheric entanglements of tuberculosis cross lines of class and caste, this book argues that the embodied, often unre-flexive, sensation of aversion and self-protection inherent in concerns for caste and bacterial contagion is connected to caste difference's biomoral components. Atmospheric responses to TB and embodied practices of managing caste are entangled. They shape each other in alarming ways. By bringing TB, caste, and atmospheres together, I suggest that TB and the atmospheres entangled with it are often read through caste's biomoral lens and its ideas about how bodies and spaces interact to create material and immaterial atmospheres with bodily, ritual, and perhaps even cosmo-logical effects.

ENTANGLEMENTS

In her magisterial study of quantum mechanics, Karen Barad uses the word "entanglement" to describe the complex set of relationships that give a particular entity an ability to both exist in itself and to do something in the world.[53] Barad's term beautifully describes respiration's iterative ca-pacity to build relationships and also exist as singular breaths. Indeed, the presence of breath often indicates life, in general, and the living individ-ual, in particular. It makes each breathing thing both part of something larger and its own unique entity—both are atmospheric entanglements.[54] Though breath might be necessary for life and represent life itself, it is also framed by socially held meanings and attunements just like any other technique of the body.[55] In other words, breath is cultural and encultur-ated. It creates us and entangles us with atmospheres and with others, as well as with pasts and futures. In breath we exist, but we are vulnerable to others, even nonhuman others. We all breathe individually together, entangling ourselves in the same air through this incessant process of ex-change. Because of breath, there is likely more of me in the world than there is me in my body. An anthropology of the contemporary must begin to consider breath and it must breathe.

Breath is unavoidable, but like atmospheres, it is not merely a substrate of life or the substance by which bodies live. The anthropologist Harris Solomon writes that "breathing *seems* deeply individuated, because it is mostly thought to be autonomic: Chests heave and nostrils flare, some-times at will, often without thinking. Yet in contexts of respiratory distress, breath must move between people, and between people and machines."[56] Solomon calls breath between and inside bodies "social breathing." Social breathing is constant, and Solomon suggests that when breath must move between people and in and through spaces, technology, and care, it raises the question of inequality.[57] For Solomon, "it is differences in these technics of bodily techniques that index how breathing becomes social—differences that are subjective and structured by inequality at every turn."[58] In this sense, breath is an ideal lens through which to think about the entanglement of atmosphere and inequality. Social worlds exude their effects into the air and redistribute those effects in the variegated bodies of breathers. Anthropologists can no longer do without it. Breath is doubly cultural and doubly entangled; forms of breathing are shaped by the social aesthetics of gaseous intake, and social difference distributes the effects of breath's environmental vulnerability unequally. Breathy atmospheric entanglements are complex and asymmetrical relational ecologies of ideas, airs, bodies, affects, bacteria, social forms, matter, inequalities, and subjectivities that make up life in Ambawati.[59] There is no being without entanglement, no life without of atmosphere, and no body without breath.

In most public health accounts of TB, the suffering subject is imagined as a self-contained individual actor for whom choice, to access or resist intervention, is an effect of self-reflection and projected futures. As self-contained individuals these subjects are breathless. Such a breathless theory of the subject is inadequate for understanding TB and inequality in Ambawati, not least because it blames individuals for systemic failures in the provision of care and the creation of drug resistance.[60] An atmospherically entangled subject might be more useful. This subject is at once an individual—capable of experiencing desire, breathing, and reflecting on and giving an account of him- or herself—and inextricably wrapped up in social and biological forms that constrain, govern, and even make possible that subject as an individual. A subject within an atmosphere is never fully self-contained or self-composed; he or she must breathe.[61] Instead, the subject is buffeted by senses, tingles, intuitions, and perhaps even whiffs of insight that come from that atmosphere rather than from knowledge or even force. At the same time, an entangled atmospheric subject's actions enter and affect others.[62]

Caste was a central atmospheric entanglement in Ambawati because to talk about an atmosphere was a way to talk about caste. Anthropologists and historians have debated whether caste as a hierarchical social organization relies on cosmological, political, or economic difference to establish and order unequal social groups.[63] In Ambawati, any one of these could be the case. Caste here is an entanglement of processes. My neighbor Ramba Meghwal is a good example. For him, caste was a personal identity but also the effect of government social categories that aimed to annihilate the discrimination of caste but reinforce its utility as category.[64] His caste allowed him to access subsidized electricity, food, and medical care (when he became sick with TB) but also required that he assert his family's history of caste untouchability to do so. Historically, caste is a way of talking about ritual purity that slips into bodily and atmospheric hygiene.[65] In this sense, Ramba contested caste hierarchy through his meticulous practice of personal hygiene and a commitment to rapidly treating his TB, which invoked contagious bodily substances that he was eager to avoid. Finally, caste organized Ramba's necessary but burdensome connection to others. It structured who could be marriage partners for his children and the web of social relations that he accessed when he needed credit and care during his illness.[66] As a subject of caste, Ramba was an individual but also governed by and enwrapped in relations beyond himself.

The atmospherically entangled subject of TB in Ambawati is also a subject of biopolitics.[67] Biopolitics, Michel Foucault argues, are politics of control that shape the possible forms that life takes.[68] These are often micropolitics of who and what counts and how they are counted. Partha Chatterjee follows Foucault to suggest that the majority of modern subjects in India experience national social participation as being governed by the pastoral state and its biopolitics.[69] This is often the case in Ambawati. In the village, citizens are governed by a whole set of development interventions, of which the public health system's TB program is one. Foucault called this form of power "governmentality," or governance by shaping milieu.[70] Governmentality structures the social and climatic atmosphere so that subjects are more likely to find conforming to, or even enacting machinations of, power as useful to themselves. In other words, it molds individuals into subjects who can thrive in particular systems of power.

Within TB's atmospheric entanglement, these are atmospheres of development and liberal participative, though anonymous, citizenship. State power uses affects, climates, relationships between bodies and bacteria, states of exception, and kinship relations to craft entangled atmospheric subjectivities as subjects and objects of politics. In fact, atmospheric care for TB, though often outside biopolitics, is not without its own entanglement with the pastoral liberal state. Atmospheres and atmospheric subjects are entangled with webs of power and significance that often evade them. At the same time, other social forms, like caste and kinship, with their own logics and aesthetics of the subject, introduce equally difficult questions of how to care for loved ones and atmospherically entangled life.

ATMOSPHERIC CARE

Our coughing and sputtering in the tea stall was a form of atmospheric attunement—attentiveness to the connections shaped by air (and other phenomena like dust or mud or forests or breath) that anthropology often considers contextual—that helped manage a world of danger and made life possible. As breathers, we all are physically—but not always reflexively—attuned to the quality of the atmosphere. In Ambawati these forms of attunement and response might best be described as what Michael Vine calls "atmospheric care." "Practices of atmospheric care," Vine argues, "call upon caregivers to forge anew spaces and structures of familial relations, even as they infuse the otherwise mundane materials of everyday life . . . with new affective and therapeutic significance."[71] In Ambawati, those engaging in atmospheric care expanded these spaces past even the limits of the family and the aerobic. He proposes atmospheric care, a concept I develop further in this book, as a way to consider how attention to the breathed environment serves as a purpose-oriented action of support and relief.[72] Vine writes, "As aerobic beings, humans must always remain open to their environments. At the same time, this openness carries with it the risk of injury."[73] Indeed, breathy atmospheric care requires openness and risk but not unidirectionality or clear intention.

People throughout this book practice atmospheric TB care that is full of affective and therapeutic significance. They fan a feverish loved one. They build a hilltop pavilion so a father can look at the forest as he convalesces. They make hospital stays possible. They attempt to discern the potential effect of clouds that roll overhead. They even attend to everyday lived spaces as part of the afterlives of loved ones killed by TB. These acts attend to the world beyond the individual. Helping to make a hospital stay more comfortable or managing the effects of air are practices that, like TB, have distributed effects. My contention, both for anthropology and for public health, is that these atmospheric components of care and social life are too often overlooked. Both fields are breathless. Much of what people in Ambawati do to live and help others live with TB would be missed if we attend to care only as a form of tactile and affective action with a clear, linear relation to suffering. Studies of care too must breathe.

Another impact of considering TB and inequality as entangled with atmospheres is to open ways to reframe the highly technocentric provision of TB care by public health institutions today. If this book offers a single intervention in the public health discourse around TB, it is that more attention must be paid to how people are providing atmospheric care for TB and how systems might better support them. Indeed, where systems do not support atmospheric caregiving, inequality comes to matter the most. Moments when health care systems lacked atmospheric care often led to poor patients being turned away from treatment or mobilizing scarce resources among families and neighbors to fill systemic gaps in atmospheric care.

In biomedicine and public health, care for managing TB in the atmosphere most often falls to the affected person. Only she or he is the person who breathes. It is the patient who must wear a mask or avoid social life. This book is a call for health systems to recognize shared breath and help shoulder this burden by building safer hospitals and creating the kinds of atmospheric conditions—clean water, ventilation, safe and affordable housing, employment, and strong public infrastructure—that have historically been associated with reduction in rates of TB. Instead of responsibilizing the patient and pharmaceuticalizing TB control, as is too often the current case, Ambawatian care shows that atmospheric approaches are the only way to control TB.[74] Thus, atmospheric approaches should be integrated into public TB care rather than castigated by biomedical institutions and thrust on the shoulders of those already struggling to get by.

LOCATIONS AND METHODS

Constituting an ethnographic location from the entangled atmospheres of Ambawati has not always been easy. One way of doing so was to position Ambawati within national frames of development and citizenship. For decades, India's social development policies left indigenous people, like Gajanandibai and Kalyan Singh, to "develop along the lines of their own tradition and genius."[75] Then neoliberalism transformed benign neglect into a palette of initiatives aimed at autonomous administration, market participation, and increased infrastructural spending.[76] These ideas reinvigorated a national and local politics of reservation, which apportions jobs and seats in government to marginalized people as tools to empower and align them with liberal forms of democratic citizenship.[77] At the same time, the health system began a strong push to build a rural primary health care system, and World Bank investment reinvigorated the national TB-control program.[78] These events have shaped the atmospheric entanglements of dust, mud, roads, and care in Ambawati. I began gathering data in 2008, about a decade after these national transformations began but mere months after they finally reached Ambawati as publicly funded TB care and a schoolteacher's position. They felt recent when I began research for this book. Indeed, these policies and their effects in this rural village anchor some of the book's ethnographic knowledge of it.

Several things about me shaped my ethnographic attention in Ambawati as well. My gender, age, race, and regional origin all framed how, who, and what I could know. As a young man, then in my twenties, I was able to build close relationships with other men my age. They were forthright about hopes and aspirations and often used language of development. Women my age, however, kept their distance. Many were young brides. Saying little to me was a way to manage their reputations and mine. Lines of gender propriety were more porous with women over thirty. They could speak to me as they would a husband's younger sibling or even a nephew. These opportunities to interact across genders typically took place in public—on verandas and roads and in fields and tea stands. Interior spaces were often no larger than two square meters, but the exterior spaces of Ambawati in which most of my life occurred were atmospheres where men tended to dominate. Even sickbeds were situated on the verandas outside small mud houses or under shades like the tea stall. Women rarely occupied these sick beds, but they often cared for their loved ones in the open air.

My age and gender also intersected with language. Most people my age could speak Hindi, a language in which I am fluent. Older people, particularly women, tended to speak to each other and to me in Mewari and Wagri, the two regional languages spoken in Ambawati. Though Mewari and Wagri are proximate to each other in many ways, they are challenging for Hindi speakers. For the first few summers in Ambawati, these languages, and which to use when, posed difficulties for me. Over time I have learned both, but in the early years this language barrier reinforced my association with the village's under-forty-five crowd.

My appearance also mattered. There was never a chance of passing as a community member. Not only am I obviously white, but I am often a head taller than my neighbors in Ambawati. My obvious racial difference caused questions and stares at first. Eventually, attention faded as those in Ambawati and its environs came to know me better (although race as economic difference and connection to colonial past was likely unshaken). At large public events, however, my friends were often as fed up as I was with the prying questions and reminders of my difference. One neighbor even began asserting that I was his aunt's son. Few believed him.

My difference was not always a liability. Everyone knew I was writing a book about TB, and neighbors often felt that it might be useful to have an obviously foreign researcher join them at sites of biomedical care. Their hope that my presence would facilitate better care allowed me access to hospitals and clinical spaces that I otherwise may not have had. Similarly, my difference as an American, and potential source of economic resources during a health emergency, occasionally made people more comfortable when accessing biomedical care with me.

It also mattered that I had grown up on a farm. Though the elite university that I attended for graduate school may have had some bearing on access to bureaucracies in New Delhi or in Rajasthan's state capital, it was my ability to talk about cows and corn, and a willingness to lend a hand when agricultural work needed to be done, that facilitated relationships in Ambawati. The farm crisis during the Ronald Reagan administration that marked my childhood in Iowa shapes my anthropological interests. It makes me keenly aware of urban-rural divides and the connections that intimate and everyday life in a rural community have to global markets and policies. Ambawati is no exception, and these concerns frame my thinking about labor and inequality there. My agricultural upbringing may also have attuned me to discussions of atmospheres as climate and weather. Similarly, the calls of jackals in the evening reminded me of Iowa's coyotes and made for lively conversations about relationships with the nonhuman.

My own interest in TB as a biomedical disease also framed what I could know. It took months for me to let go of the biomedical certainty underpinning my initial questions about people not accessing or staying in public sector care. I also had to reconsider my insistence that people should access state care, particularly as I learned of its challenges. Confidence in biomedicine was deeply ingrained in my view of the world and, to some degree, still is. One particular biomedical conceit framed my engagement with TB itself. I was too cavalier about my own risk of infection. In retrospect, perhaps I could not appreciate TB as an atmospheric entanglement until many months into fieldwork. However, my negligence also could have been an example of the deeply engrained social and political differences between people in Ambawati and me. I had the benefit of a lifetime of access to the US medical system, which could, if necessary, diagnose and treat a TB infection with precision. Thus, my underestimation of my own risk at the time might also have been entangled with US exceptionalism.

I did, however, worry that I would acquire the disease at the many sickbeds I visited, and I was careful to remain outside and upwind when I visited people actively sick with TB. I did not wear a mask. No one in Ambawati did. Yet despite years of life in Ambawati and other TB-endemic places in India, no bacteria seem to have entangled themselves with me. This may have something to do with luck, but more likely it is a result of the circumstances of my life; not living in poverty, not being a member of a historically marginalized group, and always having enough to eat probably had far more protective effects than anything else.

These geographic, political, personal, and epistemological factors contour the ethnographic location from which this book constitutes and imagines atmospheric entanglements. So do the methods I used. I spent four summers in Ambawati before beginning sixteen consecutive months of participant observation there in 2011 and 2012. Each time, I lived in a rented house in Ambawati's Meghwal neighborhood. Since that time, I have returned for another summer and continue to visit frequently and maintain contact by phone.

Over what is now a sixteen-year period, the residents of Ambawati and I have created a large set of longitudinal data about life with TB. I have spent time with twenty-two Ambawatians experiencing a TB infection: some people I had known for only a few months and others for over a decade. In each case, I spent time with those who had fallen sick, their families, and their neighbors to learn how TB affected bodies, selves, and social worlds. Often our conversations preceded a TB diagnosis and extended long after the end of treatment. With these people and many others in Ambawati, I have exchanged innumerable stories and accounts of TB and other events. I have also been invited to countless sites of healing and taken part in these rituals.

For a while, I lived with the community nurse at the Ambawati clinic. I also visited TB hospitals in Udaipur, Ajmer, and Delhi and met with TB physicians and bureaucrats there. I searched archives for mention of Ambawati and TB hospitals in state documents and to locate stories I heard in Ambawati within the court histories of Sagwai. I advocated on behalf of my friends when they asked me to, and I experienced the paradox of interacting with a broken health system while working with the village nurse to help people access care. Mostly I listened and engaged in everyday life, going to weddings, worrying over weakening friends, cutting wood in the forest, pulling weeds, studying the clouds, attending funerals, riding the ramshackle bus, squishing through flooded roads, searching my clothes for sparks, and breathing the same air at the same time as those around me. From these methods emerged a story of TB in which sickness is not always the main character but one in which it looms, often unconfirmed, over the lives of those in a small Rajasthani village.

Though I shared air and space with my neighbors in Ambawati for over a year and we continue to maintain relations of friendship, because breath moves through both inherited and noninherited sociality, my own bodily experience can be only my own. Our unique positions meant that we breathed together but differently. An ethnography of atmospheric entanglement must face methodological challenges posed by the intersection of intimacy and inequality and by the vital virtuality of atmospheres and entanglements. I have tried to address these concerns by focusing on breath, my own and others, as it comes and goes, sometimes without notice but always as a reconnection and an opening to atmospheric entanglements. Some breaths, bodies, and atmospheric entanglements can enter the nets of knowledge, I present them here as data. Some vibrate with a vague sense of possibility, and some pass through unknown but with effect. Studying atmospheric entanglements and rendering them into language is perhaps, as my grandfather would say, attempting to rope in the wind.

AMBAWATI'S ATMOSPHERES

This book is organized around seven atmospheric entanglements. Each chapter centers on a node of self, breath, meaning, matter, and bacteria that helps interpret the amorphous gathering of TB, intervention, and life in Ambawati. Three chapters—"Breath," "Air," and "Clouds"—focus on the ephemeral connections among climates, bodies, and affects made by breath and the world of gaseous atmospheres. Three others—"Dust," "Mud," and "Forests"—focus on amphibious materials that cross categories to become matter out of place. In each of these accounts, the matter in question changes state. What brings the six chapters together are their themes' imbrication in the lived experience of TB and TB care in Ambawati and the ways that they inspire a way of living with or making sense of troubled breath. The seventh chapter, "Afterlife," works to imagine an atmosphere in which vital matter becomes entangled with death and memory, breath and life. The atmospheres and atmospheric caregiving in these chapters might surprise those familiar with biomedical ways of thinking about TB, but it will become clear that those in Ambawati face questions that bioscience cannot answer. In their attempts to find a way of life with TB, Ambawatians complicate and contest bioscience's answers about TB with evidence drawn from entangled atmospheres.

Chapter 2 centers on breath. It recounts the story of one TB-afflicted man and his family as they made sense of breath, illness, and life as multiple. The family's efforts to find a cure oscillated between attending to breath as physiological, vital, and transcendent air. The chapter follows them as they move through diverse forms of relations to find care for their social breathlessness, make sense of its source, and interpret the acts that facilitated breath's stability within an atmosphere.

Chapter 3 centers on Ambawati's nurse, Suresh, and the multiple residues of state and social work that settled on his clinic (and the national TB-control program) like dust. The dust that coated boxes of TB medicine in the clinic instantiated political history alongside a contemporary global politics of drug-resistance prevention through patient control and surveillance and the passive resistance of the people who walked Ambawati's dusty roads to take the medicine. This atmosphere of dust highlights atmospheric entanglements with the past and with forms of governmentality.

Chapter 4 leaves clinical spaces for the home and focuses on managing atmospheres of air. The chapter's movement of air shows how air might be a way of speaking about caste, caste contagion, and TB. It examines how climatic and affective atmospheres connect and separate people to interrogate the susceptibilities and relations that air and atmospheric care might make.

Chapter 5 visits a TB hospital where Ambawati's mud left traces on breath, biopolitics, and global health data. The chapter considers the ways an atmosphere of mud might stick to bodies and selves, rooting individuals in place and history, as well as in failed promises of development. Mud evoked in a context of TB, it argues, serves to talk about the bodily effects of deferred futures and unfulfilled promises of progress.

Chapter 6 deals with events around a TB death due to vindictive clouds. As climatological social actors, the clouds authorized narratives that interpreted breathlessness and death as due to moral lapses like theft and adultery. Cloudy biologics helped answer questions that bioscientific stories could not—namely, why some but not others fell sick in the first place and died on a particular day. It imagines what kinds of biosociality atmospheric assemblages might allow.

Chapter 7 visits a drug-resistant TB patient who lives at the edge of the forest. It considers the kinds of uncultivated, sporadic, or even lateral ways of being in the world that a forest atmosphere might metaphorically and materially foster through liminality and reassortment. The chapter tells the story of how the district TB physician, who explains that furnishing expensive medicines to forest-usurping patients puts them "on government duty" to get well, frames a form of ironic yet dutiful citizenship.

Chapter 8 deals with disembodied breath as it entangled death and memory in an atmosphere of afterlife. Those killed by TB, though gone, live on to inhabit the world as a ghost and a mother's limp. Wheezing disembodied breath suggests that even if TB is someday controlled, it will haunt Ambawati, as it does the rest of humanity, on the moving air.

Chapter 9 sums up the book. It reflects on what more a breathy or atmospherically entangled anthropology and public health might look like. It considers the methodological, practical, and thematic openings and foreclosures that a consideration of atmospheres and breath might bring to the study of both social life and social disease.

The book's vitally entangled stories and atmospheres chart a course through Ambawati and its experience of disease and care. To start, we must leave Gajanandibai's tea stand and follow the asphalt road east along Ambawati's northern border. Then we turn south down the dirt road toward the forest and take a left at Ramba's stone well, where his granddaughter is studying, to follow another dirt track through pastureland. We pass Kesarlalji's house and that of several Meghwal families, weave between two rows of Rawat family homes, and try not to trip on the rough cobblestone path out of the hamlet that also serves as an open-air toilet. As soon as it's safe to breathe again, we pass Gautam Singh's house, his small flock of sheep, and the place where his sugar refinery once stood, then the village school, an open-air Hanumanji temple, and the village pond's dam. We traverse the earthen dam but scamper down the embankment midway through so as not to disturb the ghost who lives under a peepal[79] tree at one end. Finally, we walk the remaining hundred meters to a hamlet called Gametiya Ghara and Siddharth Singh's house. We have traversed and been traversed by a great many atmospheres along the way, but here Siddharth Singh and his small family introduce us to TB, breath, and their atmospheric entanglement on a small veranda behind Ambawati's pond.

TWO

BREATH

Do we not feel the breath of empty space?
—Friedrich Nietzsche, *The Gay Science*

SIDDHARTH SINGH RAWAT[1] AND I had been friends since my first visit to Ambawati in 2007. He was in his midtwenties, like me, and we chatted often. I looked forward to spending more time with him during my sixteen-month stay in 2012 and planned to meet up with him once I had gotten settled into the small house I had rented. Mere hours after I arrived, however, Siddharth Singh's uncle dropped by to tell me that I should visit my friend. He was at home sick. I went to see him the next day. Siddharth Singh had changed dramatically. He had lost weight, could no longer work, and coughed frequently. Many of his neighbors, including his uncle, were certain that he suffered from tuberculosis. I agreed with them and encouraged Siddharth Singh to have his sputum tested for TB. He disagreed, and for the next eight months he and his family sought treatments for other ailments.

I spent much of the following year participating in and thinking about Siddharth Singh's care. I had weekly and twice weekly conversations with Siddharth Singh and his family members about how he was feeling and what new practices or sources of care they had considered. I joined his family as they visited physicians, Hindu and Muslim healing shrines, and a large hospital. Together we completed curative rituals and everyday care at home and worked with Suresh, Ambawati's public health nurse, to facilitate Siddharth Singh's eventual TB treatment and drug-resistance testing. His health improved at times, and the apparent efficacy of a nearby

26

Muslim ghosts' shrine shook my faith in bacteria as the cause of his illness.[2] At other times, his breath would falter, and I lost sleep devising ways to convince my friend to visit the TB hospital. I worried that, without a TB diagnosis, Siddharth Singh would join the staggering number of Ambawati residents who had lost their lives to the disease in the first quarter of the twenty-first century.

In public health literature, this family, whose struggle with TB I knew so well, would have been a textbook example of delayed TB diagnosis and sporadic care seeking.[3] Siddharth Singh might have been portrayed as a patient lost in the morass of medical pluralism.[4] He might even have been identified as a resistant subject, whose unruliness led to the high rates of TB infection, mortality, and drug resistance across India.[5] Indeed, our quest for therapy and meaning did sometimes feel haphazard, random, and erratic. Public health vocabulary, however, obscures the sense of purpose and intimacy with which the family went about providing care for their breathless member. After many months I realized that I, like much of public health's literature, had missed their concern for breath and its connections.

Public health studies of patient action and I had, as Nile Green warned, "accepted [breath] as an ideologically neutral sphere of human activity . . . [that] has seemed neither to require nor reflect a context."[6] I had assumed that breath was a raw but ephemeral material life process uninflected by context or meaning. Siddharth Singh, his family, and many others in Ambawati, however, did not. Instead, breath, the vulnerabilities it created, and possible ways to manage those vulnerabilities organized much of the work our small collective did to care for Siddharth Singh. I simply had not seen it. My effort to translate conversations with Siddharth Singh and his family from Hindi, Mewari, and Wagri into English blinded me to the many words for distributed relational breath that we had been using in conversation and practice.[7] On a damp monsoon morning, however, my neighbor Memibai Meghwal helped me see my error.

A widow with four children, Memi occasionally gathered *tendu*[8] leaves and other forest products for supplemental income. Many in Ambawati collected and sold these leaves, which are used to wrap small cigarettes called bidis. Cigarette company middlemen paid one rupee for a hundred leaves, so each tangle of leaves carried home needed to be counted and organized in bundles. When the leaves were in their prime Memibai, several neighbors, and I spent mornings stacking bundles of fifty leaves on her small veranda. It was pleasant but knee-stiffening work. We stretched often.

On one break, Memi asked her nephew Prahlad to sweep the tattered leaves from the veranda. "Prahladiyo," she said, "sweep up these leftover leaves, but watch out for the animals (*praani*s) crawling there. They are also living things (*jiv*)." The animals in question were leaf-munching centipedes. Her directive contained a knot of ideas about respiration, care, and the soul that revealed a connection to even the creepiest, crawliest of things through breath. Ten-year-old Prahlad sang a snappy devotional song at the top of his lungs as he swept the leaves into a corner. After finishing, he coaxed a brown centipede from the pile and onto the end of the hand broom. He studied the insect before walking with toy-soldier-like movements to deposit it on a nearby pumpkin vine. With a leap he sat back down beside me, and our group chuckled as we resumed bundling.

I enjoyed Prahlad's performance, but I was struck by the word *praani*— breathing thing, creature, being, or person—that Memi used for the centipedes and inchworms.[9] Fishing more leaves from the pile, I asked, "Those bugs, you called them *praani*s. Do they also have breath (*praan*)?"[10] "Of course," Memi replied, "they have life-breath (*praan*). They are alive. All living things (*jiv*) have life-breath (*praan*)." She knotted another leaf bundle and tossed it aside. By calling them *praani*s, or creatures with breath, rather than animals or insects, Memi highlighted the ethical relations of similarity and care that breath as *praan*, a particular kind of animating breath that I have translated here as life-breath, fostered between Prahlad and the tiny herbivores. Their liveliness, as a sign of soul-possessing breath, meant that he ought not needlessly harm them. But it was not just any breath.

"Is there a difference between life-breath (*praan*) and respiration-breath (*sans*)?" I asked, tying a shred of bark around my bundle. Memi explained, "Life-breath (*praan*) is different. Respiration-breath (*sans*) is different, and strength-breath (*dam*) is different."[11] Prahlad rested his elbow on my knee casually, as if the three unique types of air entering and leaving the body were utterly obvious. It had not even occurred to me that breaths could be differentiated and brought into social life through their categorization. Amused by my growing bewilderment, Memi went on: "Breath (*sans*) is breath (*sans*), han, han, han, han." She panted loudly to exaggerate a filling and emptying chest. As the air that leaves and enters the body, *sans* could be heard on a sigh, seen on winter mornings, or touched by a hand placed before the mouth. It was a bodily process like respiration that, with some attunement, could be sensed, experienced, and even briefly modulated.

Dam required elaboration.[12] It was different. When our giggles subsided, Memi evoked both the chest and strength to describe it. She said, "Strength-breath (*dam*) is the work of the chest/lungs [*daman*][13] that gives strength.[14] Do you know that saying, the one that helps explain how strength-breath (*dam*) is like strength?"[15] I said that I did not, so she puffed out her chest to parody an angered man issuing a Mewari provocation: "Thane me dam ve, to bane aa jaa." She repeated it again in Hindi for me, "Dam hai to bahar aa jaa" (literally, If you have the strength-breath in you, come out [and fight]). Her parody, indicating that *dam*, or strength-breath, was force, vigor, and courage, elicited more laughter. In the weeks that followed, I learned that *dam* (strength-breath) is an airy energy, vitality, or strength that keeps the body active and affecting the world. A respiratory faculty that makes for more than a simply living body, *dam* might describe the heavy breath of labor and creation.

Memi counted out another packet of leaves and started to think about *praan*. It seemed even more complicated. "See," she said, "*dam* is respiration-breath that gives strength, but *praan* is different. *Praan* is respiration-breath that is life/sentience (*jiv*). That insect is alive just like us, so it has life-breath (*praan*)." I asked what she meant, and she replied, "You know, when you cannot breathe [*hans leno*] and your life-breath goes out [*praan nikali jaye*], you are dead. You have no more life (*jiv*). It leaves you. You are just an empty body, and your soul/self (*atma*) goes out and enters something else [*praves kare*]. Your life-breath (*praan*) goes out and your soul goes out." I asked, "So if someone's life-breath (*praan*) goes out, where does it go?" "With your soul (*atma*)," Memi answered naturally. "It goes, stays with your soul?" I asked. "Yes," Sundar, a woman in her late thirties answered from her seat in the circle. Memi thought for a moment and said, "It goes with your soul. Everything with a soul has a life-breath (*praan*). It must go with the soul and enter a new body." I pointed to the centipede inching back from where Prahlad had placed it and asked, "So if I were to kill that living thing (*jiv*), its life-breath (*praan*) and soul would go out together and enter a new thing." Memi responded, "Yes, it is also a living thing (*praani*). Its soul and its life-breath (*praan*) would go together into another thing."

Adjusting Anne-Marie Mol's philosophy of a body multiple, with its materiality and agency reframed by practice and positionality, we might suggest that Memi outlined a philosophy of breath multiple.[16] One form of breath was physiological (*sans*), one vital (*dam*), and the final cosmological (*praan*). Each of the three aerial substances could be lively and meaningful ways of connecting the body and self to the world of other people, actors, and even other versions of the self. But they drew boundaries in different places.[17] Each is an entanglement of diverse stories of life and moral stakes that weave and shimmer in ephemeral but connective lines to distribute breath—all embodied in that little centipede crawling through our bundles of leaves.[18]

The year of Siddharth Singh's sickness was replete with moments when breath's automatic and individuated fantasy fell away. It provides multiple lenses on breath, on the connections breath makes and requires even when stable. Indeed, TB-related breathing trouble reveals these respiratory connections most clearly because, as Harris Solomon suggests, "in contexts of respiratory distress, breath must move between people, and between people and machines."[19] As the family worked to move and hold each of the breaths troubled by TB, they raised Solomon's question: "When breathing is compromised, what shifts in the ways bodies turn air into breath?"[20] Their answer was simple: everything from self to body to air, language, family, and life itself was transformed and affected by breath's compromised state. Nevertheless, it was transformed even when breath was not compromised.

Sitting with Siddharth Singh through a year of social breathing, this chapter argues that breath is cultural. It cannot be effectively interpreted as universal or individual but might rather point to an intermediary form of shared particularity. If there is any hope of understanding the intersection of human and airborne pathogenic life, breath must be engaged ethno-graphically. Anthropology cannot remain breathless. Breath is inextrica-bly entangled in cultural forms and altered by practices like language, care, and bodily attention or attunement. The chapter traces each of Memi's breaths—respiration-breath, or *sans*; strength-breath, or *dam*; and life-breath, or *praan*—as they shape Siddharth Singh's care, body, and bac-teria. It shows how each breath is imbued with local and global practices that socialize air, breathing, and of course, TB. Further, it argues that, as a culture-laden connection in the world, breath presents a methodological opportunity for anthropologists to see how material and social relations are shaped during practices of social breathing and all that it is connected to. Finally, it shows how breath and social breathing particularize TB and bodies, in Ambawati and elsewhere.

Breath and its entanglements are central, but rarely considered, nodes of human diversity. By ethnographically situating breath's confluence of meaning and materiality, what once seemed a universal building block of life can emerge, not as presocial or self-evident context, but as a phe-nomenon hemmed in, multiplied, and experienced through prisms and processes of meaning, relations, and care. Care and disease also reveal themselves to make troubled and smooth breath a cultural practice in dy-namic and unexpected ways. Each inhalation and exhalation connect and reconnect breath's meanings and metaphors of life to the body anew.

SIDDHARTH SINGH'S ROTATIONS

Siddharth Singh insisted that he did not have TB, but I hoped he would eventually at least take a test. Not long after I began my visits to his sick bed, one of my prods irked him. He replied, "If you get tuberculosis, you die quickly after. I am not near death. My problem is that my rotation [*rotation*] is not happening, so my respiration-breath is strange." He was ready to change the subject, and we moved on.

I often heard others talk of their bodies as out of *rotation* when they were sick. As I began to ask questions, I learned that *rotation* was a word created from the English "rotation." People had acquired the term, like pharmaceuticals, from physicians who used mechanical metaphors of ro-tation to explain patients' bodies as dynamic interconnected systems of

organs. Mewari- and Wagri-speaking patients borrowed it with modifica-
tion. They spoke often of *rolation* as a kind of bodily circulation and tempo
or being in synch with time and the seasons.[21] I found the word's easy glide
between rotation and relation generative and wondered what a *rolating*
body might mean for Siddharth Singh.

A few days later I asked Siddharth Singh what he meant by his body
being out of *rolation*. In his answer, he described the cyclical body and
breath that he and the family used to organize care and relations. It aligned
well with Memibai's respiration-breath. He looked at the laundry drying
on his unused motorcycle and said,

> A body is like a motorcycle. It can't just have one part working, right? They
> all have to be doing their part or the whole thing doesn't run. If there is
> no gas, food, it will not run. If the gas tank is full but the spark plug is not
> working, then it will not start. If you fix the spark plug and the gas is full,
> but the tire is flat, the motor will run but the machine will not move. I am a
> perfect example of that problem. You know, we tried to use [the motorcycle]
> a couple of days ago and it turns out that somehow sand got in the gas tank.
> Finally, Mangilal [a neighbor] got the sand out and we tried to make it run.
> It would start for a few minutes. Kind of like me. I can walk around for a few
> minutes before tiring out. So Mangilal started fixing it again, and it turns
> out that the air filter was clogged. The filter was full of bits of fuzz, so the
> engine could not get air and it stalled. It is like that with the body. You've
> got to have all the things working so that wheels can turn and the motor
> runs and all. It must all be in *rolation*. My problem is that I can't get enough
> air in and out. I'm just like the motorcycle. My air, my respiration-breath is
> weak. I need to strengthen it.

Siddharth Singh's motorcycle simile is an example of what Emily Martin
suggests are capitalist modernity's mechanical metaphors of the body, but it
points beyond the mechanical.[22] In his body metaphor, respiration-breath
is a necessary but intangible part of an interconnected machine. Normal
respiration-breath, Siddharth Singh suggests, goes in and out effortlessly,
turning a pump or a piston to collect the next one in a way that suggests
that breath might be of the body and external to it. Like the clogged filter
that starved the motorcycle's engine of air and made it immobile, weak-
ened breath disturbed Siddharth Singh's *rolation*. It caused the lack of

appetite, fever, physical weakness, weight loss, and immobility that were now central to his life in bed. This body is both mechanical and inherently connected to the world. Breath in the machine opens mechanical metaphors' closed systems to others and to worlds.

As I observed Siddharth's family care for him, I noted that their attention often traversed the boundaries of an individual body. They activated external and immaterial relations as they moved social and spatial circles to bring his mechanical, breathing body back into tempo through substances and enactments. This moved, or perhaps *rolated*, respiration-breath through Siddharth Singh and his relations.[23] The family's search for honey, which one doctor prescribed as part of a regimen to soothe Siddharth's cough and steady his breathing, is an example of how troubled breaths *rolated* Siddharth Singh and his body to a place, to family, and to caste.

On an unseasonably hot January day, not long after Siddharth Singh told the story of the motorcycle, I ran into him and his mother, Nabudibai, as they were traveling to a nearby Ayurvedic doctor and decided to join them. The doctor prescribed a cornucopia of powdered herbs, biomedical pharmaceuticals, and other substances aimed at catalyzing motion within Siddharth Singh's body. Folding the packets, the physician told us that they would "help Siddharth Singh rebuild his lungs after an old infection and strengthen his respiration-breath." He insisted that the medicine be mixed with honey collected from the forest near Ambawati. "Honey from a shop will not be as good. It should be local jungle honey," he explained. We noted his advice and made our way homeward. As we slowly returned to Ambawati, Nabudibai told me that the doctor had said the same thing at their last visit and that she had "done a circle around Ambawati" [*mu akka gaon ra chakkar khatdio ho*] to see if anyone had honey. No one did.

The next day Siddharth Singh's father, Narayan Singh, bicycled to Nabudi's natal village in search of honey. There, he arranged for Nabudi's cousin to go into the forest to collect some. The next day, however, the cousin found himself embroiled in a conflict and wound up in the local police station. Days later, news of the arrest reached Narayan Singh, and he set out to visit more relatives in search of the requisite honey. This time he cycled to his mother's natal village, which also bordered the forest. With no honey to be found there, he visited his sister-in-law's natal village and learned that the man who collected honey—Siddharth Singh's aunt's uncle—sold it to a shopkeeper in Sagwai. About Narayan Singh's age and from a neighboring village, the shopkeeper gave him some honey on credit because of their lifelong acquaintance. Narayan Singh, surprised to find forest honey in the market and accessible not through family but neighborly relations, brought it home in hopes that it would steady Siddharth Singh's breathy relations to the world. He had distributed respiration-breath and the breathing body through a network of kith and kin.

While Narayan Singh moved Siddharth Singh's body and breath through more distant relations, his mother, Nabudi, did so at home. Siddharth Singh often talked of troubled respiration-breath making him vulnerable to changes in temperature. On a particularly sunny day he told me, "When it is hot, I feel very, very hot, no matter how much I pant or sit in the shade, and when it is cold, I shiver without being able to stop it, even with three quilts. My body is still out of *rolation*." Here, *rolation* was environmental, and this time the problem was not just that he could not move his breath but that he could not move his breath in a way necessary to match the shifting weather. Nabudi set to work to manage the heat and cold of Siddharth Singh's body and stimulate the exchange of breath through massage. Her practices of bathing and massaging Siddharth Singh brought atmosphere and community into another intimate poetics of Siddharth Singh's *rolational* body and breath.

As Siddharth Singh's health deteriorated, Nabudi started to bathe him where the sun beat down on the hardened layer of clay and dung pavement in front of their home. The pair undertook the process at midday, when the Rajasthani sun beat down at its hottest, so that the water would not give Siddharth Singh a chill. Siddharth Singh squatted with his boney knees pulled up to his chin as Nabudi doused her underwear-clad son with warm water and scrubbed his back in a circular motion. She often rubbed so hard that Siddharth Singh winced in pain and her bangles tinkled loudly as if they would break. After one particularly vigorous bath, Nabudi told me that she had been trying "to knock loose some of the knots in his body and help his breath's *rolation*." Physiological breath's movement between body and world was blocked by knots in the flesh. The combination of heat and massage, Nabudi hoped, would remove them to let external air in and allow pent-up bodily air out.

The physical work of getting air in and out of the body through massage fell to Nabudi because their intimacy as mother and child could enable a very tactile form of social breathing. The intimate, tactile, and public work of bathing and massaging was perhaps only possible within their relationship's capacity to return to the de-sexualized intimacy of mother and child.[24] Here, too, troubled breath reordered the relations of care between an aged mother and adult son to re-create the physically intimate relationship of loving mother and vulnerable child.[25] As the tiny sixty-year-old woman bathed her once hulking thirty-year-old son, she reorganized or rewound the temporality of intergenerational care, or *seva*, as she worked to restart Siddharth Singh's breathy *rolation*.[26] As the search for honey organized an intimate poetics of care between Narayan Singh, Siddharth Singh, and their extended networks, respiration-breath gave form and tempo—*rolation*—to the intimate poetics of Nabudi's daily care for her son.

I visited Siddharth Singh a few days after one of Nabudi's baths to see that his skin had turned black and flaky. It was even peeling off in places. He caught me studying a scaly patch on his arm and asked if he looked bad. I told a reassuring lie. As I settled on a nearby cot for our now weekly chat he explained,

> That's Mom's work. Someone told her that massages with kerosene would help with *rolation*. Two weeks ago, she asked Shantibai auntie for some kerosene, but she had run out. The day before yesterday, Shantibai auntie brought a small can of kerosene and Mom used it as a massage oil. You've seen her do those massages. Well, she gave me one and it burned like fire. I was in so much pain, but she insisted. Now look at me; I'm worse off than I was before. When Mom tried to return it, Shantibai auntie said that we should keep it just in case. Now we're burning it as lamp oil. I won't let Mom come near me with the stuff. I wonder who put it in her mind that this kerosene massage would be helpful.

A body and breath of rotating climatic yet mechanical liveliness made kerosene, with its potential to make heat and fire, a reasonable massage oil for a cold body.[27] Its effect on Siddharth Singh's skin, however, was a shock. Still, the kerosene brought more family relations into Siddharth Singh's physiological breath.

Shantibai Rawat was Siddharth Singh's father's cousin's wife and Nabudi called her younger sister. She knew that Siddharth Singh was ill, but she was busy with her own work and had not come to visit him in several months. A few days after delivering the kerosene, Shantibai came again to check on Siddharth Singh. Her daily work required that she pass by the family home, and soon she added visiting Siddharth Singh and Nabudi to her daily routine. Providing care for *rolating* body and breath followed and perhaps reinforced existing intimate circuits. The family's ability to draw on these relations for healing substances suggests that Siddharth Singh's body and its rotating liveliness was inflected by relations of familial and neighborly intimacy. In short, practices of care for breath and bodies were, like breaths themselves, *rolational* processes of give and take, intimacy and credit.

Siddharth Singh's family tried whatever they could think of to get his respiring body back in *rolation* with the social and aerial world. They did so through pharmaceuticals, humoral home remedies, and body work aimed at affecting the physiological experience of breath entering and leaving the body. In each case, they leaned on existing social and ecological relations that had a give and take of their own, some within the nuclear family, others the extended family and caste, and still others of neighborliness, credit, and patronage. These rotations through relations, everyday and exceptional, fraught and fluid, reveal a moral economy and relational affordance of respiration-breath that is entangled with relations of kinship and further afield.[28] Siddharth Singh's *sans*, or respiration-breath, was cared for by many, and care moved his breath into all kinds of relations. The family's work on breath was the relational work that Solomon has called "social breathing" and Michael Vine has called "atmospheric care," but *sans* was not the only breath they considered.[29]

ASPIRATIONAL *DAM*

On another of my visits, Siddharth Singh lamented from his cot, "I used to be so strong (*takhat*). You remember how I could throw bricks? I had so much strength-breath (*dam*). I could fight and win too. You remember.

Do you remember the time that I carried that door all the way home from the bus stand on my back in the middle of the night?" "I remember," I told him quietly. Siddharth Singh's elegy for his former brick-throwing vitality spoke what he had not said in months: he was now dying. Growing weaker by the day, Siddharth Singh could only watch as his cousins, both of whom he had taught his trade, accumulated bricks and built homes next to his mud structure. He lamented the loss of physically and economically vital strength-breath that would have allowed him to build his own brick house and achieve financial or infrastructural security for his family. A few days later, he told me that he felt stagnant, as if his dreams of growth and progress were stalled by a lack of force. Though respiration-breath still hesitantly *rolated* worldly air in and out of his body, exertion and action were difficult. Confined to bed but still breathing, he lacked strength-breath. Siddharth Singh often lamented his lost *dam*, or strength-breath, with nostalgia and a sense of unmoored and isolated ennui. As the source of action, strength-breath can be individually possessed while relationally shared. Its double meaning of material breath and metaphorical strength provides yet another biography of breath that narrates what it meant for Siddharth Singh to struggle to breathe.

Challenges associated with debility and diminished strength-breath caused Siddharth Singh to worry about himself in ways that coughing and disordered physiological breath had not. Siddharth Singh's role in the world and his family was bound up with, or anchored to, strength. His work as a builder, his ability to earn money, his openness to innovation and change, and his performance as a dutiful son and providing father all centered on strength. Or in another translation of the same word, they relied on breath.

Soon after his elegy for lost strength, Siddharth Singh began to tell me with concern that his breath was moving. I dutifully noted this as "*dam chalna*" and "*dam salno*," strength-breath moving, galloping, or taking off. Still, I found it an odd phrase. Respiration-breath was troubled when it did not *rolate*, but strength-breath was troubled when it moved. I did not understand what he meant until I entered the family's brush-fenced enclosure to see Siddharth Singh crouching in the shade on a sweltering April afternoon. He was shirtless and panting. His shoulders rose nearly to his ears before crumpling back into place and rising again. He struggled to pull in short breaths. I squatted next to him as Nabudi corralled a goat that had broken its tether. Though trying not to betray concern, she watched her son closely. I watched him too, and he rasped, "Hold on, my breath is moving [*Dab jao, mahro dam sali riya*]." *Dam*, in this short sentence, was something between a word and an inward gasp. The staccato inhalations and exhalations transformed his body as Siddharth Singh struggled to breathe and speak. Its ambiguity reminded me later of the fine and tentative line between insignificant breath and signifying language.[30]

At the time I could only think of fear. Siddharth Singh seemed convinced that the panting episode would pass and that exhalations would soon become words again. Still, I was alarmed. There was nothing I could do for my friend. I waited for his body and breath to stop moving uncontrollably and tried to remember how to perform cardiopulmonary resuscitation in case it stopped entirely. After about ten minutes, Siddharth Singh's breathing evened. He stood and stiffly made his way back to his cot on the veranda. Moving strength-breath had sapped even more of his energy and depleted his ability to act on the world physically and linguistically. I suggested that I come back the next day. He agreed that tomorrow would be better.

The next day I returned to ask Siddharth Singh about what had happened. He explained that his strength-breath had been moving and told a story about the transformation of breath, self, and labor that caused it. His autobiographical account foregrounds social breathing and susceptibilities among breath, vitality, individuals, collectives, suffering, and aspiration:

> I worked in a stonecutting factory near Kota, right? It was a great job. It paid really well. I liked it. I worked there for a year before Kumbh Singh [his son] was born and then again after coming home for a while. That is where I learned to speak Hindi and live on my own and cook for myself. It was good to live outside Ambawati and see the way other people live. I met men from all over India. The work was for strong (*dam-daar*) men. Mostly we picked up huge blocks of stone, put them on the cutting machine, and carried the slabs [away], but one time when we were lifting a stone it slipped. It slipped and I was injured badly. I was on my back for weeks. Then when I could move, I came home. After that, ever since that injury, when the clouds are bad my breath (*dam*) moves like it did yesterday.

The stonecutting factory was about six hours northeast of Ambawati by bus. Siddharth Singh's experience there, of nonagricultural work and of living in a room with five others whom he did not know, was central to who he was. It gave him the language to communicate beyond Ambawati and an entrée into a whole world of paid labor with its possible ways of being. As a first glimpse into different economic possibilities and an individualized singular self, the experience was a touchstone for his knowledge of the world and potential economic futures. It was also a time of self-making and social-relation making outside the structures of family, neighbor, and caste that guide relationships in Ambawati. With none of these familiar relations to draw on, the factory was a new way of being in nonkin relations. New social roles like coworker, roommate, or friend among strong, breathy, *damdaar* men became open to Siddharth Singh. In a context of paid labor he could forge an individual, embodied self that was characterized by speaking of and caring for oneself within relations of capital rather than community or caste.[31] He built a new kind of intimacy and social breathing there.

Although Siddharth Singh's anecdote is about the novelty of paid labor, it is also about crafting an individual and laboring self when its very center, signified by strength-breath, can and often does give out. He found himself as an individual among other individuals with unique potentials and capacities. Their work of lifting huge blocks of stone onto a cutting machine to be turned into granite tiles and slabs, however, was still a collective one. When one member of the group stumbled, Siddharth Singh's strength proved too little for the massive stone. It struck him in the chest, rendering his laboring body breathless. When Siddharth Singh was "on [his] back" he was also far from family and had to rely on coworkers and the factory patron for care. His individual strength-breath was insufficient, but the relational affordances and possibilities that social breathing crafts between friends and coworkers became obvious again.[32] Eventually, he was able to return home to heal and take up masonry, but he reentered his now shifted family and community relations as one who works off the farm. He would be changed by the experience of entering the world of laboring, with its interchangeable individuals and its intimate poetics of individualized strength-bearing breath that moved erratically when his strength waned.[33]

Observing Siddharth Singh's *dam* move and listening closely to his narrative of labored breath and wage labor evokes an ethical and relational analogue in the breathy English word "aspiration." Though Arjun Appadurai suggests that the capacity to aspire is a way of thinking or imagining new potentials that many of India's poor lack, for Siddharth Singh aspiration was as everyday as breath.[34] Breath's capacity to labor was a central part of his imagined future. It was part of being alive. This numbing of possible futures, for Siddharth Singh while he was ill and for many of his neighbors in general, was not the inability to dream. Rather it was a recognition of the limited and fleeting opportunities young people in rural India have to enact dreams and mold the future. His injury had stifled his individual and prosperous future, foreclosing a whole set of opportunities. Now from Siddharth Singh's cot it seemed that what was earlier a missed opportunity was an impossibility, an individualized future on hold.

Though a laboring, breathing individual, Siddharth was still part of a vital collective rather than one among many. His visions of a vital future were rarely for himself. Even as he turned strength-breath into labor at the stonecutting factory, he did so to send money back to Ambawati. His future strength was distributed through his children and family. He hoped for a future of comfort for his parents, new clothes for his wife, mobility and access to the market by motorcycle, a well-made house that would not collapse in the rain, and an education for his children. He even mused about sending his youngest son to college. Futurity and strength-breath were inner and outer, individual and collective potential. Though he spoke of possible futures as a networked potentiality, his breathy strength was individuated action on a network's behalf. It too was wrapped in social forms and deeply *rolational*.

May arrived and Siddharth Singh struggled for each breath. His cheekbones and clavicles protruded. His family continued to search for care and relief as the sweltering western wind made him feel as if his body was on fire. I kept visiting and prodding him to get a TB test. One hot afternoon, I passed the house and Narayan Singh called out, inviting me to tea. The older man was mending the family's bullock-drawn cultivator while Siddharth Singh slept. He needed a hand to hold the pole steady as he smoothed it with an axe. I was happy to help, and we set to work. When tea was ready, we stopped to sip the hot liquid from tiny ceramic cups.

Preparing the tools of his trade for the approaching monsoon had turned Narayan Singh's mind to his son. Breaking the silence he said,

> Siddharth Singh will have to start improving soon. I have made so many circles here and there to find a treatment. When the rain falls all of that is over. I will have to spend all my time at the plow because our land is waiting. If I do not do it and spend my time looking for treatment . . . If I do not work hard (*mehnat*) in the field and give it what it needs, then we will all starve. What will we eat if we do not tend the land [*maal*]? There will be nothing, nothing. I must care for the land because it provides for us. Siddharth Singh is sick. It is all we have, land [*maal*] and work (*mehnat*).

Though Siddharth linked his vital individual and social force to the potentials of productive individualized labor, Narayan framed strength-breath as work and agricultural reproduction on family land. The potential vitality in the soil, like the family, was multigenerational, and though Narayan Singh's somber revelation seemed like a choice between caring for and abandoning Siddharth Singh, Siddharth Singh's strength-breath could outlive his breathing body in the strength of his children and their inheritance. Narayan Singh worried that he would need to divert his own energy, action, or strength-breath to the field, no matter how difficult. His might have been another a way of attending to Siddharth Singh's vitality and the future for his family. To care for the family, even in Siddharth Singh's absence, was somehow a way to care for his son's potential to act in the world and create a vital future.

As head of that family, Narayan Singh had a crucial decision to make. Pondering it, he found himself worrying through the status of vital yet ethereal breath. The question centered on whether strength-breath abided in an individual or family body.[35] In turn the stakes of care and neglect, as well as his success as a father and member of a lineage, relied heavily on whether *dam*'s strength-breath was distributed among bodies in a series. Narayan Singh did not want to lose his son's physical presence in the family. But, he also worried that by focusing on an individual the shared strength of the family, as work and land, would suffer. His conundrum, which I could not help resolve, rested on questions about Siddharth Singh's potential to be part of the family or lineage's strength-breath without a body.

Could strength-breath live on through land's connections even when respiration-breath's relations of physical copresence were broken?

In the end, by opting to focus on his fields, Narayan Singh decided that strength-breath's relations and biography were intergenerational. Siddharth Singh's troubled strength-breath, he decided, troubled the whole family's potential and aspiration. *Dam*'s connections were different from bodily *sans*. They seemed more like complex and dynamic connections between an individual breathing self and a self that had been created by and lived within webs of kinship, lineage, and caste. As father and grandfather, Narayan Singh viewed his task as making decisions for benefit of all, which included Siddharth Singh.

Both men's practices of strength-breath were framed around the connective power of breath that shaped the relations between self and collective that extended before and beyond the present.[36] By keeping hold of the land with its connection to and potential for sustenance, Narayan Singh could care for the family, Siddharth Singh, and the children's future strength-breath. Even in his act to reduce his role in caring for Siddharth Singh's powerless body, Narayan Singh imagined an intimate poetics of caring for a living breath that extended *dam*'s vital strengthening air through relations and generations. It was social breathing indeed.

PERSISTENT, POWERFUL *PRAAN*

The looming rain clouds that Narayan Singh and I worried would mark the end of care for Siddharth Singh's physical body and its troubled breath had the opposite effect. As the monsoon neared, Siddharth Singh began to consider a tuberculosis infection possible. Finally in late May, Siddharth Singh, his mother, his father, and a cousin left home at four a.m. They bicycled to Sagwai and caught the bus to the TB hospital. There Siddharth Singh started the TB medication that would help him regain his strength and steady his breathing. The group returned later. Rain fell, and Narayan Singh hitched up his oxen to plow the family's fields. Nabudi kept bathing Siddharth Singh rigorously. We all waited.

The summer corn grew but Siddharth Singh's condition did not improve. Suresh, the village nurse, and I began to wonder if Siddharth Singh was infected by drug-resistant TB, or possibly HIV, since both infections slow or stop antibiotics' effect on the bacteria.[37] Suresh found a way to have Siddharth Singh's sputum tested for drug resistance, but the test showed that his bacteria were vulnerable to TB drugs. Still Siddharth Singh's breathing and strength continued to deteriorate. One August night Siddharth Singh was rushed to the hospital for supplementary oxygen and a rumor went around town that he had died. When he returned a few days later, Suresh and I decided that we ought to find out if Siddharth Singh's blood was HIV positive before it was too late.

One evening we visited the family together. On seeing us, Narayan Singh pulled several cots out into the breeze and called his brother Phul Singh to join us. Suresh struggled to begin a conversation about HIV, as we anxiously slurped tea. "You know I think these TB medicines are working too slowly," he said. "More slowly than maybe they should. It's possible that there is another, bigger illness that's causing the TB to stay. If he does not improve, we will maybe have to consider this possibility." Narayan Singh and Phul Singh nodded their turbaned heads gravely and said that they would keep a close watch for improvement. In the meantime, Suresh suggested that the problem may not be another illness but ineffective drugs. One of Siddharth Singh's publicly supplied anti-TB medicines was nearing expiration, so Suresh advised the men to buy it from a private pharmacy just in case. Narayan Singh did so.

I joined Phul Singh a few days later while he scared parrots away from the corn's juicy young ears. As we awaited the inevitable return of the little green birds, Phul Singh said, "Suresh is from Wagad you know.[38] People there are very knowledgeable about tantra. They have powerful tantrics among his people, so he must know about it. That must be what he was talking about the other day when he said there may be some other, bigger problem afflicting Siddharth Singh." Suresh and I had never discussed tantra—a system of occult practices and incantations, which often involves the inversions of Brahmanical Hindu practices, aimed at manipulating the material and cosmological world to bring about bodily and social change— and I thought he had been talking to the family about HIV. Nonetheless, tantra shaped the family's discussion of Siddharth Singh's illness and care. They had long worried that the illness was due to tantra practiced or commissioned by Siddharth Singh's uncle or cousin.[39]

As the burly eldest son of the extended family's eldest son, Siddharth Singh had used some of his now depleted strength-breath to physically prevent a cousin from running away with an older married man about a year earlier. The confrontation with his cousin and her family included a motorcycle chase, a public spectacle, and a shouting match. A few days after the events, Siddharth Singh began to feel breathless. He was sure that his spirit-medium uncle or his frustrated cousin had taken vengeful tantric action against his life-breath. Harmful words and emotions might float silently on a smiling uncle's breath or the sigh of a seemingly love-lorn cousin. Tantric invocations, I would soon learn, traveled on breath to imbue environments and others with the blower's power or pain.

Most accounts of tantra in South Asia focus on classical and more documented tantra with its links to sexuality, goddess worship, and rituals of inversion. Those familiar with this more mainstream and textual version of tantra might find its iteration in Ambawati closer to magic than tantra. Nonetheless, Ambawati's tantra is replete with the inversions of Brahmanical Hinduism that typify tantra. The practitioners I know inverted the Brahmanical hours of worship and even images of deities. During worship they removed their turbans, occasionally prostrated themselves feet first, and tended to venerate the goddess Kali and her attendant deity Bhairav. In Ambawati, as elsewhere, tantra is, as Hugh Urban suggests, "a shifting amalgam of fantasies, fears, and wish fulfillment" that aims to make sense of a staggeringly unpredictable world and affect it.[40] In other words, it is an incredibly informative lens on power in social life. It is also entangled with life-breath.

Though tantra in Ambawati is desexualized, its shifting amalgam has similarities to global and pan-Indian tantra that emerge in its treatment of life-breath, or *praan*, rather than semen or other bodily secretions, as the source of substantial cosmic power.[41] Breathy liveliness is central to tantra in Ambawati. Most people even refer to tantric practitioners as blowers, or those who hit with a blow (*phunk marnewale*). Many who talked of tantrics even pantomimed the tantric practice of blowing a burst of air through a tube-shaped hand to make an onomatopoeic *phunk* sound. I did not think much of these terms or gestures until Takhat Singh, Ambawati's foremost tantric, taught me the basics. I knew his sons, a science teacher and nurse, well, so when I asked about tantra, he invited me to come learn. He insisted that I visit his house, in the last hamlet before the forest, early in the morning after bathing and before eating breakfast. Though that required a nearly forty-minute walk on an empty stomach, I complied.

Takhat Singh taught me various tantric invocations, but he explained that I could not do "the work" until I completed the correct rituals and stopped eating meat. He also insisted that he could not teach me anything malevolent because he did not know those practices.[42] I was eager to learn a few basic and protective invocations even through my ritually unprepared body and breath could never do things with tantric words. Takhat Singh asked me to write the incantations in my notebook. I dutifully transcribed complicated rhyming couplets filled with curse words and sonic inversions that made little sense but could protect people from ghostly spirits, stop fire from starting, and dispel the evil eye, among other things.

During our third session, Takhat Singh explained how to move incantations into the world: "The words are as important as being able to move them by blowing. First learn this and practice it [the verse] and then say it. Say it in your mouth and give a blow and then the person will be well." "So, you just give the respiration-breath?" I asked. He responded, "Just say it face-to-face, right in front like we are sitting. But do not let them hear you say it. Say it like this, in your mouth, and then give a blow. The problem will go away." "It works when the respiration-breath goes out?" I asked again. "Yes, as the respiration-breath goes, it goes, and the person gets better. Say it, say it in your mouth and when it is finished, last, [at] the end, give a blow like this" He cupped his hand into a tube and blew out sharply to make a *phunk* sound and continued, "Just as you give it a blow the problem will go away." The words, it seems, had power but without breath blowing them out they could not enter or affect the world. They needed both soul-filled breath and human body. "Even the gods' influences and all?" I stammered. Takhat Singh replied calmly,

If you come into someone's clutches, who knows, something, someone, whatever can happen, some black magic. If someone casts a spell, then take a string and make a knotted bracelet. Put it in your hand and then say the tantra, say it three times in your mouth and blow it on the person and then say it in your mouth three more times and blow it. Then tie more knots and tie it on the sick person and it will heal. Tantras move when you blow the respiration-breath the words made.

Words and a tantric practitioner's disciplined body were at the intersection of breath as respiration-breath in *sans* and life-breath in *praan*. By moving on breath, the "magic words" became affixed to others who neither uttered nor heard them. "Until you blow, the patient will not get better," he said. Breath, it seemed, could move far more than just bacteria, and I began to feel that the strict demarcation of breathlessness caused blurring. Troubled life-breath can and did ricochet through respiration-breath and strength-breath and vice versa. Words too could take on life in breath.

Takhat Singh's words of intercession and reproach moved on his breath. They could alter the atmosphere of a place and the *praan*, or life-breath, of another, even a deity. Because Takhat Singh had training, his life-breath, his respiration-breaths, and the words on them, I learned, could invite or even oblige a deity or spirit to do what he asked.[43] He taught me that deities when entreated and goaded by the words emitted from a ritually pre-pared body have no option but to comply. "Tantra," he explained, "works ahead of gods [bhagwan u aage sale]." Life-breath with all its power was somehow accessible through ritual and cosmological preparation of entan-gled body, its other two breaths, and language.

Indeed, the family integrated Suresh and his problem of "another, bigger illness" into their worry that breathy tantra had been used to pro-voke a deity to afflict Siddharth Singh's life-breath all along. Tantrically troubled life-breath could gesture toward the dispute, its familial moral action, and disruption of family relations. To manage cosmic disorder that might extend into breath, Narayan Singh visited their family god, Bhairav.[44] Bhairav disavowed any connection to Siddharth Singh's breath-lessness. Narayan Singh found this very suspicious and visited several other gods and goddesses. They too claimed no knowledge of what the problem (*chakkar*) might be. However, deities, like humans, may have rea-sons for deception, so Narayan Singh consulted others. After our con-versation with Suresh, he got on his bike again and headed to the shrine of Nathubaoji. Nathubaoji is one of rural Rajasthan's hero deities and a hyperlocal cosmological power.[45] An ancestor who lived spatially near but temporally far from the family, Nathubaoji was a Rawat man of the 1800s. He was caught and killed by a group of landlords after stealing what some said were his own cattle.[46]

After several visits to Nathubaoji's shrine and conversations with the ancestor-deity through the medium, Narayan Singh was able to convince Nathubaoji to take up the case. Nathubaoji's role in Siddharth's collective breathing was as cosmological investigator to find out what had been troubling Siddharth Singh's life-breath. In return, Narayan Singh visited the shrine each Tuesday for weeks. His oscillations between home and shrine enacted even more breathy relations. Eventually, Nathubaoji revealed that Siddharth Singh and Narayan Singh had in fact been afflicted by their family lineage's deity, Bhairav. The very one who had insisted that he didn't know anything about Siddharth Singh's sickness or his life-breath. Bhairav, Nathubaoji said, was irked by Siddharth Singh rather than Narayan Singh becoming the family's chief devotee and had been troubling him.[47] Bhairav asserted that the generational order of things had been disturbed when Siddharth Singh's devotion surpassed the father's. Hearing of Bhairav's duplicity, Narayan Singh suspected that his brother had indeed used tantra to coerce the deity into harming Siddharth Singh. After all, the offended brother had also complained that Siddharth Singh's role in the family conflict had usurped his father as the head of the family.

Disordered life-breath, whether caused by genuine godly anger or goaded by tantra, reveals a complex set of lines connecting bodies, breaths, actions, and cosmologies. Though Nathubaoji could diagnose the source of breathlessness and open a negotiation with Bhairav, the family had to resolve its conflict with the lineage deity who was tugging (*kheenchna*) on Siddharth Singh's life-breath itself. Narayan Singh began to frequent Bhairav's and Nathubaoji's shrines, taking vows to become a chief devotee at both.

For months after Nathubaoji agreed to help Siddharth Singh, Narayan Singh visited Suresh's clinic to pick up his son's pharmaceuticals and the shrines to pray. Siddharth Singh's breathlessness could be caused by microbes *and* tantra and managed by medical *and* cosmological action.[48] Meanwhile, the family, Suresh, and I waited for the effects of the two entangled interventions. By November, Siddharth Singh was moving around a little on the farm and bathing himself. No one quite knew what to make of what was, regardless of cause or treatment, a return from the precipice of death.

As we began to talk about his sickness in the past tense, Siddharth Singh stopped looking furtively across the thicket fence toward his uncle's house as he spoke. He felt more protected from the external, possibly tantric, life-breath-affecting respiration-breaths that might be coming from that direction toward his own breath. His breathing, though still unsteady, was improving, and he began to talk again of the future in small ways. He even convinced Mangilal, the neighbor, to take him on the back of his newly repaired motorcycle to Nathubaoji's shrine. Though it would take another year for Siddharth Singh to get back to work and regain his strength, the worry about death had passed. The moral status of Siddharth Singh's life-breath and relations seemed to have returned to a state in which his breath felt his own again. Potential cosmological repercussions of his brief failure to be a deferential son and nephew had been managed. His life-breath, even if it did go to a new body at death, would not carry the negative effects of a disordered family life. His TB infection too seemed to have been cured.

BREATH CONTROL

Breath, this chapter shows, is cultural through and through. From first breath to last, breath is shaped by care, relations, and bodily attunement. It is entangled with the social practice of life with others and categories. The family's practices of social breathing, as the three diverse ways of talking about breath show, entangled each breath and breathy affliction with situated social forms like kinship, community, and labor. In this way social breathing collects and separates people, but it does so unevenly. The three unique but interconnected breaths that helped the family make sense of Siddharth Singh's breathlessness reveal that breath and its meanings shape what is at stake in a TB infection. With each of the three breaths came different ideas and actions related to breathlessness's cause and what care or relief might be. Through them, inequality, practice, and meaning enculturate breath and frame each of respiration's incessant iterations anew.

Siddharth Singh and his family, like breath itself, subvert easy narratives of control. Though Siddharth Singh did often feel alone, he talked about and worked on these feelings by addressing the troubled and tense relationships evidenced by problematic relational breath itself. TB's biopolitics of quarantine, control, observation, and isolation were replaced by practices that *rolate* breath through relations of care. The family welcomed hundreds of guests during Siddharth Singh's year of sickness, when biomedicine would have urged him and his family to control the spread of infection by turning inward. "We went through fifteen kilos of sugar making tea when I was sick," Siddharth Singh told me in the months after he'd begun to gain weight. Given that each of the family's teacups holds only about three tablespoons of the often heavily sweetened tea, fifteen kilograms of sugar represents a massive number of guests who came to offer healing, comradery, or simply their presence. Rather than limiting breath's connections TB care expanded them. Other forms of social breathing reveal themselves as at stake in practices that seem imprudent or dangerous to a biomedical gaze.

Breath made connections—similar to the powerful ephemeral connections of meaning, choreography, and space that Carla Bellamy documented in a healing shrine about two hundred kilometers from Ambawati—and locations into meaningful indicators of coexistence and ethical being. Tuberculosis's troubled breath revealed intimacies of kinship as breath lines of help and risk. One uncle searched for honey. Another uncle muttered curses under his breath. Aunt Shantibai brought heat-bearing massage oil to kick-start *rolation*. Mangilal, the neighbor, drove the motorcycle. Even the deity Nathubaoji was cajoled into providing care by invoking shared kinship and landscape. Breath's lines made shared interest, emotions, and fates possible, just as they could be experienced by an individual whose liveliness and agency was not necessarily limited to a material body.

Breath allows for contagiousness and care beyond touch.[49] It blurs lines between individuals and collectivities while organizing a whole set of categories and relations that contain an atmospheric logic different from that of the biosciences.[50] Biomedicine has its own *bios* and morality of breath. Though no longer a clear scientific index of liveliness, as Margaret Lock and Elizabeth Povinelli have separately shown, respiration is a necessary and riskily ephemeral part of life.[51] In biomedicine's optical logic breath must be made material or visible to the eye or technological apparatus. Breath's invisibility and intangibility renders it foreign in biomedical logics even when it is inside the metabolizing body. Still, it indicates life.

Breath and its connections in biomedicine are too often sources of death and danger to be disciplined rather than lived. Even TB bacteria are assumed to be more lively than breath. Biomedicine's ideas and practices related to TB, its attention to disease and patient control, and its work to contain and prevent spread through treatment make Siddharth Singh's biological breath a source of risk in a global biopolitics centered on its control. Biomedicine's attempts to isolate breath inside and contain breath outside bodies imagine a suffering self as singular and contained within a body. Thus, TB becomes an individual problem of productivity, responsibility, and isolation that can be solved through pharmaceuticals, health security politics, and quarantine rather than one of relation, climate, labor, and possibilities to be dealt with socially or, to use Siddharth Singh's word, *rolationally*.

That biomedicine's biologic of breath makes it a simple connection or vector in which body and world touch each other leads to imagining breath as one of the few ways a skin-encapsulated body can be exposed to the world and vice versa. To control breath and the bacteria that float on it is also a way to control bodies and disease. Control of breath, as evidenced by pharmaceutical treatment, sputum-based TB diagnostics, and a single-minded focus on contagious individuals rather than contagious spaces, makes for care practices that evidence very little care. These practices are a biopolitics of knowing, ordering, and controlling individuals who are devoid of the relations that caused their illness in the first place. They were, however, not the only ways of knowing, ordering, and engaging individuals in practices of social breathing.

Only in the breathless biomedical system was Siddharth Singh separated out from his context and the communion of breathing others in which he lived to make *him*, rather than the weather, the cosmos, or his clan, a source of risk. Where biomedicine saw contagion, Siddharth Singh and his family, in contrast, saw the give and take of community. With so many visitors, it's likely that the bacteria did spread, but Siddharth Singh and his family shared the work and world of breath in a way that moved bacteria and care through relations. Following three breath forms we can unfurl a whole mosaic of meanings that give TB a particularly atmospheric biological form and embodied experience in Ambawati. They reveal that despite Tim Choy's evocation of Marx and call for breathers of the world to unite, some unions and practices of social breathing are more likely than others in a world of caste, class, and unequal access to pulmonary care.[52] Some people and networks can hold their breath longer than others, whereas others cannot and will not hold out for a future of individualized breath. Breath, as Memi shows, makes difference and similitude, danger and life. It was this moral and medical danger that seemed to permeate conversation about dust.

THREE

DUST

> I am a suspect in America, but I will end up being a dust speck out in
> Mother universe. Just a dust speck. Just a dust speck moving around, and
> around, and around universally. . . . We all just end up being a dust speck
> after working and building and creating parts of humanity while being a
> suspect.
>
> —Lonnie Holley, "I'm a Suspect"

> *Chalega hathi. Uregi dhool. Na rahega panja, na rahega phool!* (The elephant
> will run. Dust will fly. The hand and the flower will not remain!).
>
> —2017 Bahujan Samaj Party election slogan

KALIBAI RAWAT VISITS THE Ambawati primary health clinic just
after sunrise each morning.[1] She silently greets nurse Suresh—who is often
puttering around his room behind the clinic—and rattles the clinic's back
door. The metal door usually swings open, but occasionally Suresh must
search for its key and remove the lock. Once inside, Kalibai opens the
shutters, retrieves the palm broom she made for the task, and sweeps the
clinic's three rooms and atrium. In the consultation room, where Suresh
spends most of the day seeing patients, Kalibai's broom picks up a scrap of
paper or empty medicine packet and a large pile of dust. She deposits the
pile in the clinic's atrium before sweeping the birthing room and empty
storeroom. Because these rooms are unused, Kalibai returns with dust but
little detritus. She combines it with the heap in the atrium before sweeping
the whole pile off the back veranda and heading homeward. After Kalibai
has left, Suresh sweeps his own room, takes a bath, and opens the clinic to

patients. Because dust is a constant interloper, Kalibai will return the next day to sweep away the clinic's freshly accumulated layer.

Dust is ubiquitous in Ambawati, and women like Kalibai sweep nearly all inhabited spaces daily. The clinic, however, is particularly dusty. It sits on a windswept scrap of uncultivated land where the village's asphalt road crosses a dirt throughfare. Bus, motorcycle, tractor, and bullock cart traffic at this intersection of soil and tar kicks up plumes of tawny dust. Once airborne, the dust makes its way through the clinic's glassless windows. Inside, particles float in the air and catch the light before accumulating in a fine layer on the floor, desk, windowsills, and shelves of papers and pharmaceuticals. Dust builds up on the boxes and surfaces that Kalibai does not sweep, mixing occasionally with spider webs. In 2012 seven of the boxes held TB medication, and each revealed the name of a patient scrawled on it. These are patientwise boxes. Each contained pharmaceuticals for a single patient to whom Suresh distributed TB medicines one dose at a time as part of TB's directly observed therapy, short-course (DOTS). Four were covered with dust. The patients associated with them had left treatment. They had been unable to submit to the fifty-four clinic visits that observed therapy requires. Three boxes had no dust. Their patients visited the clinic regularly to consume their pharmaceutical contents.

Ambawati's dusty clinic, the TB treatment that takes place in it, and the dusty boxes reveal tensions in the practice of TB care, and health care more broadly, in India. The dust accumulating on boxes might materialize the metaphorical dust of colonial forms of control that settle on the clinic. It resonates with the African American sculptor and performing artist Lonnie Holley's self-identification as simultaneously a dust speck in a larger universe and a suspect in the racially divided US South that opens this chapter. Dust and suspicion incessantly enter through the cracks and open windows despite the state's pastoral goal of using development, e-governance, and rationalization to sweep these forms of control out once and for all.[2]

Colonial-era strategies of managing life on the subcontinent, by the British government and Indian princes, were based on an uneasy anxiety about a resistant populace that might best be governed through techniques of counterinsurgency and discipline.[3] Counterinsurgency techniques, such

as settlement, surveillance, and extraction persist within DOTS. Along
with them exists a prose of counterinsurgency that interprets every action
by the sick poor as either resistant or irrational medical citizenship. Despite
DOTS's humanitarian and pastoral goals, people and bacteria subjected to
it are covered in the dust of colonial-era counterinsurgency measures. It
settles on contemporary clinics as the entanglement of care and surveillance for those in TB treatment. They make dust an apt material metaphor
for the effects of colonial projects on contemporary life with TB.[4]

Sensed but seen only after they settle, affective connections to colonial
infrastructures of control and subjectivity pervade even the new. The layers
of dust in the clinic, despite its being built in 2004 and renovated in 2010,
accentuate its desolate atmosphere. Far from inhabited parts of Ambawati
and poorly painted, the clinic has an atmosphere of abandonment similar
to what Ann Stoler and Fanny Chabrol both call "ruination."[5] Theories
of postcolonial ruination suggest that the structures of physical and epistemic domination central to colonial control persist within contemporary
forms of life and politics. Everyday events unfold or are built in the dust
of colonial practices, the remainders of which "reside in the corroded hol-
lows of landscapes, in the gutted infrastructures of segregated cityscapes,
and in the microecologies of matter and mind."[6] Ruins and residue enter
the twenty-first century as dysfunctional systems of faltering or oppressive
state care and a biopolitics that "impinge[s] on the allocation of space and
resources and on what is available for material life."[7] In other words, the
past settles on present infrastructures and breathed atmospheres as dust.

Extending Stoler's analysis, Chabrol suggests that ruination abides in
the oppressive residues of health's physical, epistemological, and political infrastructures inherited by the postcolonial state. They continue in
the contemporary, with only some repurposing, to shape life and medicine. Chabrol argues that, by allowing a health system to be in or go to
ruins, the postcolonial state has left the politics of life to private sectors,
philanthrocapitalists, and nongovernmental organizations that reiterate
colonialism's logics of health care as a tool for extraction.[8] However, ruins
as metaphors, with their emphasis on historical action and contemporary
inheritance, cannot account for failed, botched, or halfhearted attempts
of contemporary governments to build new primary care systems like

Ambawati's clinic or the DOTS program itself. New construction can veil ruination, but dust, in its persistence, brings the unsettling effects of history into even the newest of spaces and projects. Though the bricks and mortar of these new health infrastructures are (usually) sound, they are covered with residues of colonial pasts, extractive capitalism, and global inequalities of race that shape the clinic and TB itself.[9] Dust provides a material and metaphor, a "microecolog[y] of matter and mind" in Stoler's words, indicator of the colonial and coercive biopolitics within contemporary health and atmospheres.

Dust moves within or merges the categories of solid and air, culture and nature, and cause and effect that were central to the colonial project in the first place.[10] It is a product of categories that separate human space from nature, but it is more than just a cultural misfit.[11] Dust is part of an irritating world that pesters the eyes and nose, causes coughs, and makes breath unpleasant. Prolonged exposure to dust has even been shown to increase risk of TB among diamond cutters and stone mine workers by creating abrasions in the lungs.[12]

Margaret Trawick writes of such remainders in South Asia: "Remainders are reminders. Reminders of what? Of the unwholeness, the incompleteness of existence. No matter how much you try to sweep up, there is always some bit of dirt in a corner somewhere. Nothing can ever be perfect. Nothing is ever totally finished, past or forgotten."[13] Indeed, Kalibai's sweeping of the clinic eliminates some of the dusty soil that has settled on the floor, but it whips some back up into the air too.[14] Dust highlights how attempts to ameliorate the effects of earlier actions stir up these very effects, reorganizing and redistributing them before allowing them to settle back on ordinary life and the future.[15] Everyday care for TB in Ambawati's clinic is no exception. Colonial forms of governance such as surveillance, bureaucratization, census taking, localization, and controlled comportment pervade practices of TB treatment in the clinic, turning patients into unruly objects of control.[16] Like motes revealing currents of air, dust provides a way of talking about atmospheres and breath that links bodies and bacteria to the past, to colonial forces, and to politics.[17]

Built at the turn of the twenty-first century, Ambawati's postcolonial health center is not ruined, but it is dusty. This chapter follows two of the clinic's nurses and three patients, Kesarlal, Ramba, and Moti Singh, as all five are disciplined by TB treatment in the clinic. It traces the residual-filled atmospheres that extend TB biopolitics far beyond its walls. From there, it spends some time among the dusty shelves of TB medicines, active and expired. Finally, it points to the key role that dust played in keeping cutting-edge diagnostic technology out of the Ambawati clinic. In short, the chapter attends to the material and metaphorical dust that settles in Ambawati to consider how atmospheres link particular lives to the unanticipated and perhaps unimagined effect of biomedicine's entanglement of bacterial and human life with a politics of resistance and counterinsurgency.

RESISTANT LIFE AND COUNTERINSURGENCY

Drug resistance, like dust, is a residue of action. It has accompanied pharmaceutical treatment for TB from its very beginning in the 1940s, and etched resistance—a biological metaphor drawn from political life—into the bacteria's DNA and scientific discourse surrounding it. Mere months after clinicians in the United Kingdom used the first antibiotics to treat TB in 1947, some TB bacilli seemed to survive pharmaceutical exposure.[18] Physician-researchers worried that the slow or absent response by a few bacteria to the drug, which seemed incredibly good at killing them just months earlier, was evidence that they had evolved to resist the pharmaceuticals. Thus, even from the first months of treatment, TB science was inseparable from a pharmacological and bacteriological conversation about residues and remainders as resistance.

That narratives of *Mycobacterium tuberculosis*'s liveliness and treatment should be entangled with displacements and anxieties around resistance is at least partially related to the materiality of antibiotics and TB bacilli.[19] Most of the mid-twentieth-century's newly discovered antibiotics worked by stopping bacterial reproduction, but slow-growing mycobacteria like TB are not susceptible to these drugs. TB evades pharmaceutical prophylactics by simply reproducing too slowly and living too long to be affected. In response, physicians must use more toxic antibiotics that kill the bacteria directly. These drugs, however, take time and do not stop bacterial reproduction. Using them intermittently or stopping before all the bacteria are dead puts a positive selective pressure on the bacteria that remain. This is how antibiotic resistance happens. Bacilli less susceptible to antibiotic intervention not only survive some exposure to drugs but multiply when the drug is not present in the body, passing the capability to neighbors and the next generation.[20] Even if treatment resumes, it will affect only the susceptible bacteria, and the resistant ones will survive to become the dominant strain affecting the patient because they replaced the once susceptible bacilli. In this bacterial evolution, early clinicians saw the capacity to resist technoscience and its machinations.

Bacterial evolution does not necessarily lead to political resistance. Instead, a series of what Lyle Fearnley, following Bruno Latour, has called scientific displacements,[21] allowed TB science and public health to quickly naturalize resistance by imputing to bacteria an inherent and evolutionary capacity for actions once described as political.[22] Displacements are metaphors that scientists use to make sense of their objects, and resistance is an exceedingly powerful metaphor. Today it oscillates dynamically between describing political and bacterial life, to organize bacteriology and public health around preventing resistance and managing bacterial and biopolitical counterinsurgency. The result is a biopolitics authorized by a view of bacterial life as potentially resistant. This biopolitics interprets a deviation from standardized biomedical protocols by patients or caregivers as social resistance that will *lead* to bacterial resistance. It frames how all TB is treated.

TB thus represents an existential threat to the person infected by it and to pharmaceuticals in general. To subvert bacterial resistance and prevent the bacterial dystopia imagined by clinicians and technocrats, TB treatments combine multiple antibiotics and continue for many months after the patient feels better. Despite this, resistance continues. Today, pharmaceuticals, TB mycobacteria, medicine, and metaphors of governance have dialogically shaped each other to create the biologies and biopolitics of TB mycobacteria, its disease experience, and its treatment by biomedicine, but it carries the residue of decisions made in the 1980s.

When the new drug rifampicin became widely available in the 1980s, Paris-based epidemiologist-clinician Karel Styblo decided that the drug had to be combined with auxiliary drugs and a draconian surveillance measures to ensure that patients took the prescribed course.[23] Styblo insisted that patients could not be trusted to take their medicine.[24] Therefore, whereas in the past patients had been sent home with a month of medicine, Styblo's new program required a health care worker be custodian of the medicines and for patients to visit that health care worker every other day to be observed taking the medicine. In a pilot project in Tanzania, Styblo showed that the drug and surveillance program was 90 percent successful. It was cheap too. Soon the World Bank began to support this combination of pharmaceuticals and patient surveillance as a cost-effective TB treatment for the poor.[25] DOTS for TB was born. In the 1990s, the program of treatment and control went global, and after successful pilots in Malawi and China, it arrived in India as part of a major World Bank loan in 1993.[26] The program's Indian iteration, the Revised National TB Control Program (now called the National Tuberculosis Elimination Program), uses protocols developed in Europe and East Africa to surveil and care for patients in thousands of dusty clinics like Suresh's.[27] By 2001 DOTS had reached a clinic near Ambawati, and in 2006 Ambawati's first patient received DOTS from a preschool attendant.

On a visit to Delhi, I met Dr. Kapoor, one of the physicians who helped bring the program to India. He explained that safeguarding medicines in clinics rather than in people's homes was a central part of TB care. He told me that "the health system has taken responsibility for that patient—his success and his failure—because they are custodians of the medicine." He went on to explain that, in those early years, organizers had hoped that by locating services in clinics and insisting people visit daily, the TB program would not only prevent resistance but "help get people in the habit of going to services instead of having services come to them, and it would help people to have more of a relationship to the village sister [nurse], so they would trust her if they had another need." The project thus had multiple aims, not only to combat TB but to train a certain kind of biomedical subject. It was also covered in the colonial dust of a politics oriented around surveilling unruly, unpredictable peasants as a counterinsurgency tactic. In this case, the insurgent to be known and disciplined was no longer an anticolonial subaltern or unruly peasant; it was resistant bacteria and a nonadherent patient. Even those individuals whom doctors thought might have TB but were undiagnosed were, until the mid-2010s, labeled with the designation "suspect," and this kind of language pervaded conversations about TB care for decades.[28]

Though located in the same community as its recipient, a TB medicine box is never to leave the custodianship of the village nurse or some other figure of biomedical authority.[29] It is a tether, just as Styblo intended. In the vast majority of cases throughout India, these boxes remain in health centers like Suresh's, but occasionally patients receive their medicines via another government institution like a crèche, school, or townhall. Agents of the state must monitor the patient taking medicines and take action to find him or her in case of a missed dose.[30] The custodian provides the patient with her medicines every other day, blister pack by blister pack. To take medicines to a patient's home or to entrust the entire box to a family is for Suresh and his colleagues nearly unthinkable. Dr. Kapoor, and perhaps Suresh as well, is convinced that without observation patients will confuse or avoid the many months of toxic medicines, allowing their bacteria to develop resistance. Surveillance is key to pharmaceutical success and futurity, but it requires patients to stay put and submit to observation. It was neither the patients' nor Suresh's decision, but the dust of this policy, with its tactics of counterinsurgency, had settled heavily on their lives.

India's TB-control program relies on the clinic, its people, and its infrastructure to take a pastoral role in illness and life. The clinic must treat and train, cure and cultivate a citizen at the same time. Like other pastoral biopolitics, the TB-control program's framers and practices are concerned with shaping patients as willing subjects of biomedicine who go to some lengths to access and steward antibiotics and as citizens who access state resources as a path to economic and social development. Like the dust that interloped in the clinic, these biopolitics of TB coat both Suresh and his patients in a politics of care and control centered on the potential for biological and social resistance.[31] Both nurse and patient were simultaneously enacting biopolitics and being disciplined by it. Suresh's insistence that patients visit him regardless of their ability is an example. So are informal requirements like the one that required that Kesarlal stay in one place for the entirety of treatment and a generalized belief that if patients leave treatment, it cannot be restarted. Behind each of these practices lies a dialogical displacement of political and biotic resistance that make TB governance a counterinsurgency politics of control, custodianship, and surveillance.

The TB program's use of surveillance to stabilize and root mobile forms of life that power deems risky is not new. It has a strong resemblance to the colonial mechanisms through which Britain controlled groups of Indians who subverted state power over social and economic life. The state called such groups criminal tribes. After the suppressed Indian revolution of 1846, the British colonial government used legislation called the Criminal Tribes Act to surveil and stabilize mobile Rajasthanis and other potentially insurgent Indians, who the government believed to be constitutionally and collectively deviant.[32] In south Rajasthan, the Rawats' Bhil-Meena ancestors, Lambana salt traders, traveling storytellers, and others whose lives and economic practices seemed insurgent, antisocial, or illegible to colonial bureaucrats were criminalized, if not always officially, through associations with vagrancy and theft.[33] This social politics used police surveillance, residential schools, and forced localization to bring groups declared constitutionally unruly or backward into line with more governable collectives and economic forms. The postindependence state continued these practices through graduated categories of citizenship, Adivasi residential schools in southeastern Rajasthan, and government schemes aimed at knowing the population through categories.[34] Thus, the TB program's insistence on localizing patients and surveilling them occurs in the dust of these counterinsurgency laws, and it conflates insurgent bacteria and insurgent subjects.[35] It also kicks up a dust of colonial counterinsurgency that resettles in present and future lungs.

In Ambawati the biopolitics of TB echoed centuries-old attempts by the powerful to keep people in place rather than allow them to move. When TB treatment conflicted with their lives as they needed to live them, then, they discontinued treatment. Daulat Singh, for example, left treatment at the clinic twice when he needed to mediate a dispute between his sons in Kerala. Others found that the clinic hours overlapped with their daily visits to the forest for work and grazing. Indeed, the rules that required that patients attend the clinic and remain in place meant that TB services in Ambawati often remained unused. Thus, dust settled on the boxes of medicines that people refused to collect. Inspired by clinical language, Angela Garcia suggests that this refusal and an inability to engage in bio-politics is a form of "self-discharge," in which the person might be seeking "release and reproof" from institutions and technologies of the self connected to biomedicine rather than the medicine itself.[36] In Ambawati many sought such reproof and refused to live with the dust of the past. They discharged themselves of care's counterinsurgency biopolitics even if that meant sickness and death. Others, however, begrudgingly crafted a legible self.

MAKING KESARLAL LOCAL

Kesarlal Meghwal's presence in the village revealed his illness. He had returned for treatment after several years working at a gas station about three hours' travel west. Ambawati was his home, but Kesarlal was not particularly happy to be back. He was not here seeking familial comfort and care.[37] Instead he had been required to return to his official address after being diagnosed with TB and enrolled in the public TB treatment program. To continue free treatment, he needed to go where his medicines were and where he could be observed by the public health system.

It was all the result of a misunderstanding, Kesarlal told me. He had been diagnosed in the district hospital when, after coughing and losing weight, his boss at the gas station insisted that he go in for a checkup. Because Kesarlal listed Ambawati as his home address, his box of medicines arrived here. He told me later that he did not think to use the gas station's address because his family was not supposed to be living in the station's small office. Consequently, for the six months of treatment, he, along with his wife and four-year-old son, would need to live in the single-room house they had built in Ambawati. The doctor told him nothing could be done.[38] This meant not only that the family needed to move their things back home and sweep the months of dust and mice out of their four-square-meter house; but also that Kesarlal, now jobless, could not repay the money he had borrowed from brothers and cousins to build it. His wife, Dalidevi, worked as a day laborer in neighbors' fields, but money was tighter than it usually was. The creditors realized that they could not recuperate their money from a sick family member, but they groused whenever Kesarlal

came home with a treat for his son or some other item they found too lux-
urious. Kesarlal tried to make the best of things, but he was frustrated and
spoke of how Ambawati's dust had covered his dreams.

Kesarlal, like many others, often wondered aloud how I survived the
village's dust, or *dhul-mitti*: "Here there is dust in everything. How do you
manage? No matter what you do, dust just keeps coming in. I do not know
where it all comes from, getting dust in the development." I took "getting
dust in the development" to mean that dust stopped the smooth advance
of development or that even those things that were developed, like his
cement home, were constantly interfered with by material and metaphorical remainders of the past.

Ambawati is often dusty but is no dustier than nearby towns and
certainly less so than a highway gas station. Dust in Kesarlal's comment
signified something more than a fine layer of grit on his home's floor. It
was a microecology of mind and matter that indicated the inconvenient
ubiquity of failed development projects in the area. For Kesarlal, dust in
Ambawati, just as in the clinic, was about Indian modernity's unintended,
downwind effects in the hinterland. Dust explained why his life had not
gone as planned. "I am stuck here in the dust," he said often as he watched
others drive by on motorcycles, a luxury he could no longer hope for, or
when his neighbor's flour mill sent white powder up through the shin-
gles to settle on the surrounding houses. These were tools of progress and
accumulation once aspired to, but now they were simply sources of the
unrelenting dust.[39]

Writing about rural vulnerability in Karnataka, Esha Shah suggests
that invocations of dust are "metaphors replete in the expression of rural
alienation" and that refusals of dust "could even be interpreted as an act of
seeking dignity and self-worth."[40] In Kesarlal's life, dust provided a language to talk about the effects of other ways of organizing life through
ontologies that created barriers between him and the future he aspired to.
It was a metonym of the rural abjection that authorized the foreclosures of
aspiration that surveillance and settlement required of him. It also represented the unintended effects of action taken elsewhere, like the decision
to build the clinic on a dusty outcrop or to insist on sending TB medicines to Ambawati rather than a clinic near the gas station or to Kesarlal

himself. Ambawati had been left in the dust as these decisions were made. So had Kesarlal.

When his health improved enough to work, Kesarlal tried to move back to the gas station. He soon learned that if he returned to his job, he could not take the box of medicines with him. It was not lost on Kesarlal that he was tethered to the clinic by his treatment and the assumptions of fixity that its designers had inscribed within it.[41] He and his medicines were, after all, under the custodianship of the Ambawati clinic. In our many conversations, he often repeated that he knew he needed to take the medicines for six months, and that he intended to take every last one, but that visiting the clinic regularly was burdensome. He also knew that if a health bureaucrat came to survey the clinic and his box was missing, Suresh would surely lose his job. One day Kesarlal mused, "It's a real service the government is doing for us, giving us free medicines like mine. They have saved my life, but because of the rule that I must go to the clinic here, I have had to sit in the dust and wait for the whole course to be completed, even though I have a job waiting for me [at the gas station]." Indeed, the need to attend the clinic every day had stifled Kesarlal's hopes for nonagricultural work and for bettering the lives of his family. The gas station job and its steady income had underwritten the house in which he now lived, as well as providing money to send his son to school. It was a way to move toward the periurban life that Kesarlal and his wife aspired to. Now, the family bank account was empty, and their dreams were collecting the dust kicked up by the progress of others. Treatment for TB, a disease of poverty, had driven him and his family even further into destitution in a bid to prevent antibiotic resistance.

Akhil Gupta has written of governance in rural India as a fickle, just-in-time bureaucratic apparatus that often works through an uneasy and unpredictable tension between threat of abandonment (or denial of service due to a failure of legible citizenship) and largesse in the form of arbitrary exception to rules and systems.[42] Kesarlal's experience of TB's postcolonial biopolitics is an example of this tension. To access care, he had to make himself legible by staying in Ambawati, his permanent address and ancestral village. Failure to do so risked the removal of state pharmaceuticals necessary to treat his TB, even if this was not allowed in policy.

He was convinced that he could move to the city to work, but he would need to leave treatment or make the six-hour round-trip journey to get his medicines several times a week. No policy said that he must stay home or leave employment to access the clinic, but poor transportation infrastructure and communication within the health system meant that he had no choice. Similarly, his experience with other facets of the state had made him worry that his medicines would be withheld, or Suresh punished, if he did not follow the protocol diligently. Rendered suspect by TB's biopolitics of resistance, Kesarlal's role in supporting his family and his hopes for a better life were left to gather dust.

Like many of the rules governing the Indian health care system, these policies had been made by others somewhere else, in this case in Delhi, and on the basis of antimicrobial-resistance-prevention strategies developed by the International Union Against TB and Lung Disease far away in Tanzania and Malawi.[43] Though new, the program was coated with the dust of imperialist concerns about unruly, resistant, mobile Indian peasants, backward subjects who imperiled everyone by refusing to abide by treatment.[44] This was not Kesarlal, who for his part, simply wanted the mobility and potential for wealth that he felt twenty-first-century life promised him.

RAMBA'S HABIT

Each Thursday after his midmorning meal, my septuagenarian neighbor Ramba Meghwal retrieved the empty blister packet he kept wedged between a clay tile and the teak rafter of his small house, put on his white plastic shoes, and hiked up his dhoti before cycling down the dirt road to the clinic. There, he would sit on one of the consultation room's plastic chairs or crouch on his haunches in its door frame chatting with others until his turn came. With little room for privacy in the clinic, those waiting often did so around the person engaging in consultation.

When Ramba's turn came, he sent an empty medicine packet spinning across Suresh's desk with some triumph. Suresh caught it and returned it to the large white box of tuberculosis medicines marked in Devanagari "Ramlalji Meghwal, Ambawati Jageer." He pulled a new packet containing a week's worth of medicines from the box and, if time permitted, put a check mark on the pink paper that recorded each dose of Ramba's six months of treatment. Medicine collected and chat complete, Ramba stowed the medicine in a used soybean seed bag he carried with him. Then he visited the Ambawati bus stand to run weekly errands or chat with friends before returning home to graze his goat and pull weeds from the small field he shared with his wife, widowed daughter-in-law, and granddaughter.

Arranging his life around collecting medicines and submitting to treatment surveillance was the cost of accessing the government's free medicine, but it was not always easy. The first two months of his six-month TB treatment required Ramba go to the clinic for medicines every other day. During these early months, Bhanwaribai, his wife, made the two-kilometer walk to the clinic because Ramba could not. DOTS rules required that he consume the medicines in front of the nurse, but this rule is often broken. Instead, people visit the clinic to collect the medicines and take them at home with food and water.[45] In Ramba's case this exception was particularly necessary because he was to weak to reach the clinic. Soon, with treatment, his health improved. He began to go to the clinic more often and eventually felt strong enough to take his old bicycle. Eventually, he took charge of the trips altogether. He could cycle to the clinic while Bhanwaribai walked.

From the third month of treatment, the number of pills needed to treat Ramba decreased from four tablets every other day to three. Now, in what TB technocrats in Delhi and around the world call the continuation phase of treatment, Ramba could pick up a week of pharmaceuticals each Thursday.[46] Though he felt well and no longer coughed, he continued the weekly clinic visits and shopping trips. He had little money to spend and even less of a habit for consumption, but he enjoyed the opportunity to sit with the other old men who gathered under the bus stop's banyan tree to discuss karma, crops, and the comings and goings of younger men and women. He had, in his words, "gotten in the habit of going to see Suresh every week." These weekly visits continued until Ramba finished every pill in the box. Because he had no TB symptoms and a sample of his sputum revealed no bacteria, Suresh declared Ramba officially cured by sending the pink paper to the district hospital.

Clinic visits were not a particularly burdensome habit for Ramba, but they were examples of the biopolitics of life and imagined pharmaceutical futures that enter the clinic and accumulate in people's lives and experiences of care.[47] India's nationally standardized TB treatment protocol, which Suresh and his patients follow, is part of a global politics of suspicion toward people afflicted by TB. Suresh watches his patients take their medicines, not because they are expensive, but because they are precarious; their potential to fail or be rendered obsolete by drug resistance means that the public clinics must manage those who access them. A politics of bacterial and human life ensues when the imputed resistant characteristics of bacterial life are mapped onto the political subjectivities of the people afflicted by them.[48] It reveals the sociological management of a pharmaceutical gap.

The vertical TB-control program organized Suresh's care as much as it organized Ramba's weekly habits. In fact, Suresh was as much an object of biomedicine's discipline as an agent of it. He found himself conflicted when providing care, preventing antibiotic resistance, and protecting pharmaceuticals.[49] The locus of programmatic and clinical pastoral attention—pills or people—was never quite clear. Health workers like Suresh were stuck between the role of a community health nurse, who should insist that people come to the clinic for care, and that of a vertical program worker, who, through direct observation and the threat of denied care to the unruly, must ensure that TB patients like Ramba take all their medicines to avoid the growth of drug-resistant bacteria.

The project asked Suresh to provide what Lisa Stevenson calls "anonymous care" to all who arrived at the clinic, care that insists on the erasure of the patient's context.[50] Although this was clearly a fiction, Suresh tried to imagine that his patients' relations, biographies, and identities did not matter beyond the relation of citizen to bureaucratized system. All patients were to be treated the same, no matter their ability to attend the clinic or tolerate the medicines or embody biomedicine's ideals.[51]

With identities in abeyance in the clinic, Suresh and Ramba could be slotted into the structural roles of caregiver and care receiver, observer and observed, custodian and ward, recorder and recorded, but like the dust that had to be swept out each morning, the world outside the clinic would not go away. Though the health system had taken responsibility for Ramba and aimed to train him to go to the clinic for care, it left the work of actually coming to collect the medicines to Ramba despite his age and physical condition. Ramba had to find a way to traverse the physical and social distance from his home to the clinic, and upon arrival, had wait his turn despite being the eldest man there. If some part of a patient's biography prevented attendance at the clinic, care was challenging, anonymous, or otherwise problematic. Suresh too was both anonymous and not. He was expected to act in a way that imagined him as divorced from his context, despite his position as a member of the indigenous community and his desire to provide care for the poor in his community.

Indeed, anonymity extended to pharmaceutical treatment. Though Ramba's name had been hastily scrawled on the white box of TB medicines that sat in the clinic, the pharmaceuticals it contained could have been for anyone. All adults received a standardized set of medicines, adjusted only if they had been in TB treatment before or if their treatment had no effect after many months.[52] Pharmaceutical standardization and anonymization of care meant that social and bodily differences were controlled for and could not work their way into the clinic or its care.[53] Difference did, however, enter the clinic as side effects endured by some but not others or as unwillingness to submit to anonymization. Such deviations were indexed by the dust-covered white boxes, scratched with names, on the clinic shelves. The irony of the anonymity of care was that, despite standardization, one person could not take another's medicine. When a course was ended prematurely, the box remained as a silent reminder of the failure to be disciplined. It could go to no other. The namesakes of the dusty boxes had been too entangled in relations, responsibilities, or roles of life and labor to heed the call of the anonymous clinic. The TB program's bureaucratic temporality and protocolized care, its relations of adherence and immobility, and its biopolitical subjectivity of citizen and antibiotic steward were more than they could bear. These patients had left TB treatment, but Suresh hoped they would return. Until they did, their boxes gathered dust.

MOTI SINGH'S DUSTY BOXES

Moti Singh Rawat was a frequent clinic visitor for years, but after several rounds of unsuccessful TB treatment, he decided to stop. When he told his son and me about the decision, he explained that he was "tired of going all the time to the clinic and getting injection after injection. It has been years of this, taking medicine for a while, getting better, and then falling sick again." He coughed and continued, "I keep taking medicine and doing what they say, but nothing happens. I have to just keep taking it. 'I've had enough,' I said that to the sister. I gave it to her in writing. I would not take that TB medicine anymore. It wasn't doing any good and I feel okay. I can do anything I like."

It is likely that Moti Singh's bacteria were resistant to treatment, but they were never tested. Instead, he was treated three times with the same drugs or one additional drug. This was in accordance with the national policy at the time, but eventually Moti Singh had had enough.[54] Leaving TB treatment did not, however, mean that he had left the clinic entirely. About a year after ending TB treatment, Moti Singh visited the Ambawati clinic early one morning to manage a problem of dust.

As he approached the clinic, Janaki Malviya, who was the nurse before Suresh, bustled outside to meet him. I was enjoying the sunshine and a chat with Hansa Singh Rawat, the community secretary, as Janaki hustled up next to us. She spoke to Moti Singh: "Ah, you've come back, have you? Finally ready to admit that you were wrong to leave treatment? Who is to say that the government will start your medicines again?" Typically a bit acerbic (but caring), it was hard to tell if Janaki was joking or venting her anger. "I'm not here for the cough, madam. I'm here because of my machine," Moti Singh replied, pointing to a dusty white plastic box that hung on a lanyard around his neck. "It is not working very well. I think maybe it has a short in it or something. Probably the dust has gotten in. It is hard to hear again." The box which he usually kept in the breast pocket of his shirt was the receiver for a hearing aid. Its white wire coiled upward over the top of his ear and inside. He had gotten it two years earlier at a camp for people with hearing difficulties. In fact, Janaki had suggested he go there. That was why he had returned to see her when it malfunctioned.

"I don't know anything about it," Janaki replied. "There's nothing I can do for it. Maybe you can take it to the community hospital if you want. What does it matter if you refuse to take your medicines anyway? You don't have any confidence in me. Besides, you are going all around the village spreading TB. Better to try to live than try to hear." Unaccustomed to being addressed in this way, the kindly man was startled. "Ah, yes, okay. I'll go to Sadri then. Maybe they can get the dust out of the box. I do not even have TB. I thought this was a clinic for the people," he grumbled as he ambled away. "He has to have TB," Janaki said in Hansa Singh's and my direction, "Probably drug-resistant TB by now. The old man has been in and out of TB treatment so many times. He's terrible about taking his medicines. Some people, I think they just want to live as they choose or die. They will not do what it takes to be healthy." Janaki hitched up her sari to return to the clinic across the dirt yard.

A year and several months later, Moti Singh and his wife went to the bus stand to sell a few loads of hay. Then they returned home, ate dinner, and made their cots to go to sleep. Moti Singh did not feel well. He woke up around midnight, coughed up a large quantity of blood, and died. Almost everyone agreed that Moti Singh's was a good death. Its swiftness raised the potential of his return as a ghost, but its lack of protracted pain indicated moral uprightness and a good future for his soul. Of course, neighbors continued to talk in hushed tones about how Moti Singh had long been in TB treatment and how, after years, he had officially withdrawn from treatment. Others had done this too and died more painfully from the disease. Sitaram Dholi and his brother Laluram had both wasted away after ending their treatment. So had Rai Singh Rawat after fleeing the TB hospital, and two years later Lal Singh Rawat would die in the same way.

Their dusty funeral processions were the unintended consequences of actions taken in the clinic on behalf of a global TB-control paradigm aimed at preventing resistance and protecting antibiotics. In some cases, individuals felt that they could not return to treatment after having left: recall Janaki's admonition that the government might not let Moti Singh restart his medicines. Moti Singh's resistance to the treatment paradigm was a more convenient explanation of his continued cough than iatrogenic antibiotic resistance. He was not particularly resistant to medicine, though. The problem was in policy. A policy decision, which required that he prove multiple years of unwavering submission to the treatment surveillance paradigm before he could access a test for resistance or the medicines that might treat it, had lived effects in Ambawati. It connected global discourses of antibiotic resistance, bodies in Ambawati, colonial techniques of control, and bacteria to Moti Singh's body and bacteria, but he was not alone. In many cases patients who submitted to the paradigm but did not improve experienced a programmatic failure to swiftly deal with antibiotic resistance. This changed in 2012 when public sector treatments for drug resistance began in earnest that very year, but drug resistance had spread widely precisely because people were obliged to take years and years of the same medicines before being granted access to a test for bacterial resistance.[55] Of course, this continues to be attributed to culture and patient resistance.[56]

The pastoral politics of providing free hearing aids to the poor but leaving them without a maintenance plan is analogous to the provision of surveilled medicines to prevent resistance without a plan to routinely test for resistance; both are simulacra of care dusted with residues of control. Moti Singh did not resist biomedical intervention; indeed, he went to ask for help with the dust in his hearing aid. The difference between the two white boxes centered on utility and trust in patients. He did desire the positive effect that biomedical intervention could have on his life but was cheated of that result in the case of TB treatment.

However, even his failed TB treatment and Janaki's admonitions did not keep Moti Singh away from the clinic. He returned to it often, but the potential risk of drug-resistant TB infection that he represented for Janaki meant that she met him outside its walls and often with the exhortation to restart treatment again. In short, the dust stirred up by failed treatment and potential antibiotic resistance continued to settle on Moti Singh's life, health, and the bacteria in and around his body for the years that followed. It pulled his breath, body, self, and even his death into a much broader biopolitics, belying the cruel irony of Janaki's charge that he failed to desire wellness. He did not represent a resistance to biomedicine as much as self-discharge from TB's biopolitics of surveillance and biologic of resistant life that relied on colonial understandings of the value of life, counterinsurgency, and the necessity of surveillance.

MEDICINES TURNED TO DUST

Janaki Malviya served the Ambawati clinic for four years along with her husband, Jai. Jai was a trained physical education teacher, but, like many trained teachers, he struggled to pass the Rajasthan public service exam and win a teaching position in a school. Until he did, the pair lived off Janaki's salary as a general nurse and midwife. The nurse who preceded Janaki had insisted on treating people in the room she rented with her husband at the Ambawati bus stand. She didn't want to travel all the way out to the clinic. The clinic was far from other homes, and the previous nurse always said she was afraid to walk back and forth to the clinic because that required passing Ambawati's speakeasy and myriad potential snakes. It was never clear if these snakes were material or metaphorical.

Janaki, however, broke the lock on the health center and spent the first few weeks of her tenure sweeping and scrubbing the four-year-old but never-used building. Janaki and Jai avoided serpentine problems by moving into the room behind the clinic. The fastidious pair could regularly be found in the clinic, Janaki treating patients as they arrived and Jai keeping her company by studying for his exams at the clinic's westerly windowsill turned desk. Slowly people began to visit the health center for treatment because they had confidence that Janaki would be there after their long walk. The dusty clinic eventually came to life even though the medicines on its shelves were often in short supply.

Just as the national TB program provided basic TB care, another program called the Chief Minister's Free Medicine Initiative provided the clinic with an essential set of medicines to distribute free of charge. However, their supply was intermittent and Janaki, like Suresh after her, would often practice a pharmaceutical bricolage with the medicines she had. In many cases, Jai would need to make a trip to Sagwai on his motorcycle to buy medicines from the pharmacy there. This was particularly common for injectable and oral antibiotics, which were in short supply because of both cost and antibiotic stewardship initiatives.[57] Though Janaki distributed the medicines at no cost and injected all medicines for free, she asked her patients to reimburse the cost of the medicines that Jai brought from town.

This mix of free and for-payment pharmaceuticals, though necessary, was often confusing for Janaki's patients (and the resident anthropologist). Everyone managed their confusion by ignoring the situation, until several dust-covered boxes of unused medicine on the shelves brought things to a crisis. According to Janaki, the medicines in several of these small boxes had passed their expiration date. Thus, one evening, following government protocol, Janaki collected them and took them to the dust pile out the back door of the clinic and set the whole thing alight. A passerby saw her burning the medicines, and a scandal quickly ensued. Rumors spread like wildfire: the village nurse was burning the free medicines in the dust pile and taking money for others!

Lighting dust piles on fire is a relatively common practice in Ambawati. In fact, I was once admonished for not burning the pile of dust that morning's sweeping had amassed outside my home. I had not even considered burning the pile until Ramba's wife, Bhanwaribai, crossed the road with a glowing ember from her stove to set the whole thing alight: "Burn it, son. It burns. It keeps things cleaner if you burn it." From then on, I would, like my neighbors, occasionally burn the dust and detritus pile as part of a dust-related hygiene regimen.[58]

Janaki's burning of the pharmaceutical dust pile, an act she felt compelled by hygiene and regulations to complete, created frustration about bureaucratized biomedicine's unfulfilled promises and the austerities of antibiotic stewardship programs. It seemed to my neighbors that Janaki had been burning "their" medicines for one of two reasons: many said that she aimed to profit by selling medicine and wanted to eliminate free alternatives; others contended that she had burned them to hide the fact that she had not been doing her job. The very nurse charged with rationing medicine to people, giving them just a few pills at a time in order to preserve public supplies and antibiotic efficacy, was now burning those medicines she had safeguarded. Their frustration with the policy became focused on the administrator of the system.

For Janaki, she *was* doing precisely her job by both giving medicines in small doses and burning those that had expired rather than distributing them. That these had ended up in the dust pile was due to a struggling health system that supplied medicine in large shipments and refused to let them be used for people other than the patients they were designated for. Like the health system itself, the dust-covered medicines were an example of the progress made to bring pharmaceuticals to village clinics, as well as the unintended consequences of being at the tail end of lines of supply and control that often allowed them to expire before use.

That Janaki should burn the medicines she had been asked to steward for the whole village after requiring that people constantly travel to the clinic to get a few pills at a time was a perceived betrayal that the village council could not leave unaddressed. A few days later the enraged, and perhaps inebriated, village mayor arrived at the clinic. All present agreed that he berated Janaki for burning medicine that ought to have gone to sick Ambawatians, for failing her charge, and for frequent dereliction of duty. The next day, Janaki traveled to the subdistrict hospital and resigned from her post. Before nightfall, she and her husband had packed up the room behind the health center and left. Three days later Suresh arrived.

By trying to manage medicines the best she could, Janaki ultimately received the blame for a rationing system that dates to the birth of biomedicine on the subcontinent. That medicines had made it this far was a feat achieved within living memory. To burn them was to reveal the betrayal of a local promise in service of a global one. That so many with TB had died because of this biopolitics of protecting pills from people made their destruction seem even more of a betrayal. Pharmaceutical expiration, and the dust that the boxes gathered, was an effect of the biopolitics to which all were subject. This would not be the only biomedical failure credited to dust.

DUSTY TECHNOLOGY

While I was busy with fieldwork in Ambawati, the World Health Organization (WHO) and global health delivery experts were agog with hopes that a machine smaller than a desktop computer would revolutionize TB diagnosis and perhaps end the epidemic all together. The machines, called Xpert, tested sputum and other samples for tuberculosis bacteria's RNA. By searching for the bacillus's genetic signature, the machines could diagnose

TB in a sample with as few as ten bacteria in it. Older microscope-based methods needed thousands to provide a positive result. The machine could also simultaneously identify resistance to the key drug used to treat TB, rifampicin. In western European and North American hospitals, the machines identified over 95 percent of TB-positive samples, diagnosed drug resistance in two hours rather than two months, removed the potential for microscopist error, and identified almost 40 percent more people in need of treatment than the microscopy method.[59] Moreover, researchers were certain that the machines could be used to the same effect at the point of care in clinics like Ambawati's throughout the developing world. Xpert promised a revolution in TB diagnosis and care.[60]

Dust, however, quickly dashed these hopes. It infiltrated the machines and reminded everyone of the challenges underfunded clinical spaces posed to global health's highly technologized interventions. Discussion of dust first occurred in WHO-coordinated pilot project reports on machines sent to clinics like Suresh's in Africa and Asia. Though they did not initially send machines to India, project organizers did test them in Pakistan, Bangladesh, and Nepal. The results of the project were frustrating. Within two years, 42 percent of all the project's machines had failed. Half of those sent to Nepal needed to be replaced, and none of those sent to Pakistan and Bangladesh functioned after twenty-four months. One report's authors diplomatically wrote, "Many module problems seemed to be clustered suggesting that other implementation issues, such as irregular power supply and currents, dust build-up, overheating, and staff quality control may have contributed to the failures."[61] More privately, they worried that dust and poor clinical infrastructure had done the machines in. Discouraged, they began to wonder if the meager human and technical infrastructures of clinics like Suresh's would render the new tool useless. Perhaps dust would quash TB's molecular revolution before it even began.

A second pilot study, this one testing the machines in urban and rural hospitals in India, found that Indian dust did cause serious problems with machine functioning and accuracy. These researchers wrote, "It was further observed that majority [*sic*] of temperature associated errors was related to inadequate exhaust of warm air from the equipment either due to clogging of exhaust fan filter due to dust or inappropriate positioning of equipment."[62] However, they reassured readers and policy makers that most of these problems could be solved by cleaning each machine's fan filter and maximizing air flow around it. With this solution in hand, their research accelerated the use of molecular technology for TB in India's public and private hospitals. India's TB-program leaders and its international donors soon placed multiple machines throughout each state. However, despite the hope that this technology might reach Suresh's clinic, which functions as the area's point of care, it was not to be. Ambawati's clinic did not receive enough patients and was far too dusty, no matter how fastidiously Kalibai swept. Instead, it would be stuck with older "appropriate technologies" that were less able to diagnose TB and asked to submit to the regimen of monitoring in order to prevent drug resistance.[63] If such a test is needed today, patients take their sputum samples several hours by bus to access an Xpert machine. Like airborne bacteria, dust as an airborne matter stood in for the dangers that rural atmospheres and neoliberalized infrastructures posed for health development projects so effective elsewhere.

PICKING UP DUST

As "microecolog[y] of matter and mind,"[64] dust's is an "unfolding and pro-cessual materiality."[65] It is a residue of other forms of biopolitics and forms of organizing life that swirls uncontrollably in the present and defies attempts to manage it with newer, even more technical entanglements of life and action. In Ambawati, dust is a betwixt and between by-product of modernity's triune of mechanization, mobility, and medicine that irritat-ingly reveals the unanticipated consequences of each. Dust's presence suggests that the clinic and other trappings of modernity have not lived up to their promises of human mastery over the natural world's uncertainty. The pastoral state, democratic liberalism, and a biopolitics of pliant engaged subjects of health were, after all, charged with controlling and eradicating TB in India[66] while replacing a hierarchical social and political life char-acterized by caste with an egalitarian society of merit and democracy.[67] In Ambawati, these transformations, like dust, are somehow stuck midway or hanging in the air to irritate lungs. Democratic liberalism has assured Dalit and indigenous farmers of their equal rights as citizens but requires an iterative performance of poverty, naivete, and incomplete liberalism to access them.[68] The pastoral state built a new clinic, but the clinic often seemed to steward its medicines and surveil its TB patients. Its medicines are covered in dust.

When entangled with aerial materiality of breath, dust reveals atmospheres that stretch the self outside the body and sentiment and into a medical and political climate marked by human and bacterial counterinsurgency. Like the other amphibious materials and metaphors in this book, dust highlights how postcolonial biopolitics of TB and breath are precarious, dynamic hybrids of political and biological concerns in which one term never totally dominates the other. In air full of dust, we breathe the past and future. Thus, TB care is neither wholly colonial nor wholly decolonized, neither wholly fostering biological life nor wholly entrenched in an agonistic politics of counterinsurgency and resistance. Instead, the public clinic is full of an amphibious and shifty postcolonial politics of life, self, and health best characterized by pervasive dust rather than ruination. Dust specks float on the air that people breathe and cover pharmaceuticals. They enter and make particular bodies suspicious remainders and reminders of colonized pasts and precarious futures. Sometimes, however, the dust mixes with water to create mud and adhere bodies in place.

FOUR

AIR

Hawa men udho mathi!
Kaam karo an khao.
Rakhi-dora bandva ra dhyan raakh ja.

(Do not fly up in the air!
Work and eat.
Be careful with whom you build relations.)

—Goddess Narsinghi Mata
Vijaydashami 2012, Ambawati[1]

FOURTEEN-YEAR-OLD KHEM SINGH RAWAT rarely left Pipliya
Ghar, a hamlet of Rawat families about a half kilometer from Ambawati's
clinic. Though I would eventually know him with some familiarity, I first
met him as a silent caregiver for his father, Bheru Singh. Khem Singh
quietly observed each time I visited Bheru Singh, who was debilitated by
tuberculosis. Though Khem Singh said little, Bheru Singh often looked
at him before commenting, "He does not say much, but he takes good
care of me." Khem Singh seemed unaffected by the compliment and kept
waving the scrap of cardboard he used to fan his father. Khem Singh was
too small to lift or bathe Bheru Singh, and he did not cook. Still, Bheru
Singh insisted that he was a good caregiver. I found this perplexing because Khem Singh's care rarely fit with the tactile body work that I had
identified as caregiving. It was only later that I realized this monotonous
and incessant fanning was an example of what Michael Vine calls atmospheric care—a diffuse and multidirectional attention to and management

77

of the atmosphere, of breathed air.[2] Atmospheric care took up most of Khem Singh's day. Far from inconsequential, it shaped the air in which the family lived and the course of his life.

Families like Khem Singh's did much to manage air and comfort those afflicted by TB. Practices of circulating air around sick neighbors and family members highlight how infections, among other things, can permeate an atmosphere. These circulations make nontactile care work, like fanning, as essential as feeding or searching for medicine. Indeed, they require a distributed attention to the physical and moral states of both sickness and health. Atmospheric care that manages air's potential contagion and comfort also reveals central shortcomings in pharmaceuticalized TB care. Pharmaceuticalized TB care, epitomized by directly observed therapy, short-course (DOTS), underestimates atmospheric care as care and ignores the ways that its meager atmospheric infection-control measures replicate caste-based practices of social marginalization. Because of these blind spots, aerial atmospheric care, which was so important that Khem Singh left school to provide it, falls to family members.

Air is the context in which life and TB infection happens. It is the most obvious stuff of atmospheres. Aerial atmospheres are made up of atoms and particles and microbes and plants and people. Air can desiccate an already dry field, pass signals of clandestinely smoked cigarettes, or trouble bodies. On festival days Ambawati's air was filled with incense and excitement. On Holi, the festival of colors, these were layered with liquored breath and bawdy song. Most evenings the hearty airborne smell of cooking chapatis altered moods and imaginations of what was possible, but occasionally the stink of a dead water buffalo left to decompose upwind of the Meghwal neighborhood was a pungent reminder of formerly casted roles. Material and affective entanglements or atmospheres—in Ambawati often spoken of as air or wind (*hawa*), weather (*mausum*), or atmosphere (*vaatavaran*, which comes from the Sanskrit word *vaat*, or "air," and *aavaran*, or "covering")—can be sensed, altered, and inhabited even by more than humans. Air's atmospheres might also be affected by words and emotions. Habits and predilections, Kathleen Stewart suggests, can waft across a community's atmosphere to "pick up density and texture as they move through bodies, dreams, dramas, and social worldings of all kinds."[3] A place's air can affect people and their ways of being, as they did Khem Singh, just as people's actions within them shape and alter atmospheric airs.

Air can be a fickle, nondeterministic, tentative, and risky connection that affects people just as it can be affected by people. It seems intangible, but Khem Singh taught me that air is constantly touched by human practices. Our breaths and actions socialize air. Air is not empty space; it is a conductor that subverts boundaries. Air allows breath to move in a diversity of shapes and directions, so Ambawatian work on tubercular or other airs might reveal ways that people shaped an amorphous plume into something manageable. Timothy Choy has called the outcomes of such management "air's substantiations" and urged anthropologists to bring these processes to ethnographic attention.[4] People like Khem Singh did atmospheric work to substantiate insubstantial air. Taking this work, as atmospheric care, and its effects seriously might reveal how aerial relations connect and separate people who find themselves in the same place and time. As Choy writes, "Thinking more about air, as not simply taking it as solidity's opposite, might offer some means of thinking about relations and movements between places, people, things, and scales that obviate the usual traps of particularity and universality."[5] Examining some of the atmospheres that air and air work substantiate, this chapter highlights the atmospheric substantiations and futures people aim to build or maintain from amorphous and potentially dangerous air. Along the way it reminds ethnographers of atmospheres that they too are peopled and powerful.

As I observed Khem Singh and others I learned that managing air might both provide care and enact atmospheric distinction. Air is a medium through which contagions of all kinds move, creating a shared atmosphere of intimacy or circuits of separation, sometimes to the same places and people.[6] Choy calls these intimacies and separations air's "poetics of difference."[7] Air's transformative potential, it seems, is tempered by existing relations and differences.[8] Air's potential to subvert boundedness, burst bubbles, and shift over space and time is tantalizing, but permeable bodies and selves are rarely and unevenly desirable.[9] Social structures often work to prevent such aerial subversions. Khem Singh and the others in this chapter foster and foreclose these airy connections through atmospheric care that extends far beyond illness. Managing air and transforming or substantiating it into atmospheres might be one way of domesticating unpredictable but already social air.

Worlds outside Ambawati are similarly replete with practices that substantiate air and form distinctions within atmospheric systems, resources, and even airspaces.[10] Atmospheric connections between people and air occur in Indian philosophy, classical Chinese medical texts,[11] Greek and Hippocratic theories of ecological and moral miasma,[12] and German Romantic theories of climatic nationalism.[13] In all these theories, the climate has agency. It makes boundaries and connections, as a natural frame on the social. Janet Greenlees shows, however, that air came to be a matter of social concern in the late nineteenth century when it was enclosed by walls in buildings, factories, and cityscapes to move toxins and proclivities between classed rather than cultured bodies.[14] The air of colonial and postcolonial Delhi too, Asher Ghertner demonstrates, was shaped by dynamics of privatization and protection that connected and separated air along lines of social difference.[15] Ghertner shows that enclosing or separating air was central to delineating colonial social categories and limiting the risk of commingled colonizing and colonized bodies in spaces where air could move heat, toxins, and bacteria. Air-conditioned cars, elite working and living spaces, and the unequal capacity to manage air's infectiousness and potential exposures still imbue air with social inequality. Indian modernity's enclosed air loses its agency and mobility, adhering to a particular social group or class who breathed it.[16]

Air in Ambawati has a double meaning: like other entangled atmospheres it is both an environmental material and a synonym for caste in place. It is not surprising, then, that an aerial poetics of difference in Ambawati should enmesh caste and TB. Within a social world divided by inherited caste like Ambawati, connective breath and air's proximal relations exist within established frames but also blow between them. Airborne bits of bodies, words, sicknesses might allow caste and caste contagion, as both substance and affect, to float in the air, moving among and into people in unexpected ways. Air work is perhaps always caste work, imbuing atmospheric care and Khem Singh's fanning with a whole set of meanings. It seems that in Ambawati a peopling and casting of the air makes it a conduit of more than mere bacteria. Perhaps practices of atmospheric care and distinction feel pressing because air and atmospheres can be filled with soundless but powerful connection to places, people, and selves that must be managed.[17] Forms of connection are built and broken by atmospheric care over and over again, and when these substantiations intersect with a TB epidemic both social change and tragedy can ensue. This raises the stakes of pharmaceuticalized TB care's practices of individualized mask wearing in lieu of other forms of collective atmospheric attention.

Atmospheric air work and connection, though invisible from the biomedical perspective, was central to TB care in Ambawati. This chapter centers on Khem Singh Rawat, the fourteen-year-old son of parents afflicted by TB. Khem Singh was obligated to care for Bheru Singh, leaving school in the sixth grade. Next, it considers another connection between air and place by recounting the exposures that brought me to a healer and air worker. Then it observes the entanglement of caste and TB care enacted by a health worker before considering air and caste more deeply. Finally, it returns to Khem Singh two years later as he finishes six months as a migrant laborer, affected by the air of another place, to reveal a changed atmospheric self. Altogether the chapter reveals a set of social relations created by air that imagine a body and atmosphere not through its boundaries but through its connections or susceptibility to the world. Air, I argue, connects place, person, and body in ways that reveal another set of breathy relations between caste, subjectivity, and TB care. Air helps interpret TB's impact on Khem Singh's life and make sense of his otherwise overlooked atmospheric care.

FANNING AS CARE

Khem Singh's childhood was punctuated by a series of tragedies. When he was ten, his mother fell ill from tuberculosis. Her health improved with treatment, but just two years later his father Bheru Singh became ill with the same disease. He became sicker and sicker until he was bedridden. In both instances, Khem Singh stayed home from school to care for his ailing parents. Though still a child, Khem Singh took on the role of caregiver.[18] He continued attending classes intermittently when his mother or grandmother could work around the house. The family ran out of money as Bheru Singh's health deteriorated. In a desperate attempt to stay afloat, Khem Singh's grandparents and mother went to work in nearby poppy fields. They did backbreaking but comparatively well-paid labor extracting poppy sap to be turned into morphine.[19] With all three adults away earning money to pay for treatments, Khem Singh left school for good. He stayed home to watch after Bheru Singh and his siblings. "We would have taken him to the poppy fields with us, but he has never done it before," his grandfather Dhan Singh once remarked. "Probably if he breathed in the poppy field air, he would have gotten too affected by it. He would have run away to fall asleep in a ditch. It's better if he stays here to take care of his father." In a parallel formation of air and comportment, the old man was worried that the intoxicating properties of the poppies would move through the air to affect Khem Singh. Unlike his elders, Khem Singh did not have a lifetime of experience with the poppies that oozed raw opium.[20] I was worried about exposure to TB, which was perhaps inevitable anyway.

For months, Khem Singh stayed home caring for his Bheru Singh. Alongside the fanning Khem Singh was a dutiful caretaker. He served food when his father was hungry, made tea throughout the day, heated bathwater if Bheru Singh felt well enough to bathe, and attended to the family's remaining animals. He spent much of his day, however, fanning Bheru Singh with a piece of cardboard box. Khem Singh spoke little to visitors and silently, if a bit awkwardly, went about his chores. Not quite a child, but not fully grown into an adult body either, he often positioned himself on a mud platform that supported one of the house's rough-carved teak posts. There, he fanned and listened to adults' conversations or stared off into space. Perhaps he had been lulled by the constant fanning: back and forth, up and down.

One day, Dhan Singh looked toward his grandson as we discussed the effects of TB on their family. Though he said nothing in front of the boy, he seemed to gesture to the weight of Khem Singh's burden. Later, Dhan Singh privately explained that when the family decided on how to care for Bheru Singh. They felt that of the three children, Khem Singh was least cut out for school. And he had already failed a grade while attending his mother. "He will make a good farmer, I think," Dhan Singh said, "He's not much interested in other things. School suits Shambhu Singh better.

Besides, I could never trust him to stay here. He would run away and play, but Khema will do just as he's told." Khem Singh's younger brother, eight-year-old Shambhu Singh, was more active, constantly getting into mischief. It was hard to imagine Shambhu managing the laborious and often boring care work that Khem Singh took on. Dhan Singh felt that the taciturn Khem Singh would best help the family at home, keeping Bheru Singh, the sole earner of nonagricultural income, alive. Later, "when things are easier, we will try to find Khem Singh a job or send him back to school," Dhan Singh explained. For now, caring for a sick family member was more urgent, and Khem was fit for the task. The decision seemed to weigh on the old man's mind, nonetheless.

To me, the choice between education and fanning seemed cruel. I felt that fanning was a pointless enactment of palliative care as Khem Singh waited for Bheru Singh's improvement or death. But over time, it became clear that the silent act of fanning was part of a larger project of care based on managing his father's air. The end of Khem Singh's education because of the family's poverty and an unresponsive health system was tragic, but the silent act of fanning as a gesture of care was as important as feeding, washing, and comforting Bheru Singh.

Fanning was a way to regulate the climate for Bheru Singh, whose body was unable to adjust to it. From the first days of his illness, Bheru Singh felt especially susceptible to the weather, often experiencing intense fevers and chills.[21] On hot days, he felt as if his body were on fire, and he visibly shivered with a pleasant evening breeze. As his family and friends noted, the illness had caused his body difficulty keeping external air and temperature out. From his perch, Khem Singh kept on waving the piece of cardboard in an attempt to cool Bheru Singh through May's hot midday sun. Khem's fanning moved and regulated temperature as well as the internal and external air when his father's breath could not.[22]

Khem Singh's fanning was comfort work. It kept flies from landing on and pestering Bheru Singh, and it provided a breeze to cool the hot summer air as it moved across his father's feverish body. In a way, Khem Sing's fanning created a bubble around Bheru Singh to protect him from winds and pests that rode in on them.[23] But this was performed by rearranging existing air, not excluding or encasing it. Fanning worked on and moved body and world. It assumed that the sick body did not end at the skin but was susceptible to the influence of the air around it. Khem Singh kept *rolation* going by moving external air in hopes of aligning Bheru Singh's internal air. In other words, atmospheres inside and outside the body commingled. Khem Singh's constant fanning was akin to breathing for Bheru Singh.

Khem Singh's fanning was also a way of managing the effects of air on others. Though primarily a way to comfort Bheru Singh, fanning also moved the air, ridding the family's air of microbes and blowing possibly tantric breaths off course. In this way, managing air highlights its connectivity and the need to break its potential bonds without enclosing it. Instead, Khem Singh helped air on its way, moving air permeated or socialized by people into the world. Though certainly not implementing tools to avoid the caste-affecting influence of Bheru Singh's air—as his son this would have been impossible anyway—the fanning might also have been a way to protect the rest of the family from illness that could leave his body on air.

In the fourth month of Bheru Singh's bedrest, I arrived to find his cousin Ganpat Singh Rawat tinkering with a small electric ceiling fan. Ganpat Singh's home was next to Khem Singh's, and neither had an electrical connection despite a wire passing not far away. Ganpat had decided to use some of the money he earned as a bicycle mechanic to buy the small fan and a spool of electrical wire for his neighbor. He put the fan together and rolled out the wire, striping one end and hoisting it onto the high-voltage line overhead. A few minutes later and a few more twists of the wire and the little fan that was now hanging from a rafter in Khem Singh's house began to whir. Bheru Singh, who was sleeping at the time, stirred under his thin blanket, and Khem Singh, who had been helping with the project, set to feeding the family goat. Ganpat Singh's work—buying, installing, and electrifying the fan—created a new infrastructure of atmospheric care; managing air could be taken on by technology, and Ganpat had provided it.

The electric fan was a great relief to the family. It helped Bheru Singh feel more comfortable through the hot days and kept mosquitos at bay at night. It was, however, reliant on forces outside Ambawati. The voltage passing through the overhead lines fluctuated throughout the day and at times the little fan would whir with such speed we all wondered if it might detach itself from the rafter. Other times, it would barely have enough energy to turn. In still other moments, the electricity would not flow to Ambawati at all, and Khem Singh returned to his position against the pillar and waved the piece of cardboard again. The mechanical wind was beyond complete control, though it could be worked on with wrenches and wires. Khem Singh's slow and steady motion could only partially be replaced; the little machine could not be relied on to do the air work that Khem Singh could. When breath faltered air had to be kept moving through other means. Harris Solomon has called this intersubjective and technological work of moving air in and out of bodies social breathing.[24]

Though monotonous, his fanning comforted and protected Bheru Singh while making the home a little safer for the rest of the family by adjusting the conduits of air that might move Bheru Singh's bacteria, misfortune, or breath onto others. That Khem Singh had to leave school to do so meant that the misfortune had changed his life. Air and care made Khem Singh and Bheru Singh's lives inseparably connected in ways that kinship can only describe as material inheritance and social obligation.

Khem Singh's fanning is an intimate act of atmospheric care. It connects him to Bheru Singh and separates them. It might better be imagined as a dyadic interaction between him and his father. He was managing the ways that air from bodies permeated places and the ways that air from places permeated bodies. The atmosphere of the house, where Bheru Singh was dying and his own future uncertain, was heavy. It was full of worry and the work to adjust it was somehow both important and invisible.

Fortunately, over time and with medicine, Bheru Singh's health improved. Slowly he began to move around and care for himself. Around the time of Khem Singh's sixteenth birthday, when a distant cousin from Surat came to recruit restaurant workers, Khem Singh packed his two shirts and two pairs of pants to take his chances in the big city.[25] His grandfather Dhan Singh was right: they had found a job for Khem Singh when Bheru Singh was well. But Khem's constant fanning and its effect on this life course raise an important question. What else might move through spaces and bodies on air?

VAYARA AND UNHEALTHY AIR

Air, danger, and affects can be entangled even without bacteria. When I too fell sick, I learned that atmospheric care can include the ritual management of exposure and disgust as well. In March I caught a head cold that lasted over a week. I hoped to avoid the clinic, so I asked my neighbor Meera Devi Meghwal for a remedy. She suggested I boil a few neem[26] leaves in water. A neem tree grew in front of my house, so I boiled some of its lush green leaves into a soapy-tasting tea. The infusion failed to remove the blockages from my sinuses.

A few days later, Meera's husband, Chainram, called me over to announce that I likely had a case of *vayara*, or air's effect. Unfamiliar with this word, I asked him what it meant. "It is what's happening to you," he responded flatly. "It's when your body is stiff, and your head hurts, and your nose is full," he went on. "Ah, so it's the Rajasthani word for a cold (*zukaam*)?" I asked. "No, it is different," he responded. An elementary school teacher, Chainram was acquainted with my questions about Rajasthani words, and he went on, "It's not a cold. You don't seem to have a cold because you're not coughing and it's the wrong weather. I think you have *vayara*. It happens a lot when we are exposed to a bad smell. More often to men than to women, but everyone gets it. Probably you got it from a place like the public toilet in Sadri." Meera agreed that this was the likely source: "I never go there." She added, "Its air is terrible. I cannot even stand near it without feeling nauseous."

Sadri's public urinal was an acrid place. Located near the bus stand, it was often the last place men visited before catching a minibus or motorcycle out of town.[27] The men's urinal was a windowless brick shack. Inside were a few dividers, a terrible stench, and a shallow ditch along the back wall draining out to the gutter. The lower portion of the mauve wall was covered with caked-on urine of unknown age. A few cigarette butts, chewing tobacco packets, and other detritus lined the urine-covered floor, adding to the urinal's nauseating sensory profile. Most who entered tried to hold their breath from the time their foot touched the first stair until well away from the facility. I certainly did. As Chainram and Meera bemoaned the public toilet, its odor seemed to permeate the gentle breeze blowing across their veranda.

Chainram explained that a visit to the urinal and its noxious air had likely altered my body's *rolation*, causing *vayara* and its discomfort. "You know, people go inside when necessary, and no matter what happens, one takes in that smelly air. It goes inside the body and causes all kinds of trouble. Most often it causes *vayara*, so your body stops *rolating*." "What's the treatment for *vayara*?" I asked. I was willing to try anything to clear my sinuses and breathe easy again. "You have to go see Sajjan Singh. He can take care of it," Chainram instructed. "But I barely know him," I said. "You don't need him to do much. You just sit in front of him relaxed, with your legs out long, and he puts some wind on you."

First, Chainram used the Rajasthani composite verb *vayro naakno*—to pour, drop, or inject air to describe the treatment. Then, to be sure I understood, he used the Hindi equivalent *hawa daalna*. Though the Hindi equivalent confirmed the Rajasthani, it invoked images related to the composite verb's most frequent use: to put air in a tire. My mind wandered to inflated clowns at cheap car washes and Michelin Man bodies. As they continued, our conversation disabused me of my ideas about an inflatable body. In their explanation, air could be a carrier of both smell and danger. It could move in and out of the body not only on breath but also through air. Air could be managed through purposive action, as with a tire pump, but also with a fan.[28] It was a version of this manipulation of air that Khem Singh was undertaking for Bheru Singh that they suggested I try. "Have you seen people doing it with a bunch of neem tree branches before? Maybe you've seen Dhoni's father with a grass broom near a water buffalo?" Chainram asked.[29] I had seen both but taken little notice. Neem was the same leaf Meera had suggested I use a few days before. Neem trees' dense shade was often appreciated for its ability to cool the air. Perhaps Meera had suggested the neem leaf tea as a way to work on my body's air.

"He puts wind in?" I asked, continuing to think of inflating a person as if a tire. "Yes, he says some mantras to his special goddess, Kalika Mata, and uses a broom to move the air.[30] People use neem branches when they don't have a broom, but most experts use a palm or grass broom." I was perplexed about the bad air in the public toilet, the neem tree, the brooms, the putting in or injecting of air, and what Sajjan Singh, a tantric, would do for an illness that seemed to fit with Ayurvedic and Chinese medical ideas of bodily and worldly winds.[31] I had more questions for Chainram and Meera, but Sajjan Singh emerged from his house, and Chainram set off to visit him. I followed. I wanted to understand the relation between air inside and outside the body. Moreover, I was tired of feeling congested.

Chainram opened the gate to Sajjan Singh's cactus-fenced field, and we crossed the prickly barrier. "Sajjnaba, Andy is sick," he called out, "I think he has *vayara*. Can you put some wind on him?" "Let's see," Sajjan Singh responded. "Sit down there comfortably with your legs outstretched." I did as I was told and sat on the ground in the open field. I bent slightly at the knees to keep the bottoms of my feet on the wheat-stubble-covered ground. "No, all the way. Sit comfortably," Sajjan Singh said. I complied, but worried about my position with the bottoms of my bare feet facing the whole village. He said nothing more and went into his house to get the hand broom tucked in the rafters. Chainram moved to the other side of the succulent fence and Meera watched from even farther away. I was surprised that Chainram had moved away. Most healing action in Ambawati is collective, and people huddle close to see and hear. *Vayro naakno*, I learned, usually happens away from others to avoid the aerial effects of their bodies and promote air movement. Besides, Sajjan Singh's tantric power to heal and harm was the stuff of neighborhood whispers. No one wanted to be unnecessarily caught up in it.

Before the *vayro naakno* process, Sajjan Singh and my interactions had seldom strayed from a brief hello or "How is your field growing?" Now I was alone with him, and I worried that he might make a claim to a truth about me and air that I could not contest. What would he tell me or others about the relationship between the external air and my inner state? What would be the social effects of his air work? What of the goddess?

Sajjan Singh returned but did not reveal whether he sensed my trepidation. He squatted near my legs and began whisking the air.[32] After several minutes he spoke aloud, but not to me. "Yes, mother," he said in a tone that suggested he had called the goddess on the telephone to chat. "Yes, everything is fine. It is nothing serious. We've put some wind on him. Okay, I guess you can go now. Talk to you later." Sajjan Singh stopped whisking the air and turned to me: "You'll be fine. Don't worry. It's been taken care of. You can go." A bit startled, I got up to leave. I dusted the soil off my pants, thanked him, and turned toward home. Sajjan Singh concluded by saying, "The air will be better soon, don't worry."

As I shut his gate and blew my nose, I wondered which air Sajjan Singh referred to. Would internal or ambient air improve? I resolved to ask Chainram, but soon changed my mind. My question relied on a fallacy of my own making. I had been seduced into thinking that air within the body is separate from air outside the body.[33] Sajjan Singh had been whisking up an atmosphere that revealed connections that crossed the boundary between body and world. Rearranging the air in my body and in the world, Sajjan Singh was doing boundary work with air that subverted the separation of gaseous and impermeable solid matter. The body that could puff up as if a balloon attached to an air pump was not at play. The body Sajjan Singh worked on was connected to worldly air and transected by breath. Habits, feelings, and desires could float and move on air to enter the body. Even could disgust imbue air with ethical and embodied characteristics. In turn air entered the body, bringing the world and its inhabitants with it. My body was permeable and prone to invasive winds, thoughts, and desires that may not always have been rooted in my reflexive individual self. Indeed, this had been the source of my worry about Sajjan Singh revealing some part of me that I did not know.

By brooming the air Sajjan Singh was working on atmosphere, body, and self all at once, across what had seemed a skin barrier. My troubled breathing and Sajjan Singh's air work to correct it highlighted the ways that climatic and affective atmospheres interact with bodies to localize breath in difference and move through social structures. Local air made for local breath and its own constellation of local biologies and local biologics, lively connectors of life and lives, in which air and breath were meaningful. At times, atmospheres gather people into a shared affect of solidarity and at other times spread isolation as suspicion, introspection, or fear of contagion. In both cases they require care.

ON NOT SHARING AIR

On a very hot day in September, Manju Meghwal, a family-planning health worker, stopped in my neighborhood to find out whether any women were newly pregnant. Suresh, the local nurse, joined her. When they arrived, Suresh parked his motorcycle at my house and came in to ask for a glass of water: "Buddy, we've been doing this survey all day, and I'm dying of thirst. Can I have a glass of water?" I grabbed a glass and filled it. Suresh drank enthusiastically, but when I offered a glass to Manju, she refused. I bristled, assuming Manju had been concerned about the cleanliness of my waterpot.

Suresh and I chatted while Manju visited the front gate of each house in the neighborhood and called out to its occupants. As she did so she was barely recognizable with her hair, forehead, nose, and mouth wrapped in light cloth. After she finished, she returned to my house and insisted on leaving immediately. She stood by the motorcycle waiting for Suresh, as my neighbor Ramba Meghwal sent over tea. He visited Suresh frequently to pick up his TB medicines at the clinic and wanted to extend a small gesture of hospitality and reciprocity to Suresh and Manju. The four of us sat under the neem tree in front of my house and had tea, but Manju did not touch hers. She kept her hair, mouth, and nose covered, which made drinking tea impossible. Suresh and I poured the lukewarm tea from Manju's cup into our own and quickly drank it. Though it was clear to everyone that she had not touched her portion, we hope to hide this embarrassing sign of social rejection. Suresh and I subtly exchanged sidelong glances: rejected water and tea were practices of caste purity, which we both viewed as unacceptable.

Before she left, Manju took me aside. "You should not live here. It is not safe," she warned. I was astounded, and assured her that I was perfectly safe. Manju replied, "No, the air is not good here. All of these TB patients. It cannot be safe. You will surely get sick from the air in this neighborhood, just look. In every house there is a TB patient. You should move as soon as you can so that their air cannot get you." Her covered face and hair, her denial of hospitality, and her anxiousness to leave, it turned out, were acts of atmospheric purification, but they felt like caste purity practice. After she left, some of my neighbors asked me why she had been disguised; they found it odd that she would cover her face as if she were riding a motorcycle while walking about town. I said that I did not know. Manju's tactics of managing airborne contagion was enmeshed in a caste-like reaction to a place's people and its air. It was a closure, an atmospheric care of the self.

The air of the Meghwal neighborhood was, in some respects, dangerously permeated by TB. Most houses had little ventilation, and even when they did, everyone lived near family members and neighbors who were sick with TB. The clinic and TB hospital, however, were no less dangerous, neither were the local bus nor the village tea stall. Manju's response to air was a layering of possible responses to bacterial and caste contagion. Bacterial and caste contagion is concerned with subtle or microscopic properties moving from one body to another through proximity, on surfaces, and through the air. As in many of the contexts where TB is common, health workers like Manju and Suresh have no tools to protect themselves.[34] Infection-control measures in clinics and other public spaces lag far behind other countries. The ultraviolet lights that kill airborne bacteria and the strong ventilation systems that pull bacteria-laden air out of clinics in Europe and America do not exist in rural India. Left to her own defenses, Manju managed bacterial contagion with the set of strategies readily available to her, managing caste contact through avoidance, consumptive taboos, the refusal to enter homes and intimate spaces, covering her body, and breathing through a cloth.

Manju protected herself in her way, and I in mine. I too worried about the effects of my neighborhood's air and worked to manage it by meeting with sick friends like Siddharth Singh outside where the breeze might blow away our bodies' breathy connections. I also followed my own immunity-inspired routine by eating healthy meals and sleeping well. I worked on controlling the risks of shared air by taking actions to manage my skin-enclosed body, whereas Manju and others avoided contagion by limiting their exposure to particular airs themselves. The trouble was that practices aimed at avoiding caste pollution and bacterial contagion overlapped. They made managing TB seem discriminatory because caste contagion was also airborne.

Both Manju and Khem Singh's air work operated through a poetics of difference framed by social processes and the differing ways that air and breath could distribute risks and effects of TB through bodies, lives, and practices. Khem Singh's entangled atmospheric care and kinship whereas Manju's mingled atmospheric care for herself and caste. Though shared and necessary for life, air cannot be an assumed universal. It is enwrapped in local poetics of difference like caste and exposure despite its mobility and ephemerality. Air was a metaphor for the people who lived in it and their potential to negatively affect others, particularly outsiders like Manju and me. Becoming too much like my neighbors might be dangerous not only because I might fall ill with TB but because I might pick up other habits.[35]

CASTED AIR

When I went to the nearby town of Sadri people often asked me how I managed Ambawati's air. I was struck by this purported pneumatic difference between the town and village just ten kilometers apart. The air in both places seemed quite similar to me. I learned, however, that air could be a euphemism for caste. Many town dwellers often imagined Ambawati as a dangerous, dusty, low-caste place, and by asking of the air in Ambawati they could gesture to subtle contagious substances, like caste. They even located caste in a particular atmosphere. People wondered how I managed to remain separate from these things. The truth was that I did not remain separate.

My neighbor Chandra Meghwal worked in Sadri, and Ambawati's aerial effect on his comportment was a constant topic of conversation with his boss there. One day as I waited for a bus back to Ambawati after visiting the community hospital in Sadri, Chandra showed his boss and me a shirt he bought on a rare trip to Udaipur. About twenty years old, Chandra, like other young people in rural India who aspire to the sartorial image of material success, had an interest in fashion.[36] As his boss studied the shirt, he said, "Ah, nice shirt. Don't let the Ambawati air take hold of it. It will surely be ruined." The shop owner often contrasted Ambawati with his own small town's mercantile modernity by calling it a crass and dusty place full of unrefined indigenous people who harmed everything they touched. Still, I was flummoxed by the comment. Referring to Ambawati's air might have been a way of talking about the dust and humidity that did often settle into clothing, fading and weakening it. The boss might also have been suggesting that Ambawati's wind would literally blow the shirt away. Perhaps his connection among air, caste, and theft used air to stand for its Rawat inhabitants' storied, and nearly always unfounded, propensity

for theft.[37] Or the boss could have been suggesting that the shirt would at-
tract airborne tantric ire, which might cause the shirt or its wearer to come
to harm. It is most likely that he had intended all three meanings, alluding
to the intangible effects of caste as atmosphere and comportment. Rather
than saying "Do not let your defiling neighbors touch that nice shirt,"
which was his intention, the boss metaphorized them with air. Because the
people had the potential to soil him through caste, so did the air in which
they lived and breathed.

At home in Ambawati I asked Chandra what his boss had meant.
After all, Chandra had been standing behind the counter organizing hair
scrunchies when his boss suggested that his home, or at least its air, had
the capacity to endanger or defile things and people it touched. "What
did he mean today about your shirt and the air? He's worried about dust,
right?" I asked Chandra. "Maybe," he responded with some thought before
continuing, "I think he meant that maybe someone here would steal it or
touch it and make dirty fingerprints or something. He's always talking
about how Ambawati's air is full of bad habits, especially when he is angry
with me. It's his way of doing castism (*jativadi*) without saying it. You've
heard him say all those unkind things about Rawats. When he talked
about our village's air, he meant don't let Rawats and us [Meghwals] touch
it or something bad will happen to it. Just like when he jokes about how
he says Ambawati's air has touched you when you do something like us."

The effect of caste on Ambawati's aerial atmosphere was an ever-
present theme in Chandra's interactions with his boss. If he was late for
work or missing from the shop for too long, his boss would remark angrily,
"He will always be from a village environment, no matter what I do for
him. The Ambawati air has marked him." Air, place, behavior, and caste
could play out together as a kind of inherent quality of personhood. This
essence could be emitted from a body and spread to others and atmospheres through breath. Air, like caste, was contagion that might at any
moment slip between bodies and alter bodily states and temperaments.
Though Chandra knew not to be late, at times Ambawati's unreliable air,
in the form of a broken-down bus or family obligation, overtook him. In
response to his boss, Chandra took extra care to manage his appearance
and clothing, protecting the shirt in a closet and his person with various

creams and coverings, to avoid the influence of the Ambawati air. The good condition of his shirt was his proof that it was possible for an individual to transcend the effect of caste and place by managing air.

Joel Lee's attention to caste, smell, and disgust in response to Gopal Guru and Sundar Sarukkai's tactile phenomenology of caste suggests that caste experience extends beyond the touching body to move in and through affect and atmosphere.[38] Inspired by the Dalit intellectual Omprakash Valmiki, Lee advocates for an understanding of caste that engages it by attending to signs that might indicate or mark a particular caste group in everyday life.[39] In Ambawati, it is air and its quality that provides what Lee so beautifully calls "the affective structure of caste." When following his lead, an attention to atmospheric care's entanglement with caste can incite a methodological "attentiveness to contradiction and circumlocution, as well as to non-verbal signs like silence and gesture, may guide us toward insights altogether at odds with the 'final word' of authorized discourse" on caste.[40] Breath and enigmatic yet casted air point to other ways that caste might be experienced and felt, but they also point to ways that caste and bacterial contagion overlap to make casted tubercular atmospheres and affects. The shopkeeper, it seemed, could both contest the tactile nature of caste hierarchy and reinforce what he saw as its clear effect on Chandra's subjectivity through air.

In the incident with the shirt, a place's air became a way of locating that place's people in a hierarchy of hygiene and caste. Protecting oneself from the air of another came to present a way of thinking about caste and bacterial contagion. Ambawati's atmosphere touched Chandra and Khem Singh. It shaped who they were and what they were exposed to, from TB and tantra to soap and poverty. Uneven exposure to air's dangers seems all the more problematic, particularly for those susceptible to the affective effects of airborne caste. Yet it made Manju's self-oriented atmospheric protection feel remarkably alienating.

ATMOSPHERIC PLACES AND SELVES

Khem Singh's grandfather Dhan Singh searched for air's effects on people, animals, and others. Connections of air, place, and comportment interested Dhan Singh. They shaped the ways that he interpreted his grandson who returned from the city and the ways he thought about his son's care. "He has been touched by the city air," Dhan Singh suggested half approvingly and half critically when once shy Khem Singh returned from Surat a little more talkative after six months cutting onions and kneading flour in a restaurant. Surat's air was more than just its climate. It could stand in for and entangle all the factors that had affected Khem Singh: the people, their urban lifestyle, inequality, the presence of money, and the need to keep his wits about him. To reduce Surat's urban atmosphere to something simply climatological would be foolish, and Dhan Singh was no fool. The old man knew that both people and climates make atmospheres; atmospheres mediate the relationship between selves and spaces and become infrastructure that connects human, environmental, and geological aspects of a place.

The ability to avoid a place's air was limited and Surat's air was contagious. It touched and entered the boy's body to make new similarities and differences, whether Dhan Singh or Khem liked it or not. When I asked Khem Singh what he thought about his work and the big city, he responded with more words than he had spoken to me over the two previous years combined. "At first it was very hard work. I was not good at cutting onions and rolling chapatis. Now I can roll as many as you want with time to spare. Also, they have so many things there. All kinds of soap: one for dishes, another for clothes, another for hands. They have everything you could want if you have money." Indeed soap was also a common indicator of social changes. Ann Grodzins Gold has argued that soap is "an early harbinger of a pressing, addictive bodily need for an imported consumer good."[41] It is a new way to manage adhesive atmospheres and selves. A few hours' bus ride north of Ambawati, one of Gold's conversation partners put the connection between soap and status well, saying, "Like we see that he washes with soap, he washes his clothes with soap, and we feel envy, and try to do the same. But you have money and I don't, so I get even poorer [from spending money on soap]. For this reason some farmers are in tight circumstances."[42] Soap and TB had both, through the two airs, entangled with Khem Singh and his role in the family. As with Gold's interlocutors, air, futures, and roles in a family had a shared affective charge and were deeply personal. Still, the intergenerational effects of air were

complicated. Dhan Singh connecting Khem Singh to the city's air, growing up, and soap points to a moment of making and managing futures and
consumptive selves.

Amazed by his response, I asked if he would go back. "I will stay for a
few months here and then we'll see." Dhan Singh broke in with a toothy
grin, "See I told you Surat's air has touched him. He's grown up." "He will
go back for sure," Bheru Singh added. The bloodline of a grandfather, son,
and grandson became entangled with breath and air, relations had been reordered. The child was now the breadwinner in a marketized atmosphere.

Surat's wind had blown money into Khem Singh's pocket to help pay
some of the debts his family accrued during Bheru Singh's long affliction
with TB. This fiduciary role and Surat's air, most people agreed, had a
role in making Khem Singh an adult by contributing to the family. They
spoke little of the actual money but much of its role in reworking the relations that Ambawati's atmosphere had created for him. Khem Singh's new
character reflected for his grandfather an iterative but important change
in the young boy. "He has become a man," Dhan Singh once said. "Look,
now he even talks." This understanding of air as a force that moves and
changes people helps us see the self as affected by place, in contrast to an
understanding of people as hermetically sealed. It also shows how atmospheres connect and separate people through their multiple contagions.

My friends in Ambawati were concerned with a notion of self that is
inflected by floating affects that challenge the ideal of a fully interiorized
self as much as they challenge a fully interior or exterior atmosphere.[43] It is
not the sentimentality of air that animates social life but rather the shared
problem of permeability to infection, to others, to external ideas, to dust,
to words, to unaccounted-for desires. Indeed, Khem Singh's new audacity
and interest in soap seem to have floated in on the Surati breeze, contagious as they rippled through the family's intimate and economic futures
in the same ways that his father's and mother's illnesses had.

FLYING IN THE AIR

Places have airs that touch people, creating an atmosphere of distributed
subjectivities, tastes, desires, habits, illness, disfunctions, temperatures,
and temperaments. These too affect people, making the air of a place,

for keen observers, a way to talk about the fickle self and others' actions. A. K. Ramanujan suggests that "even space and time, the universal contexts, the Kantian imperatives, are in India not uniform and neutral, but have properties, varying specific densities, that affect those who dwell in them. The soil in a village, which produces crops for the people, affects their characters (as liars, for instance, in E. V. Daniel's village)."[44] Though I never heard people speak of the effects of soil on themselves and others, they often spoke of air in this way.[45] Rather than being an inert gaseous surrounding or context, a place and its airs can and do affect people who dwell in them. The air of a place, many told me, can make an association between people and place in which neither has determinant primacy.

It is not a far leap, then, to see how TB and the atmospheric care it requires can come to imbue both a place and people. That aerial atmospheres might move caste, bacteria, and proclivities among people raise the stakes of atmospheric care and cast a harsh light on pharmaceuticalized TB care's work to manage TB through containment. Air, it seems, evades containments to hitch a ride on breath and on people. Through affliction and other intimacies, it also makes poetic connections and differences among existing social lives. Khem Singh's father was afflicted by TB, but atmospheric care also shaped Khem Singh's life course, exposing him to Surat's marketized atmosphere. At the same time, India's TB-control program could not support atmospheric care and did little atmospheric care work. It is not impossible to provide fans or UV lights to families. It is also not impossible to further facilitate development of electrical or clinical infrastructures to aid the early diagnosis of TB. It is, however, impossible to do this with pharmaceuticals. Though air can and does move among permeable bodies and we must all attend to it as climates change, TB need not be part of this atmosphere and it need not be enmeshed in caste. It remains so, however, because of a series of biomedical failures to think atmospherically. Instead, atmospheric care might look like the antisocial and stigmatizing masks that Manju wore to ineffectively protect herself.

Atmospheric factors—social, physiological, climatic, and cosmological—determine opportunities and exposures. The air had to be right for Khem Singh to leave Ambawati, and so did his father's breath. The aeolian alignment of father and son suggests what air can teach us as breath and atmospheres. They evade a fixed biopolitical understanding of how the world works and how airborne infectious disease shapes social practices of caste and kinship. The everyday relations of intimacy and poetics of difference that give life substance can be disturbed by air, yet without the mobile connections and contagions it contains, these intimacies become stagnant and even dangerous. To think of air as bounded is to imagine human experience as if only inherited social structures might facilitate connections, but air, like breath, is not bounded. It is constantly moving and connecting people. It also must constantly be worked on. One must tend to air and be careful of the relations it might make to other people and to bacteria.

Throughout this chapter air has subverted human management while still being colored by a very human poetics of difference and boundary making. When we approach the air ethnographically, it is more than an empty medium in which pernicious substances move. Air might be better considered a set of pneumatic possibilities, or atmospheric entanglements, that can be adjusted as a way to shape its unending potential for connections and distinctions. However, this management of air and self is by no means simple. Imagining a future in dangerous air is prone to failure, danger, and infiltration. Aeolian practices of distinction and care certainly did change the course of Khem Singh's life and perhaps Dhan Singh's hope that his grandson would stay in Ambawati as a farmer.

As the fanning of Sajjan Singh and Khem Singh suggests, atmospheres are not just porous. They lack the very boundaries imposed by modernism, instead creating attunement, meaning, and sensory self-making in a world defined by subtle gradients across space and time that make some forms of life possible and foreclose others.[46] Nonetheless, atmospheres are meaningful to people in Ambawati. Atmospheres mingle with internal processes like desire; hot air makes for a hot mind. The wind can carry behaviors and ethics from one person to another in a manner far more ambiguously than contagion that moves, often by touch, from one person to the next, it can also bring things in from far away or carry away tantric words.

By attending to the ways that practices of atmospheric care and distinction shape breath and inequality, we see that atmospheres are both affective and material. Atmosphere and air, though open to intervention, are connections through which contagion, danger, and hope can flow into selves, bodies, and things. Perhaps to speak of caste through the poetics of air is indeed a poetics of difference making that reveals our shared predicament of being unequally vulnerable to something as necessary, planetary, and elusive as air. Air is filled with affect, bacteria, and other entities, but it also carries clouds, another ephemeral and amphibious substance, which have the power to touch aerially porous bodies, causing pain and bringing rain.

FIVE

MUD

What I was born in was mud, girl.
— Goddess Mariamman, quoted by Margaret Trawick,
Death, Beauty, Struggle

DAULAT SINGH RAWAT BALANCED on the seat of a bicycle that his son Mukesh and wife, Dholibai, walked homeward down Ambawati's dirt road. Monsoon rain had swamped the red clay road, and after a long day at the clinic Daulat Singh was too weak to trudge through the morass. When he saw me, he waved a prescription and twelve capsules in frustration. He cursed the minimal attention he received at Sadri's government hospital. "Damned doctors," he said. "They did not do anything, just threw some pills at me and sent me back to this mud. We are going to get admitted at the big hospital tomorrow. Will you come with us?" he asked. I agreed to accompany him. This chapter follows him from mud to hospital and back.

Daulat Singh blamed mud for his sickness. Months earlier, when I had asked him why he thought he had fallen ill with what appeared to be tuberculosis, he replied, "It's this village of mud. You should have seen it when I was a child. There was mud up to everyone's thighs. Now it is a little better, but my body is tired from all this mud. So, I am sick." I do not think he meant this entirely literally, though. Like the other atmospherics in this book, mud is indicator, anchor, and medium of embodied critique. Whenever talk of development occurred or politicians passed through Ambawati, community leaders called for an asphalt road and used the mud road as a sign of delayed development. For months each year, leaders often lamented, no vehicles could reliably access a large part of town. It became impossible to buy or sell grain or building materials. Even ambulances dared not attempt the road. Roads and drainage programs, Ambawati's denizens argued, would allow easy movement and development. They were also the purview of the state.

The mud and tuberculosis in Daulat Singh's "they . . . sent me back to this mud," I suggest, highlight the unfulfilled promises of health and development, with their aspirational capacity to organize and categorize spaces and bodies, that the state made to people in rural Rajasthan. Mud was anathema to development and mud's presence revealed, to Daulat Singh and others, a slew of absences like roads and sewers and responsive medical systems that composed their vision of what it meant to be developed. Mud was a sign and a cause of stalled development, and it was atmospherically entangled with Daulat Singh's body to cause TB.

Mud, development, and inequality are viscous and inseparable in Ambawati, Indian anthropology, and public life. Mud houses in Rajasthan tend to cluster in marginalized castes' neighborhoods and evoke the present's discriminatory past. Moreover, activists and development scholars evoke mud-walled homes as indicative of their residents' poverty and marginality.[1] In their accounts, a mud home stands in for unfulfilled development, or "backwardness," a political category used to identify whole groups, particularly castes, as disoriented or blocked from the present and future.[2] Mud in lieu of pavement and bricks might signal development's unachieved work of atmospheric care. Its presence locates Ambawati and its residents as stuck somewhere between modernity and backwardness. Stuck did seem to describe Daulat Singh's experience.

Daulat Singh used a Mewari word, *kheech*, to describe Ambawati as a village of mud, but he and others sometimes used the Hindi word *khichar* too. Both mean more than just wet earth. They describe an entanglement, a sticky jumble akin to mud or muck; something less disgusting than feces [*goo*] and less fecund than soil [*maal*].[3] *Kheech* slips between liquid and solid, soil and supplement. Thus, mud is matter out of place and a dangerous category error.[4] When we reached the hospital the liminality of mud and TB allowed Daulat Singh to move between the political and social indicators, like backwardness and poverty, that the institution would use to locate and stabilize him in a biopolitics of TB. As a member of the village of mud he too could be a mixed-up subject of care, sometimes asserting himself as a developed subject with a right to care and other times as a subject of development in need of care. Each time he did so he entered and enacted the TB hospital's biopolitics differently under a different name with a different social and political history.

In its own way, the TB hospital that we would soon visit was, like Ambawati and its mud, an essential anachronism. It was both necessary for care and governance and a place out of time. Hospitalization for the duration of TB treatment has been viewed as impractical in India since the 1950s,[5] but short stays in TB hospitals were common until health reforms in the early 1990s shuttered TB hospitals and sanitoriums across the country. Guided by a broader World Bank critique of hospitals as expensive and discriminatory, designers of India's Revised National Tuberculosis Control Program eschewed TB hospitals in favor of standardized care in primary health clinics.[6] Similarly, antique equipment, old buildings, and copious paper forms gave the hospital an otherworldly atmosphere. Along with minimal infection control, they revealed that the TB hospital was of little concern to twenty-first-century Indian public health.[7] Still, it did biopolitical work by instantiating the state, categorizing people, and documenting their diseases before sending data onward toward Delhi.

Hospitals have been fertile ground for ethnographic inquiry into the training of citizens of biopolitics. Ethnographies have shown that hospitals are sites where physicians and patients negotiate thresholds of birth, life, and death;[8] diseases are constructed and treatments and diagnoses are situated and improvised;[9] and people undergo a transformation into patients or physicians.[10] The hospital saved Daulat Singh's life, but its atmosphere of care was mixed up with states of exceptions, calls to confess an identity, and work to reveal TB as right to care. Each of these were uncomfortable and uncertain. Daulat Singh, his family, and I all modulated his identity and history in ways we thought would help him access care. At times we even lied, perhaps foiling biopolitical aspirations to know disease and patient. Much of our slipperiness around Daulat Singh's identity and treatment history was to conform to the TB hospital's role in both healing and training productive citizens, but it risked bacterial resistance too. As Alice Street writes, hospitals have a "paradoxical capacity to be at once sites of 'total' biopolitical management and places where alternative and transgressive social orders emerge."[11]

Connections to Ambawati's mud and its effect on Daulat Singh's breath followed us through the hospital's hallways, mixing up the hospital's attempts to frame Daulat Singh's subjectivity and provide care. We found, however, that we were not the only culprits leaving muddy tracks on the hospital's ideals of transparency and rationality; like mud, money and physicians gummed up the wheels of rationalism and routinization. Mud and TB, as Daulat Singh exclaimed that day, are an atmospheric entanglement that reveals how development, or its lack, gathers bodies and selves in a knot of labored respiration, languished hopes, and bacteria that the hospital could not cut. Like mud, the TB hospital, this chapter shows, is a site of both biopolitical revelation and subjective slipperiness. Concerns that seem far from TB weigh it down, acting similarly to "the muck of ages" that Karl Marx suggested clings to bodies and the future itself.[12] Mud as indicator of progress not quite achieved also clings to TB care in the hospital, where the family would soon spend nearly a week.

MOBILITY AND MUD

As we walked homeward, Mukesh recounted the day. That morning, Dholibai had pawned a heavy piece of her silver jewelry and asked the neighbors to keep an eye on the family's adolescent daughter and livestock. The trio was headed to Udaipur's TB hospital, an old sanitorium now run by the city medical college. At the crossroads, however, they decided to visit the closer Sadri Community Hospital instead.[13] After a ten-kilometer bus ride, they reached the Sadri hospital. There the doctor gave Daulat Singh antibiotics, a pain killer, and an appointment to return the next week. They had hoped he would be admitted and tested for TB, but he had not been. With what seemed like no other option and unable to wait any longer, Daulat Singh and his family decided to return home for the night and make the three-hour bus journey to Udaipur the next morning. I had agreed to join them, but as I packed a small bag that evening, I considered why they had invited me. I knew the family well and they knew of my interest in TB, but some part of their invitation was likely in hopes that my presence would catalyze better care or provide a financial backstop if things got out of hand. I was happy to be both of those things if necessary. I was already mixed up in many lives and illnesses, and I wanted Daulat Singh to live.

Rain softly fell the next morning as I made breakfast and then slid down the bemired red clay road to the bus stand. Rain continued to fall as the seven a.m. bus came and went. The bus stand's pond and the road's many puddles overflowed, but there was no sign of the family. Mukesh called near eight. His voice sounded worried. The family had prepared to leave but could not arrange a motorcycle to carry Daulat Singh from their house to the bus stand. The neighborhood drivers, he explained, were afraid of losing traction on the slick road. Daulat Singh could not walk in the rain and the mud was too deep for a bicycle. We decided to try again the next day and I slogged home. Mukesh called an hour later. He explained that because the rain had stopped, we should catch the eleven a.m. bus. It was nearly eleven, so I crisscrossed the waterlogged fields as a shortcut to the bus stand. My sandals filled with wet soil, their weight doubling as I trudged through the fertile mud. My shortcut, the most direct path, took twice as long as the flooded road would have.

I eventually reached the tea stall near the bus stand. Each monsoon Gajanandibai shields the tea stall and a small patio with a bright blue tarp. This year, the tarp's two teak sapling supports had taken root. Nourished by the mud that weighed Daulat Singh and me down, they sprouted roots and leaves, refusing to transform from tree to lumber. That morning, the tarp's center sagged so deeply with accumulated rain that the saplings seemed ready to snap. A group of people huddled under its weight, enduring the risk of a deluge and the smoke billowing from beneath the teapot. I ducked inside to find Daulat Singh, Dholibai, and Mukesh. "Good! So, you are coming." Daulat Singh rasped as I arrived. "Of course I'm coming." I responded, shaking the grime from my pant legs.

Soon the Sagwai-bound minibus came splashing through potholes toward the bus stand and our journey continued. Travel quickly affected Daulat Singh. He struggled to disembark the bus in Sagwai, where we would catch one of the publicly owned long-distance buses that plie the asphalt highway connecting Mewar's market towns. Daulat Singh's breath rasped as he walked, and he coughed phlegm from his lungs as we waited under another bus stand tarp. Soon, we were on the bus and lucky enough to find seats. Thirty minutes later the bus entered the Mewar plain and left the last village within which the small family had social relations.

Now away from home, Dholibai pulled back the veil that had covered her face since leaving the house. Soon Daulat Singh curled up across their seat to rest his head in her lap. He slept all the way to Udaipur, waking only occasionally to wheeze and spit phlegm out the window. The easy intimacy of Daulat Singh's head in Dholibai's lap marked our movement outside the relational geography of Ambawati, its kin connections, and an order of things that required the performance of disinterested intimacy among family members.[14] We had left some of the relational strictures that Daulat Singh would tell me were indicative of the land of mud.

Mukesh and I ate peanuts as the monsoon-soggy landscape bumped past. He told me that he had accompanied his cousin's wife to the hospital a year earlier and "knew a little." He would guide us to the hospital and through its circuits. We reached Udaipur and crammed into an autorickshaw. I tried to remember the route as the auto circled the famous Fateh Sagar Lake, passed a cove of pink water lilies, and followed the road inland. We ascended the hills that ring the city, and eventually a tall white spire reminiscent of temples in eastern India emerged. I wondered about its purpose until the rickshaw sputtered to a stop at its base. It was a crumbling white clock tower and gate; a faded memento of a colonial-era TB sanitorium built on this once wooded hill far from the city. The clock's four faces, two in roman numerals and two in Devanagari, were stuck at 3:18.

Beyond the gate, about ten low buildings of standard government architecture and color—peach—dotted the hillside. Though the grounds were overgrown at their edges by lantana, touch-me-not, thorn apples, cat's claw, and milkweed, there was no mud in sight. The roads and paths connecting the stone buildings of the hospital were asphalt. Yellow and black curbs marked the boundary between grass and street. We were not in Ambawati anymore. People, some with handkerchiefs and scarves tied across their mouth and nose, walked the green lawns that spread over the flaky red soil. Some had set up shops selling fruit, vegetables, or tea. Still more people were cooking and eating on the hospital grounds. Some were

visibly sick, their bodies whittled by TB. Others looked healthy but fear-
ful. They accompanied sick family members. Still others walked with purpose. Perhaps they had been here a long time. Many proceeded as we did,
slowly and unsurely in the ordered, parklike atmosphere.

Dholibai spread a blanket she had made from old fertilizer sacks, and
we waited outside the outpatient ward and intake building.[15] The rickshaw
driver had directed us there, explaining that the doctors would arrive at 4
p.m. Soon, a young man strode up confidently. "What are you doing?" he
asked. Mukesh explained that we were waiting for a doctor, but the man
shook his head: "Today is Sunday. The hospital closed at noon. No one will
come back. You will have to wait until tomorrow or go to the emergency. It
is over there." He pointed up the hill vaguely. "You could go to the doctor's
house too. If he is home, he can admit you, but he will take 200 rupees to
admit someone after hours."

Forlorn, we walked to the emergency ward. The mud had delayed us.
What if the doctors did not admit Daulat Singh? Where would we stay
the night? Why did we not think of Sunday? An unspoken tension grew
as we walked slowly, stopping often for Daulat Singh to catch his breath.
I resisted the urge to carry the slender man to our destination. We found
the emergency ward and a nurse in a white polyester sari. She asked what
we wanted. Mukesh said we needed to see a doctor to admit his father.
Covering her mouth with the end of her sari in a gesture of self-protection,
she asked how long Daulat Singh had been coughing and if they kept their
house clean. Mukesh answered that their house was clean, and Dholibai
grumbled, hurt that her domestic labor had been questioned. Dholibai
pulled her veil down further over her face for the rest of the interaction
and sat fuming. The nurse left to find the doctor. When she came back,
she sat in the sun outside the waiting room door as far from us as possible.

The nurse's question and covered mouth may have gestured to the
double marginalization of caste status and mud that Daulat Singh's troubled breath could evoke.[16] She had implied that mud, or at least mixed-up
matter, and troubled breath had a close disordering relationship that were
worth staying away from.

The nurse's question about hygiene invoked the mud we had left
behind. Managing mud and maintaining hygiene is, as Sarah Pinto has

shown, a marker of caste hierarchy in contemporary rural India.[17] More-over, processes of exclusion and marginalization, no longer acceptable on the basis of caste purity, are now expressed and enacted through a language of hygiene and self-protection from germs or smells.[18] Keeping a disordered house, the nurse seemed to assert, might reveal impurity and lack of progress that came with TB.[19] The nurse's question suggested that Dholibai's role in a new hygiene-based hierarchy was to manage aspirations of mobility by mediating mud's fecund and filthy potential. That her husband was sick and that we had arrived at the hospital with rural accents after a long disheveling bus ride opened the question of hierarchy and hygiene.[20] The nurse's gesture signaled that bacterial contagion and caste pollution overlapped. Their boundaries were slippery in the controlled space of the hospital and complicated its imagined atmosphere of care. They would soon become even slipperier.

SLIPPERY STORIES

The young doctor seemed startled when he entered the darkened waiting room. A family from the hinterland and a lanky Caucasian man were unexpected. Standing a few paces away from Daulat Singh, he asked about appetite, persistent cough, weight loss, and fevers. Finally, he asked if Daulat Singh had been sick with TB before. Daulat Singh quickly said no. "You've never taken treatment before?" the doctor asked again. Daulat Singh replied again, "No, never." "Are you sure?" the physician persisted. I knew he had and spoke as the doctor stood over us, "Doctor, a lot of people in his neighborhood have TB right now. Several have started on second-category and [multiple-drug-resistant]-TB medicines." I hoped this intervention might nudge the doctor toward testing for drug resistance without exposing Daulat Singh's lie. Daulat Singh had started treatment twice before. Both times he had been called to South India to mediate a conflict between his sons there and left treatment in Ambawati.

Unfazed, the doctor asked a series of questions and Daulat Singh answered. "Name?" "Daulat Singh." "Father's name?" "Kartho Singh." "Caste?" "Rawat." "Age?" "About fifty." "District? Block?" "Sadri." "Village?" "Ambawati." "Religion?" "Hindu." "BPL?"[21] "Yes. "Ever treated for TB before?" "No." "For sure?" "For sure." His questions answered, the doctor admitted Daulat Singh. Daulat Singh would have a bed down the hill in Ward Three, but he needed to get a sputum smear and chest X-ray the next day. Until then, the doctor told us, he would receive only pain relievers. Before walking away, the young physician thrust three forms into Mukesh's hand. "Show them to Ward Three's nurse and the hospital intake nurse in Ward One," he instructed before walking away.

I had made a split-second decision to support Daulat Singh in conceal- ing his previous treatment because I had a vague sense that revealing the information would risk a denial of care. For the next few hours, I wondered why I too felt compelled to lie and inject opacity into the doctor's diagnos- tic work. It was one of several slippery stories of disease progression and identity we told to access care that seemed nearly out of reach. This one occluded a central part of Daulat Singh's disease experience, and it might even have contaminated the rest of his care. Our omission concealed infor- mation that could guide the physician as he selected tools to reveal Daulat Singh's body and illness to the hospital's medical gaze.[22] Had we disclosed Daulat Singh's earlier treatments, the doctor might have chosen diagnos- tic tests that revealed drug resistance or prescribed a different course of treatment suggested at the time to mitigate potential drug resistance.[23] We arrived on a Sunday and felt precarious visiting the emergency room to ask for care as an exception. It felt possible that Daulat Singh could be rejected, at least until morning. Spending the night outside or returning to Ambawati would have been too much for Daulat Singh. None of us wanted to be turned away. We tried to fit the mold of exceptionally pliant and deserving patients to access what seemed a spotless hospital.

We descended the hill toward Ward Three and found a whitewashed and pillared hall containing three rows of white metal beds. Sick men filled the beds and their attendants the floor, but the nurse's office was empty. Seeing our confusion, a woman told us that he had left on his mo- torcycle. We took a seat on the polished cement floor and the antiseptic smell of floor cleaner filled our nostrils. As time passed and with no sign of the nurse returning, Mukesh and I set out back up the hill to Ward One.

Ward One, mauve colored and half-moon shaped with partitions be- tween each pair of beds, is reserved for seriously ill patients, those with multiple-drug-resistant (MDR) TB. Two deathly sick men and their attendants occupied each bay. It was dark and smelled musty, unlike open and airy Ward Three. Mukesh and I searched the ward, passing ninety full beds to return where we started. Finally, we found an office with an open door and pulled curtain. We drew the curtain a bit to find a man sleeping on the desk. Mukesh roused him and we learned that he was the nurse. He took our papers, opened a pad of forms, and leafed through a large red account book. He asked the same questions the emergency doctor had. Mukesh answered, but a little differently. "Are you the patient?" "No, my father is. He is waiting in Ward Three." "His name?" "Daulatraj." "Father's name?" "Karthalal." "Caste?" "Meena." "Age?" "Maybe fifty." "District, block, village, phone number?" He handed us the new form and told us that Daulatraj Meena had been registered. "Go to the outpatient clinic promptly at nine a.m. The crowds grow as the day wears on," he warned as we left.[24]

Daulat Singh's name, his father's name, and his caste had all shifted from form to form. Father and son used different politics of identity to secure a place in the hospital. Father obscured Ambawati's mud and social marginality by asserting status as a holder of citizenship rights. Son highlighted the mud, backwardness, and caste to ask for care as a member of a group with special access to the state's pastoral care.[25] Mukesh's responses transformed the family from Rawats, or "forward" landlords, to indigenous, or "backward," Meenas. The state had designated Meenas as in need of particular development aid owing to being "shy of contact" and having "primitive traits" and "backwardness".[26] They made Daulat a double entry in some columns and a single in another, mixing forwardness and backwardness, development and "primitive traits." One patient became two people, two castes, and two statuses within the state's political hierarchy of castes.[27]

This confusion moved through information systems, slipping forward to Delhi and onward. Father and son had asserted two mutually exclusive proper names and caste identities for Daulat Singh. Both muddled the hospital's caste-category-based statistics taking, and each employed a different technique to present a subject who he felt merited care. Though the other data made it likely that this was the same person, the jumbled identity injected opacity and doubt into the hospital's confessional biopolitics of accounting.[28] In addition, Daulat Singh's earlier treatment records lingered in other ledgers at other clinics to make their way toward Delhi too.

Daulat Singh and Dholibai were asleep when we returned, and the nurse was nowhere to be found. Mukesh and I waited on the floor in silence. Our trip to Ward One with its dark rooms and desperately ill patients had thrown us. An hour later, the ward nurse arrived to find the four of us on the floor. He attended to patients and settled into his office. Exchanging sidelong glances and a tentative "let's go," Mukesh and I rose to knock on his door. As the nurse looked up, Mukesh thrust the papers at him. "We have been admitted." The nurse took the papers, opened another large pad, and asked the same questions. "Name?" "Daulat Singh." "Father's name?" "Kartho Singh." "Age?" "Maybe fifty." "Caste?" "Rawat." "Phone number?" A third entry occurred. This one followed the pattern of identity or subjectivity that obscured Daulat Singh's indigenous status and Ambawati's place within the large hill tract of southeast Rajasthan while highlighting a long history of more flexible kinship relations between Rajputs and people who lived near forests.[29] The difference between the men's sense of which self to confess—indigenous person or landowner—was part of an assertion as a particular form of citizen to the right to care. Mukesh asked for care as a marginalized person, but Daulat Singh's account of a citizenship as a landowning elite made claims to care as an already full citizen. He entered himself into pan-Indian and nationalist histories of mainstream Hinduism's spread but lost his connection to the muddied history of indigeneity in south Rajasthan.[30]

Form full, the ward nurse tore out the two new sheets of paper and took the old ones. These were Daulat Singh's treatment forms. "Go early tomorrow to the outpatient clinic and pay for the X-ray. This form is for the sputum and this one for the X-ray. Do not confuse them," he ordered. Mukesh had a sixth-grade education and command of standard Hindi, but he was still anxious about the forms. They were in English. Together, we notched the corner of one so he could distinguish them. Along with the papers, the nurse handed Mukesh a small glass bottle with Daulat Singh's patient number written in permanent marker. He explained that we must collect Daulat Singh's first morning sputum in this container. Then he explained that there would be milk and sesame seed mush for Daulat Singh twice daily, but nothing for Mukesh or Dholibai. We listened, realizing that we had not eaten since morning. Finally, the nurse handed Mukesh some medicines and told us to go and take bed number forty-eight at the end of the ward. This bed had a massive hole in the mattress. As we searched for a new bed, the nurse arrived to tell us that one of our forms was unsigned. Mukesh and I went back to the emergency building to get the signature while Dholibai and Daulat Singh found a new bed in the middle of the hall.

Mukesh and I soon returned to the ward. Everything would have to wait until morning, so Dholibai and Mukesh readied for a night on the floor near Daulat Singh's cot. Understaffed and under-resourced, the TB hospital, like many others, requires people like Mukesh and Dholibai to sleep on the floor next to their loved ones to care for them.[31] Patients and their families spend as long as two weeks in these open wards, surrounded by people suffering from an untreated and contagious airborne illness that kills millions each year. Such exposure to physical and social death in order to access care is a constitutive part of modernity, rationalization, and the hospital itself.[32]

We agreed that an American guest spending the night on the hospital floor would cause too much commotion. I would take the bus to Udaipur and return early the next day. Mukesh accompanied me to the bus stop. As we walked, he pushed half his money and the family's Below Poverty Line card into my hand, saying, "It is open here, and I will have to sleep in the ward. I cannot let anyone steal this when we sleep. Take it with you and bring it in the morning." I cached the document in my backpack and the bills in my wallet. Next, I asked Mukesh, and perhaps myself, why we had not told the doctor about his father's previous treatment. He replied, "They would have yelled at us and sent us home. We came all this way. We needed to get Father admitted. They would have told us to go back to our local clinic and get the treatment there where we had before or get a referral. But we are here, and he needs treatment here first, so we could not tell the doctor the truth." Indeed, when we felt it necessary, all four of us had performed Daulat Singh as an ideal subject of biopolitics worthy of care. Dholibai had asserted hygiene. Daulat Singh had asserted political power and compliance. Mukesh had asserted his right as an Adivasi to access development and health projects aimed at equity, and I had asserted need and risk. We four were a jumble of concerns for respectability, development, and risk as we moved through the hospital's discipline with its confessions of self and subject. For its part, the hospital—with its states of exception, multiple entreaties to confess the self, and unmediated exposures to life-threatening bacteria—reveals the messy limits of a pastoral hygienic Indian state.[33]

As I rode on the ramshackle minibus to Udaipur, my mind whirled through the day's activities, but mostly I thought about how badly I needed a shower. It had been a sweaty, exhausting day, and my American anxiety about bacteria urged me to scrub. My own theories of contagion suggested (erroneously) that a hot bath might remove a tuberculosis infection picked up at the hospital where exposure seemed inevitable. On reaching a cheap hotel, I filled the bath bucket to the lip with hot water and began splashing away. The hand pump in Ambawati emitted only tepid water, and this was my first hot bath in weeks. The warm water loosened layers of dirt and dust from my skin and hair. A stream of muddy water trickled toward the drain. Ambawati's mud had traveled on and marked me too.

ADHESIONS AND EXPOSURES

My phone rang at five thirty the next morning. It was Mukesh. Anxious, he asked when I would arrive and told me to come quickly. He needed the BPL card. I rushed to Udaipur's Delhi Gate and waited for the bus to the hospital. It was six a.m. No bus came. At six thirty autorickshaw drivers arrived to begin their day's work. Still no buses. One driver had equipped his vehicle with an impressive speaker system that boomed *sufiana kalam*, a popular form of Islamicate devotional music. As the second song finished, I decided to spend a hundred rupees on the bespeakered auto. Aspiration and speed, after all, are expensive. We sped away as the singer, Chhote Majid, sang of the veiled, opaque nature of a God he knew existed. Half listening, I reflected on the day's tasks. We needed to find TB hidden in Daulat Singh's body—something we were already convinced was there but needed to expose technologically. It was something like the God that Chhote Majid and other Sufi theologians suggest is present but behind a screen.

The driver stopped at the hospital gate, and the music still echoed as I walked to Daulat Singh's ward. My friends were visibly shaken. Dholibai was talking to herself and to me about not knowing what to do and how three patients had died in the night. She pointed to an empty bed with a large oxygen tank next to it, but Mukesh paid her no attention. He asked me to see the nurse with him. In the nurses' office a middle-aged woman looked up as I pulled the BPL card from my bag. Mukesh stammered, "See, we have a BPL card. It means we do not have to pay for the medicines you gave him this morning." The woman found their BPL number and registered it in her book, telling Mukesh she would need a photocopy. "Okay, fine." She turned back to Mukesh, "So, now that you have this you should go early to the outpatient ward to get the paper that tells you to get the X-ray. They will take seventy rupees, but not from you. Show your BPL card. You do not need to pay it." Today the family had engaged another kind of biopolitical category, that of people in poverty soliciting the health care system's role in poverty alleviation. This time they had a card as proof.[34]

It was not yet seven thirty, but Dholibai had already repacked, and Daulat Singh was seated on the bed's edge. We set off more than an hour early for our appointment, but we were not the first to arrive at the outpatient building. Dholibai spread the cloth, and we settled in among those waiting. A middle-class family ate breakfast on the building's paved driveway. On its stairs, two nurses chatted about their evening meals. A young man stood near a pillar. He recognized our accents and the five of us struck up the easy kind of conversation shared among people waiting an indeterminate time. Mauz was from a village relatively close to Ambawati. He had lived at the hospital for a while as an MDR-TB patient and returned today for a six-month checkup, sputum sample, and chest X-ray. Mukesh asked questions about where to get food and which of the doctors were particularly good, and Mauz told us about the hospital and its routine.

Soon another man arrived. He removed the large lock connecting the chains binding the glass doors. A nurse called out playfully, "Oh, Kamal Singh, you're right on time." It was ten minutes past nine. As he and the nurses disappeared into the building, Mauz and Mukesh followed. They were greeted by a shout from Kamal Singh, "It's not open yet, *yaar*, let me wash the floor once."[35] Kamal Singh mopped the floor inside the building and out, and almost as if they knew the freshly disinfected floor had not yet dried, the doctors arrived. One scattered the middle-class family and their picnic breakfast to park his car in the building's ambulance bay. He bustled in and we all followed.

Mauz was first in line. The doctor filled out another form with its now routine questions. He asked Mauz's name. "Mauz." "Last name," the doctor continued. "Harijan," replied Mauz. On hearing this casted surname, which associated Mauz with ritually polluting work like cleaning human feces, removing small animal carcasses, and herding pigs, the whole family was startled. They had suddenly found out that this man was an untouchable, and what Sundar Sarukkai has called the "affect of untouchability" washed over them.[36] Mauz gave the man at the desk some money and hurried to his X-ray. As he passed, Dholibai pulled her veil tight over her head and Mukesh stepped a pace back to give Mauz a wide berth. We chatted no more. The fluid boundaries of the body and its subtle substances that could occur outside the village where identities were less predictable snapped back in place, not for fear of TB—we were already exposed to bacteria—but for fear of crossing the caste barrier that affectively separated sticky mud and stinking feces.

An inscriptive practice that asked patients to assert or confess a self to the hospital, just as those Daulat Singh and Mukesh had completed the day before, revealed a danger of caste pollution greater than drug-resistant TB. The anonymous rational bureaucratic care aimed at looking inside Mauz's body and identity had revealed caste again. Perhaps it even reinscribed caste on bodies associated with sticky substances. Caste was far more of a feeling than a structure; TB and caste contagions moved in subtle unseen lateral ways with their own lines and risky connectivity. Caste difference was an affective sense of disgust or potential disgust.[37] It inhabited the most rationalized of spaces and the small family's hesitancy to be exposed to caste's contagion sat in sharp relief to the millions or trillions of TB bacilli that floated through the hospital's air unconsidered and unabated. Perhaps connections between caste and contagion had guided Mukesh and Daulat Singh's own confessions of caste.

We retrieved Daulat Singh's X-ray slip and left the cavernous room to climb the hill again. Dholibai steadied Daulat Singh all the way. We reached the X-ray and sputum-test building, but the technicians had not yet arrived. As we waited, Daulat Singh asked Mukesh to take him to a small bridge nearby. Wheezing racked Daulat Singh's small frame before he grabbed the bridge railing and vomited a white foamy substance into the stream below. It seemed that this might be an emergency, but he finished and regained composure. As he caught his breath, the X-ray technician arrived, and a line formed. We stood outside the X-ray room, and Dholibai began again to tell her story of the night before:

> Three, three died in the night. The one right next to our bed, he died. We were sleeping on the floor. There was so much coughing in the ward. I awoke and there were so many people by his bed. The doctors tried to help him, but they could not. They brought all kinds of machines and tanks but nothing [helped]. They hooked the tank to his face. His wife, she cried out and cried again but nothing. They could not save him. He vomited so much blood, and then they all left. In the morning the Harijans took his body away. Two others, they went too, in the night like that.

We fell into silent reflection after Dholibai's story. The night's events had revealed that the TB hospital, despite offering hope for a caring atmosphere, also exposed people to death and potential abandonment. Though the hospital aimed to help people like Daulat Singh and his family, the specter of death that hovered within it showed that even there some TB patients cannot be saved. Furthermore, exposure to the deaths and castes of strangers was unsettling. Having been so close to three strangers in the moment of their deaths exposed Dholibai and her family to what Jonathan Parry has called "death pollution."[38] No amount of disinfectant could remove this danger, more subtle and potent than mud or disease, that imbued the hospital. Death had permeated the ward despite its strong smell of disinfectant.

The X-ray technician's shout pulled us back into the world of the hospital and its medical contagions. "You, you're next, hurry up," he bellowed. Daulat Singh walked into the large room with black painted walls. The X-ray tech told him to mount a stool behind the stand holding the X-ray film. "Take off your shirt," the technician ordered. With a cough Daulat Singh removed his shirt and handed it to Mukesh. "Don't cough in here," the technician barked. "First thing in the morning, and they're already coughing on me." The cough created an obvious atmospheric connection to TB and Daulat Singh that the technician hoped to avoid.

As Daulat Singh stood boney and shirtless in front of the X-ray machine, the technician gave another command, this one dripping with contempt, "Take off those *mala*s (necklaces made of sanctified materials) and look over here." A devout man, Daulat Singh hesitated. He cautiously handed Mukesh the necklaces and draped his arms over the frame's props as instructed. The tech stood behind the large conical X-ray machine and snapped the image. He told Daulat Singh to get down, put his shirt on, and come back that afternoon. Mukesh and Dholibai were upset. "But if we do not have the X-ray, how will the doctors start treatment? They will not start. It will be another day here and no treatment. Another night here," Dholibai said as we walked out of the X-ray area.

Next, Mukesh and I crossed the dark corridor to a wide table in the sputum-testing area. Its canvas cover blotched by years of iodine spills, the table held a collection of small sputum-sample bottles anchoring test order forms like paper weights. Most contained a greenish-yellow lump of freshly coughed sputum. Mukesh and I placed Daulat Singh's two jars of bacteria-laced sputum on top of the form we were told was to go with Daulat Singh's samples. We left the samples, once part of Daulat Singh's body but now clearly separate, among the others in this biohazardous jumble of glass jars. The lab attendant told us that the doctors would have Daulat Singh's results the next morning.

Deflated, but with our day's work complete, we walked down the hill. About halfway we took a break on the curb. "Why can't the man do it faster? He only had a few. Why would it take all day?" Daulat Singh grumbled. "They will never start treatment. All the nurses say they can do nothing until there is an X-ray. Now the X-ray man will not give it. He just wants money. He would give it faster if we paid him." As we sat on the curb, another woman who had been spinning the same circles in the lab came over: "You can get the X-ray now if you give him 200 rupees."

"Thank you, but we'll wait," Mukesh said. "Leave [the X-ray] lying there where he took it," Daulat Singh snapped in frustration.

We rose and went back to the ward. As Daulat Singh settled into bed, Mukesh asked a young man caring for his own sick father about the X-ray. After a brief conversation, Mukesh called to me, "Bhaiya, let's get the X-ray." We started up the hill again. Mukesh vented his disappointment: "It's supposed to be free with a BPL card, but look, it took 400 rupees ($7.20) to get the head of the hospital to sign a form after you left last night. The nurse said I had to go to his house and get him to sign another form. He would not [sign] without a little extra money. And now look, here we go. Off to give the X-ray man another two hundred so he will do his job." I replied, "We could just wait. Anyway, they will not have the sputum test results." "No, we need it now. Maybe if they have the X-ray, they will start my father on the drugs, and he can start getting well. We need the X-ray." Off we went to bribe the X-ray technician.[39] This time we would expose something of our own.

Before he went into the X-ray tech's room, I handed Mukesh 200 rupees change from my wallet. He could not give the X-ray tech one of his 500 rupee notes lest the man take it all. Waiting for my friend to pay another bribe, I read the sign on the wall. In three languages, Sanskrit, Hindi, and English, it read

न त्वहं कामये राज्यं, न स्वर्गं नापुनर्भवम् ।
कामये दुःखतप्तानां प्राणिनामार्तिनाशनम् ॥

अपने लिये न मैं राज्य चाहता हूँ न स्वर्ग की इच्छा करता हूँ मोक्ष भी नहीं चाहता ।
मैं तो केवल यह चाहता हूँ कि दुःख सेटेप हुवे प्राणियां की पीड़ा का नाश हो ॥

I do not want for myself kingdom, or heaven, or even freedom from rebirth.
I desire to end the suffering of beings that are in anguish.

The lofty sentiments of the Mahabharata's generous king Raja Rantidev rang hollow. Mukesh was behind that very wall paying a public employee to hand over the free X-ray. When he emerged, the X-ray was still wet. We stood in the warm morning sun waiting for the film to dry. A pair of hefty men and a desperately thin couple waved their own "expedited" X-rays in the sun too. Soon the outlines of Daulat Singh's rib cage emerged. A few minutes more and Mukesh and I could begin to see the white smudge-like cavities that TB had carved in his father's lungs. Perhaps the spots in Daulat Singh's X-ray and his symptoms would allow the doctors to start him on treatment, if only to reassure Dholibai before night fell.

We returned to Daulat Singh's ward before the hospital physicians finished their rounds. The doctors were clustered on one side of the ward. Mukesh walked to a nurse. He chose one who did not have a handkerchief tied across her mouth. Handing her the X-ray, he told her that he had gotten it early. She slid it inside the chart near Daulat Singh's bed and went back to her work with other patients. As soon as she had done so, the ward nurse announced that no attendants were allowed in the ward during rounds. Mukesh and I went off to the hospital's grimy canteen for a lunch of overpriced lentils and mealy chapatis. Mukesh was certain that his father would start treatment soon. He explained that the canteen would be the family's biggest expenditure because, even though Daulat Singh's treatment was free, he and Dholibai needed to provide everyday care and to eat. Access to free physicians and biomedicine for Daulat Singh was expensive because this infrastructure of care lacked the staff to do much caregiving.[40]

Our presence in the hospital as caregivers blurred the lines between order and disorder. We blurred them even more as we muddled through the hospital's bureaucratic attempts at accounting. In the process, we sullied the many forms of knowledge that the hospital aimed to create. We muddled the counts of patients that would be sent to Delhi and onward as data that would legitimize expenditure. We subverted seemingly transparent bureaucratic systems of anonymous care by paying bribes and expedition fees. Mud in the hospital's processes of hygiene and scrutinizing a rationalized body exposed other expenses and logics at work, corrupt and otherwise. The processes that made the hospital and Daulat Singh's body transparent to science and the state made spaces in which practices and materials crossed categories to remain opaque or even invisible.[41] Often they were hidden behind walls adorned with lofty sentiments.

The sputum report did not come back by evening, and despite the X-ray the doctor could not start Daulat Singh's treatment until the next day when sputum results arrived. They revealed what symptoms and the X-ray already made clear: Daulat Singh had TB and a relatively high number of bacteria in his sputum. He would stay another four days in the hospital before returning home to start the directly observed therapy, short-course (DOTS) from the Ambawati health center a third time. The hospital cleared the murky opacity of the body and its sticky substances, but it was still unclear if the bacteria in his body were resistant to the antibiotics that he would take for six months. He was lucky: this time, he completed the course of medications and was declared cured.

MEANWHILE, BACK IN THE MUD

I assumed that as Daulat Singh's breath and strength steadied he would talk less about mud, pollution, and contagion. I was wrong. Several months later the mud had hardened and dust whirls moved across the fields of corn stubble as we chatted at his house. I asked Daulat Singh what had happened to cause his illness. He responded a bit sharply and repeated what he had told me in the soggy months before our visit to the hospital, "I live here, that's why. You should have seen this place when I was a child. There was mud up to your waist. There was so much that you could not even move. So much that once the lord had an elephant that got stuck in the mud so deeply that they could not pull it out and, after trying for three days, it died. Everything was difficult, how could all this mud not cause the breaths to move a little." I had heard the elephant story before, but never thought much of it. After visiting the hospital, however, a story of mud so pernicious that it could trap even an elephant seemed to hold new meaning. Had Daulat Singh and Ambawati's mud also trapped the biomedical elephant, foiling its attempts at linear progress and organizational power?

Perhaps, just as the kingly sovereign power's pageantry and authority wrapped up in the elephant had been no match for mud, so too did the biopolitical pastoral state's health care system struggle. It bemired itself deeper and deeper in inequality as it aimed to use rationality, triage, pharmaceuticals, vertical-control programs, and other schemes to address questions of development, caste, and airborne infectious disease. It certainly revealed the limits of the hospital's capacity to enact the biopolitical processes often associated with institutions or provide atmospheric care.

Meaning remained messy. Daulat Singh and his family hoped to reshape the atmosphere that entangled his body with mud's confusing metaphors and connections by visiting the hospital. Dholibai revealing her face was a first example of this transition out of Ambawati and into something else, like the nation or the region, with its own affective and care atmosphere. They hoped that its institutionalized atmospheric care as food, attention, and support might be the opposite of TB care in Ambawati, where it had been reduced to pharmaceuticals, but they had to provide this care themselves far from home in a confusing technological space. We quickly learned that even TB hospitals are betwixt and between sites stuck between older ideals of caring spaces and the pharmacueticalized TB's call for their closure.

The TB hospital, at least as experienced by Daulat Singh and his family, is far from a total institution that shapes or modernizes the forms of life within its ambit.[42] Instead, it is open to the world and requires an immense amount of hidden care labor by families. By asking families and patients to do the atmospheric and tactile caregiving themselves, the hospital loses much of the organizing and homogenizing power it may never really have had. Though atmospheric care could have been possible during the heyday of sanitoriums before antibiotics, the neoliberalization and pharmaceuticalization of TB care in the 1990s meant that hospitals already strapped for resources were working against financial and policy priorities.

Despite Daulat Singh's hope, the hospital was a context or infrastructure for treatment but not care. There simply was no money for infection-control measures, or for safe places for Mukesh and Dholibai to sleep, or a digital X-ray machine, or the salaries to pay for more nurses to provide atmospheric care there. Instead, the hospital with its pillared halls, metal cots, and red polar fleece blankets could provide only the context for atmospheric care that lay attendants like Mukesh and Dholibai would provide.

It was so busy managing the basics of diagnosis and treatment that it could not afford to implement necessary practices of care. Development, as Daulat Singh imagined it, was indeed delayed.

The TB hospital was only modestly successful in its attempt to craft citizens. Its capacity to render bodies as transparent purifications of biological facts or objects of charitable care was troubled by the action that we hoped would represent Daulat Singh as a docile citizen deserving of exceptional care. Our management of mud and attempts to create atmospheric care in the hospital shows how patients must craft certainty and order by performing hygienic, constrained, and certain selves in that context. This was not easy, and we tried to secure access to an elusive atmosphere of care with the help of money and performances of bureaucratic subjectivity, but it seemed to recede constantly before us, leaving only a sticky mess to get through. In the process we revealed that the hospital with all its markings of hygiene, order, hierarchy, and progress was still anything but transparent.

By entering the hospital, we hoped that its combination of imagined development and medicine could create an atmosphere of care capable of managing mud. The hospital did create a clear representation of what was happening in Daulat Singh's body behind the muddiness of social and physical life and eventually provided pharmaceuticals, but even its revelatory capacity was troubled by slippery identities and corruption. Even under the ordering impetus of X-ray, a total institution, and public health hygiene, his bacteria and their effect on his body remained murky because of our collective tactics to mitigate the risks of being matter out of place in the hospital. In other words, mud and TB revealed a connection to Ambawati and matter out of place that persisted in marking Daulat Singh's agricultural and insufficiently developed status even as we visited the hospital, and he was aware of this.

Regardless of whether the elephant in the story could stand in for sovereign power or Daulat Singh himself, mud or muck is the medium through which Ambawati and TB entered his body and breath. Mud even made breath feel like matter in the wrong place and time instead of a smoothly functioning unnoticeable phenomenon. The hospital that he hoped could provide atmospheric care to shake this weight loose, however, could not function without his wife, his son, and perhaps his friend supplementing pharmaceutical care with atmospheric care. Our time at the hospital had been a kind of hide and seek that hid some of the atmospheres that connected Daulat Singh to Ambawati and revealed others. Air, it seemed, was everywhere and unbounded.

SIX

CLOUDS

How can a cloud, a conglomeration of watery air and radiant smoke, carry
a message, such as it is taken by one with intellectual organs?
—Kalidasa, *Meghdoota*

SHANKAR SINGH'S TAWNY-COLORED MUD and stone house sits
midway between Shantibai's and Siddharth Singh's. A few paces off the
road that snakes past the Bhairav shrine, the village crèche, and a large
peepal tree, the squat structure overlooks Ambawati's pond. Shankar
Singh spent the winter and spring months of his sickness on a string cot
under its eaves. He watched as the pond, like his body, slowly shrank. One
of his sons puttered around the house, but silence there threw the hubbub
at Siddharth Singh's into sharp relief. Even though the men were cousins
and afflicted by the same malady, few who visited Siddharth Singh's bedside entered Shankar Singh's brush-fenced yard. Those who did were neither relatives nor concerned neighbors. They were healers. The nurse coun-
seled Shankar Singh about TB several times. Mohit, the Bengali doctor,
stopped to administer intravenous fluids.[1] Circular burns from treatments
to unblock bodily flows dotted Shankar Singh's chest, and his neck, ankles,
and wrists were tied with the colorful strings of tantric intercession.

Despite these interventions Shankar Singh's illness continued. He endured a racking cough, weight loss, and frequent fevers. Along with these
everyday discomforts, he struggled to breathe and experienced particularly
intense pain whenever wispy yellow clouds appeared. In May, just weeks
after the pond dried up, these troublesome clouds crossed the afternoon

123

sky again. Shankar Singh's chest heaved. He gasped, but this time breath's exchange of bodily and worldly airs failed. He died. That evening, Shankar Singh's sons and a few nephews carried his body to the cremation ground at the edge of the forest. The crowd of mourners that usually accompanies biers did not follow. Most people kept their distance from Shankar Singh, renowned as a thief, womanizer, and scoundrel, in death as in life. The next morning, as word of the meager procession spread, Dhudhi Singh summed up the event. He announced, "The sons struggled even to find people willing to carry their father's body to the cremation ground. A few men carried his body, but clouds carried away his life."[2]

Several days later, Shantibai invited me by for a snack. She was one of Siddharth Singh's frequent visitors but, despite being Shankar Singh's elder cousin by marriage, she had avoided him. As we caught up, I asked her why people who knew that Shankar Singh had TB often said that clouds had carried him away. Her response echoed Dhudhi Singh's. Ladling out a bowl of white corn and buttermilk porridge, she explained that wispy yellow clouds called *gawada* or *gawadiya*—we might call them cirrus in English, though I have not seen them cross North American or European skies with quite the same hue—have a negative effect on morally and physically injured bodies. *Gawada*, she estimated, had aggravated injuries that Shankar Singh acquired because of unsavory conduct.

Blowing on her porridge, she explained, "The clouds' upward pull (*uthaav*) cause internal knots (*gaanth*) to swell and cause pain. These swollen knots block the movement of breath through the body." Clouds blocked Shankar Singh's breath, excited it in unpredictable ways and carried it away. "That's why his breath moved so much at the end. The clouds pulled on it, but it was stuck" Adding a phrase I would soon hear often she said, "After all, he had stolen many things and taken many beatings."

Shantibai's account of her relative's death suggests that *gawada* clouds reach down to enter bodies and tug on breath. *Gawada* clouds enter all bodies in their atmosphere, proximity, or shadow, but their connection to Shankar Singh was particular. They brought pain only to bodies bearing traces of morally dubious action. Tugging at knots caused by physical and moral injury, the climatic and social atmosphere that *gawada* instantiate can create swellings that block or constrict the body's air, breath.

Gawada also color the moral experience of and atmospheric care for TB. Their effect freed Shantibai from her obligations to attend to him in both life and death. In the stories around Shankar Singh's death, the messages that *gawada* brought about his moral state conveyed to his relatives and neighbors that care for him was no longer a necessary part of kinship. Though people likely had a sense of his moral failures and found including him in kin and collective practice irksome, *gawada* cloud messengers confirmed their suspicion. By externalizing his internal moral turpitude their effects on his breath legitimized what some might call social abandonment or stigma. Though perhaps an opportunity to think more about social abandonment and TB, Shankar Singh's atmospheric entanglement with clouds, I argue, provides an example of how the entanglement of TB and an atmospheric phenomenon reconfigures social roles and responsibilities to some afflicted by TB.[3]

Gawada create new social collectives and reconfigure existing ones. Paul Rabinow suggests that collectives centered on biological states are the effect of biosociality, "a circulating network of identity terms and restriction loci, around which and through which a truly new type of autoproduction will emerge."[4] For Rabinow, these collectives coalesce around the risk of bodily pathology, like the risk of being affected by clouds. *Gawada* too make biosociality. They can reconfigure existing ways of being together, like caste and kin, much as they did for Shankar Singh.

Writing of the impact of genetics on social life, Rabinow suggests that "older cultural classifications will be joined by a vast array of new ones, which will cross-cut, partially supersede, and eventually redefine the older categories in ways which are well worth monitoring."[5] Clouds, like genes as a language of risk and the occulted internal, reveal a reconfigured sociality or biosociality. In it, Shankar Singh's breath is connected to clouds and TB to make a new collective that reshapes the ties of kinship and caste that often frame atmospheric care. Clouds are, then, an atmospheric entanglement within which biosociality has the potential to jostle or recombine breathy and social connections. They might even shape accounts of TB deaths due in part to an absence of collective atmospheric care.

Shankar Singh had experienced many of TB's sentinel symptoms—shortness of breath, persistent weight loss, fever, cough, and lack of appetite—and in the days following his death, his neighbors discussed the likelihood of TB affecting his body. They even highlighted Shankar Singh's stubborn denial of the nurse's TB diagnosis and his occasional coughs of blood. When conversations turned to the cause of his death, however, they often followed Dhudhi Singh and Shantibai's general outline. Because of his thievery, the flossy yellowish clouds "carried away," or killed, Shankar Singh, not bacteria.[6] TB, it seemed, laid a foundation of suffering, but the clouds' effect on breath and biosociality were responsible for his demise that day and his meager funeral.[7]

Though many clouds pass over Ambawati, *gawada* are a particular subset of the more general category of cloud, or *vaadara* in Rajasthani. Other clouds tell other stories, but Ambawati's cloud watchers have few romantic notions of looking at clouds as a process of imagination. Few view clouds and see dragons that turn into house cats or fluffy cotton ships. Instead, they see a stable active materiality rather than a passive screen on which human imagination might map whatever it liked. Clouds are mobile and ephemeral with an agency and substantiality of their own. They have things to say about rain and drought, when to cut grass and plant seeds, and who people might really be. Their ephemerality has real material consequence in the way that people interpreted and responded to them. As I learned more, I realized that the co-occurrence of TB, *gawada* clouds, and breathlessness might reveal social life's connections to material, moral, and political atmospheres.

Clouds as social actors that connect people to each other and to places have a history. The classical Sanskrit author Kalidasa's epic poem *Meghdoota*, or Messenger Cloud, describes a missive-bearing cloud not as metaphor but as fact. In the poem, a cloud acts as envoy crossing much of north India to relay a message between an exiled demigod and his spouse.[8] The magisterial poem resonates with the *gawada* in several ways. First, *Meghdoota*, like *gawada*, carries information. Second, both *gawada* and *Meghdoota* communicate the emotional and physical state of someone punished for "having been negligent of his charge, and having had his greatness set to decay by his master."[9] Third, *Meghdoota* and *gawada* acquire and use the landscape's characteristics as guides across the subcontinent. Landscapes, Val Daniel points out, are laden with the characteristics of the people who inhabit them, they mark *Meghdoota* too as it fills and empties across the landscape.[10] Maybe *gawada*, like the *Meghdoota*, can even say something about or acquire characteristics of those who live and breathe in a place to connect people who are otherwise socially distant.

Like air, *gawada* clouds are climatological participants in life. They lend their *bios*, or liveliness, to the biosocial collectives around TB and breathlessness. They are tactile and sensory atmospheric agents with their own breathy and moral life that can have the potential to connect with the world. Their entanglements with human bodies—through effects like retributive pain that is as nebulous, uneven, and shifting as clouds themselves—gave atmospheres their consummately affective, palpable, and shared characters.

By providing a message about Shankar Singh's internal moral state, *gawada* enter and adjust his atmospheric connections to others. In Shanti-bai and Dhudhi Singh's accounts of Shankar Singh's death, *gawada* can be both messengers who reveal a hidden moral status and vengeful enforcers of moral and social orders. As revelatory social actors, *gawada* could create categories of sufferers and set the tenor of suffering's moral interpretation. Though everyone knew about Shankar Singh's moral failings, for others whose breath was affected by *gawada*, failures to manage the self and its desires were usually less obvious and perhaps even unknown.

They may even influence the ways that TB can move through his social and breathy relations. They gave shape to the exclusion that marked the social atmosphere of Shankar Singh's illness. Public health scholars might call this exclusion stigma, but it is part of a larger atmospheric entangle-ment that connects and disconnects people. In that sense, cloud messages give breathlessness its experiential shape, tenor, and affect. They shadow the intimate poetics of TB and TB care in ways that left Shankar Singh's house empty while Siddharth Singh's was inundated by guests, despite both men having the same family and same contagious disease.

Clouds also answer hard questions. Despite a rich literature on risk factors and social determinants, biomedicine and public health cannot clearly locate the origin of a particular individual TB infection.[11] Nor can these texts clearly explain why some people who are infected with TB bacteria sicken and die whereas others do not. In the face of questions like

Why me? and What did I do to deserve this suffering? clouds lend TB their story. As moral indicators and shapers of nonfiliative sociality, clouds connect inner selves, moral practice, and atmospheres in ways that form new collectives or risk groups. Like other risk groups, the collectives or biosocialities that shared cloud affliction creates can bring people together across bounds of caste, gender, age, and class. They often require people to reflect on their actions, desires, and selves in uncomfortable ways. Thus, *gawada* entanglement is an example of what Marilyn Strathern has called "recombinant" relationality.[12] Sarah Pinto has glossed such forms of recombinant relationality as "making relations out of relations" and "unmaking relations out of unmade relations."[13] Indeed, *gawada* can do both. Clouds and TB make new recombinant and atmospheric connections to others who place and time have already connected as neighbor and sometimes family. They also unmake relations out of strained relations, like those between Shantibai and her husband's cousin Shankar Singh that actions had already strained. Cloud messengers and their recombinant potentiality could even legitimize practices that left Shankar Singh uncared for and unrelated but still kin and neighbor. Clouds, it seemed, provided a central atmospheric for making sense of how breathlessness occurs and to whom, as well as how practices of atmospheric care are distributed or withheld. They also guide the social work of discerning whose breath is dangerous or contagious and whose is not.

Focusing on an atmospheric entanglement of breath, clouds, and ethics that shapes Shankar Singh's life and death with TB, this chapter shows that clouds' mobile, recombinant material forms organize discussions about bodily and breathy connections. Viewing the clouds with two cousins, it attends to *gawada*'s differentiating effect on relations. Then the chapter enters a conversation with Prem Singh, who shows how people wrestle with *gawada* messages about the physical, atmospheric, and moral lives of those they love and those they do not. Next, the chapter rejoins Daulat Singh to consider clouds and his TB infection before an expert on such things, Vardhaba, helps me make sense of overlaps and disjunctions of clouds and bodies. The chapter ends by framing the intimate social relations of clouds and care for TB as one of the atmospheric entanglements people use to explain the unexplainable. In sum, the chapter argues that clouds might provide alternative ways of understanding breath's connections to contagious atmospheres and of organizing the limits of care.

TIGER'S CLOUD BIOSOCIALITY

Most of my fieldwork travel was on foot, so I usually kept my eyes trained downward, searching the village paths for snakes or thorns or slick places or friends. Though I watched for perils below, many of my neighbors were attuned to clouds, their messages, and their dangers. Despite collective attention, *gawada* sightings were rare. As I began to look upward, I noted the small round puffs that crossed the sky in summer, the large dark thunderheads, and the low-hanging blankets of premonsoon clouds. When each passed, I pointed upward, asking whoever was nearby if these were *gawada*. Each interlocutor would chuckle and tell me that they were not the ones. Sometimes when *gawada* did pass overhead, I only heard of them only after they departed. Other times people said that their bodies hurt, so *gawada* must be passing somewhere but we could not see them.

Eventually, however, *gawada* and I intersected. Tiger, Roshan, and I were sneaking to Sagwai for *pani patase*, a tangy snack often called *golgappa* or *pani puri*. Many young Ambawatians who migrated to Mumbai, Mangaluru, or Surat made and sold this snack there. One had returned with a sky-blue pushcart to supply the Sagwai bazaar. A lover of salty snacks like these, Roshan raced the three of us on a single overloaded motorcycle down the asphalt road from Ambawati to town. About halfway there, he shouted to his cousin Tiger and me over the wind and the motorcycle's engine, "Look there, the *gawada* are passing by. You can be sure that in six months it will rain. You could give it in writing. It's certain to happen." I tried to take a mental snapshot as we zoomed toward town. A few wispy, almost diagonal, yellowish clouds passed over fields of flowering soybeans. These clouds' color was unlike any I had seen, and though perhaps cirrus, they were arranged in twisting diagonal helices across the open sky.

The *gawada*'s messages were important to Roshan. He pointed to their presence as incontrovertible evidence that rain would arrive. He was even willing to "give it in writing" that rain would follow. In a context where written claims attain an air of truth, as well as the potential to end up in courts as evidence, Roshan's comment that one could write down the cloud's message meant that the rain they predicted was not potentiality but fact.[14] Certainty in agriculture is elusive for both keen cloud watchers and those well acquainted with the most advanced meteorological technology. For Roshan, their timing presaged opportunity and encouraged planting. He welcomed their insight.

Later, however, as our trio stood by the *pani patase* cart gulping down crispy bite-sized orbs filled with potato, lentils, and tangy sour chutney, Tiger returned to the cloud sighting. Between bites he said, "The *gawada* are out, I had better be careful of my breath. At least we know that the monsoon will come next year." I was surprised to learn that Tiger too was touched by the clouds. I asked him what happened to make him worry about *gawada* and breath. He recounted an injury acquired by falling off the back of the milk truck, which doubled as a school bus. "We were going to school on the milk truck, and I had been playing the clown, dancing like an idiot, you know. Dinka chinka, dinka chinka,"[15] he said. After a few pelvic thrusts, he continued, "When the truck hit a bump. I fell right flat on my back, and it knocked the wind out of me." He elaborated, "It was a hot day, and the *gawada* must have been about. From then on, my breaths move when the *gawada* pass. I was being a fool that time, you know. Now I'll need to be careful to keep them steady." That Tiger's breaths moved too, likely due to asthma, surprised me. Tiger did not have TB symptoms, but TB had killed his father and breathlessness evoked this history. He made sense of the *gawada*'s effects on his body in the same way that people with TB and other forms of breathlessness did: the confluence of clouds and breathlessness were reminders of foolish or felonious deeds. As witnesses and prophets, clouds might entangle past and present comportment with the self. They drew a line from previous impertinence to current attention and the possibility of future pain. That same line connected him to the father he vaguely remembered in a new and troubling way. As we ate our last bites, Tiger concluded, "The *gawada* have an effect on me, but not so much as others. It is good to have the rain they will bring in six months. Just like everything, they bring opportunity and harm, those clouds." Unstable entanglement between clouds and bodies, Tiger seemed to suggest, can harm at one moment and create opportunity in the next. Rain would fall on both cousin's fields, but in that moment the *gawada*'s presence caused Tiger to be careful with his breath, avoid exertion, and be ready for a wheezing attack. Potential and actual pain could be the climatic price for both childish carelessness and the rain that *gawada* carried.

Though worrisome for Tiger, the *gawada*'s presence for Roshan was purely beneficial. They did not affect his breath. He listened to Tiger's story with only minimal interest; there were snacks to be savored. Still, Roshan was particularly careful on the road back home. Wasting time and gasoline on sneaking to town for street food was a dalliance. An accident in the *gawada*'s presence could have lifelong physical consequences. It also risked revealing our inability to withstand a desire to shirk work and consume expensive empty calories in town. Fastidiousness in action, moral uprightness, and control of the self was a way to prevent uncontrolled breath in the future, just as a problem with steadying breath might make modulating the self and desire difficult. Roshan was careful not to entangle us further with the perceptive clouds and give them no reason to share messages about us or our trip. Roshan wanted to avoid joining Tiger.

The *gawada* separated the two friends and their ways of living in the world despite bonds of family, caste, age, and village. Clouds and their messages troubled the bloodline that connected Roshan and Tiger, but even more ominously, they threatened to connect Tiger and Shankar Singh whom kinship, caste, age, and location separated. Clouds temporally distributed the effects of a shared climate on particular bodies and created new groups around experiences of having a body and a past. Through breathlessness, the *gawada* were part of Tiger's body and subjectivity that said something about his identity that he could not manage. They provided new, if troublesome, markers of identity and ways of imagining those similarly affected as somehow like oneself.

Moralizing climatic message-bearing clouds make social groups around a quality of breath and personhood. Their collectivities even have an affective power to shift substance-based categories, such as caste, and raise questions about past and future action. By creating temporary, ethereal collectives around the self they might also reveal atmospheric entanglement's social capability. Tiger is separated from his cousin Roshan by the twisting amber clouds, just as Shankar Singh is cut off from kin and caste mates. Clouds are amphibious, moving between categories, atmospheres, bodies, and landscapes to make new, often unruly, connections.

The *gawada*'s effects on his body placed Tiger in a group with Shankar Singh despite differences in age, education, caste, aspirations, and political party. Because both shared a susceptibility to clouds, the concurrence of breathlessness and *gawada* reorganized the poles of identity to bring them together, no matter how physiologically and socially uncomfortable or unstable that grouping might be. In this way, cloud breathlessness is akin to other biomoral processes like paternity or caste, but unlike these formalized relations of inheritance, the relations that clouds create are nebulous. Clouds are morphing morally charged sources of ascribed, but not inherited, biosociality. They cross boundaries of lineage, caste, and age to connect Tiger, now an upright schoolteacher, and Shankar Singh, a long-dead thief.

In her analysis of biosecurity and bird flu, Celia Lowe uses "clouds" to describe amorphous rhizomatic entanglements full of connections that subvert logics of filiation and categorization through their capacity to change shape, their refusal of clear origin stories, and their capacity to be made of innumerable entities.[16] People, like Shankar Singh, Tiger, Roshan; clouds; and TB bacteria are among these innumerable entities entangled in the biomoral ecology that *gawada* substantiated in Ambawati. Though unique, each entity becomes entangled within or made up a *gawada* cloud of bacteria, self, weather, morals, social categories, and futurity itself. Of clouds' capacity to engulf others and blur boundaries, Lowe writes, "Just as a collection of genomes that may appear in the rapidly mutating swarm technically known as a quasi-species cloud are heterogenous and unpredictable, so, too, I found were the bodies, narratives, and politics that appeared in the multispecies cloud surrounding the naturalcultural [*sic*] event known as H5N1."[17] Cloud-entangled breathlessness created new heterogeneous and unpredictable categories and collectives. Prophetic clouds and their categories might avoid or reframe the forms of lateral filiation that make up relations among castes, people, and kin. They might also offer a new view of uninherited moral sociality, one into which clouds and breath could interpolate Tiger and others.

PREM SINGH AND CORRECT MEN

Several weeks after Shankar Singh's death I visited Prem Singh Rawat, another of Shankar Singh's distant cousins. As we relaxed on a string cot below a massive peepal tree filled with squabbling green parrots and a single monkey, our conversation quickly turned to clouds and Shankar Singh. Prem Singh and a man I did not know recounted the connections that breath could make to moral economy, weather, landscape, and pathology. By talking about the nebulous relations between action, place, and suffering that clouds can create, Prem Singh discussed the *gawada*'s capacity to reveal the internal moral qualities of people they trouble.[18]

Prem Singh began our discussion, saying, "The clouds come out and because of that, if somewhere, someone has been injured, blood builds up and the clouds pull it up. It starts to throb." The man sitting with us interjected, "When clouds come out they give heat. Then from heat what happens is that blood cannot rotate." Prem Singh continued, "Blood gets blocked and throbs, and then someone says, 'My back hurts, my chest hurts, my head hurts, my arm hurts' [or wherever he was injured]. The bad clouds have come out and it hurts. It hurts, meaning the blood has stopped and is throbbing. That's it."

"What about people who experience strength-breathlessness? How is that connected to clouds?" I asked. "Don't we have a *daman* [lung-chest-breathing apparatus] inside?" Prem Singh explained, "That chest suddenly moves quickly, because of the clouds. So he says, 'my breaths move, my breath moves [*dam sale, has sale*].' There must be an injury in the chest, so it moves fast [throbs] because of the clouds, because of the heat." "From the heat?" I asked. Prem Singh considered: "The *gawada* clouds are about when the wind is hot. The lungs, they begin to spasm all of a sudden [*hapak hapak ekdam kare*]. Because of that, because of some problem, like when our head pounds, there must be some 'mistake' in that too. Because of that mistake the breaths move. If he were a correct man (*sahi admi*), it would not happen."

I asked him more directly about the effects of the *gawada* on Shankar Singh: "People say that the clouds took Shankar Singh away. How is that?" He laughed. "He took a lot of beatings," Prem Singh reflected. "Yes, because he stole," he finished. The other man intervened, "Yes, he was a thief." "People really beat him. That is why his breath moved (*dam chalta tha*)," Prem Singh responded. "His breath swelled[19] when the clouds passed and that's why. His breath moved from being beaten." Becoming more interested, the stranger continued the interview for me. He asked, "Why, Kaylanba, Shankar was a thief and fought and because of that his strength-breath moved? "Yes, from that he got in this situation," Prem Singh said. "He was not a correct man [*how manak*]."[20]

The men used clouds to think about and interpret moral and bodily states. An atmosphere capable of discerning good and bad men emerged from the confluence of clouds and breath. Clouds reveal or even know a mistake in the body and self through their capacity to interact with or even become breath. They might even pull out the internal, moral self for all to see and discuss. It seemed that clouds could affect only some—namely, those who had bodily "mistakes" and were not "correct" in an aesthetic, economic, physical, or ethical way. To be a "correct man" was as moral as it was material.

Injury, both men suggested, was central to cloud-initiated breathlessness, but the source of the injury mattered. Though everyone is injured during a life, it mattered that Shankar Singh's injuries occurred because he was often caught stealing, and thus beaten. Stealing from the neighbors and swindling his brothers revealed what the men described as Shankar Singh's inability to engage an ethical economy. Cloud affliction supported this view. It was even rumored that Shankar Singh had been hit in the back with an axe in the forest during a flight. This was likely his chief injury. Other beatings also happened in the forest when he tried to steal goats and a woman's jewelry. He was even thrashed in Ambawati when he made dishonest business deals and tricked his cousins. These were, in his neighbors' opinions, beatings in the name of justice and correction, but they did not take. Shankar Singh's beatings, many argued, caused knots and thickenings in his injured body that clouds could agitate.

The injuries and thickenings that clouds pulled on were not simply physiological ones; they raised questions about all who had them. Thickenings' presence and the consequent effects of clouds on Shankar Singh's body as breathlessness were messages confirming that he was a morally and physically incorrect man. In Ambawati, this incorrectness was an affect and way of being that was more contagious and more pernicious than bacteria. Aversion to this moral contagion likely explained Shankar Singh's family's resistance to visiting him during his illness.

Though Prem Singh's "correct man" comment sent me into a revery about clouds as arbiters of a self's morality, the stranger asked another important question: "Say, Premba, what about Daulat Singh who lives behind the pond?" Daulat Singh also suffered from TB and struggled to breathe. Prem Singh reflected for a minute and said, "Yes, he must have been beaten for something, but he is good man. Maybe he drank too much alcohol." With that we each fell into our own silent reflections about correct men, injury, and the people we knew. Only the chattering parrots broke the silence overhead. That is, until one fell out of the tree, stoned from eating too many poppy seeds.

The conversation and the silence afterward hinged on the problem of knowledge and categories created by clouds that enter bodies to prophesy through breath. Clouds and TB-disordered breathing revealed something about Shankar Singh and Daulat Singh. For Prem Singh and the stranger, cloud-associated breathlessness and pain confirmed what they already knew about Shankar Singh, but they raised questions about Daulat Singh. Prem Singh and the stranger found Daulat Singh a good man, but the clouds, their conversation assumed, had an insight or ability to discern a moral quality that they did not. Prem Singh's evocation of alcohol grasps at an answer, but it was a feeble evocation of alcohol to signify untempered desire. All three of us knew that Daulat Singh was not prone to drink in excess.

When pressed Prem Singh struggled to think of a mistake, violence, or dalliance that could make Daulat Singh's breath accessible to the clouds and connect him to those with breath affected by clouds and desire. Daulat Singh's persistent experience of breathlessness, or *dam chalna*, and apparent moral fortitude had raised unanswerable questions about his righteousness, exposure to punitive violence, management of aspiration, and clouds. Of course, I thought I knew something else that linked the bodies of Shankar Singh and Daulat Singh: bacteria. We had reached a limit. I decided to ask him.

Daulat Singh suffered with TB for years, but finally his health began to improve after a sojourn in the Udaipur TB hospital. Since our time there,

we had met twice weekly for months, so I raised the topic during one of
our conversations. As we chatted over cups of black tea and lemon leaves, I
asked, "Do you also have *dam chalna?*" I made no reference to Prem Singh's
comment about uprightness, but Daulat Singh told me the story of his own
injury, obedience, history, and trouble catching breath anyway. He said,

> Yes, my breaths move. They have for a long time. I have worked very hard
> all my life. You should have seen the mud here when I was a child. When I
> was a young man, I fought with my father too. I had been doing some wrong
> things, and once he really hit me. He is a big man. You have seen him. He
> is much bigger than me. The biggest man in our extended family, and he hit
> me several times with a bamboo stick on my back. He is tired now but then
> he was strong, and he hit me hard. I ran away. I could not catch my breath,
> but I ran. I ran past the last house and into the forest. I was hurt very badly.
> I stayed there for maybe a week. I just ate what I could find, and I hid there
> so he would not beat me more. Finally, I had to go home. My wife was
> there, and she was very young. I went home and got her, and we moved here
> [almost a half kilometer from the hamlet where Daulat Singh was born] and
> built a small hut. You know the kind, with a few sticks and cut branches and
> leaves for shingles. We built it in the old way, and she nursed me. After a
> while, I could do all my work again, but we stayed here, and now for many
> years when the *gawada* come out my breath *(dam)* moves.

Daulat Singh, like Tiger and Prem Singh, recounts a relationship between
cloud, forest, correct behavior, and his physical symptoms that was made
meaningful by *gawada* messages and revelation. When the clouds come
out, his "breath moves." In other words, he related his struggles to breathe
to filial disobedience.

   In another recombination of kinship, clouds, and illness Daulat Singh
rooted his individuality and separation in familial violence. He emphasized
that his father was a strong man who used violence as a corrective, while
also mentioning the bumps and bruises that a life of demanding work and
mud have given him. By telling a story about clouds, Daulat Singh might
have located himself as an individualized subject of violence—a beating by his father and the political economy that mud and manual labor
represent—and highlighting his individualized desires. Troubled breath
and *gawada* came together to root his atmospheric suffering in individual

actions and desires. He accepted the *gawada*'s insinuation of having not been a correct man by locating himself in a moral and political economy that punishes whatever his bad behavior was by making him feel weak. Trouble and individuality set in when clouds prevent the going and coming of breath and block the world inside the body.

Exposure to breathlessness along with retributive human and cloud violence brought Shankar Singh, Tiger, and Daulat Singh into a commune of incorrect men, but Prem Singh had been in his share of fights too. He was even hospitalized following a particularly violent tangle with a neighbor over land. To Prem Singh, the land was rightfully his, and though he lost the fight, the beating was not due to his own failings and was thus unjust. When I asked him if he had problems with clouds and breathing, he told me with some pride that he did not. His body and breath's imperviousness to clouds was evidence of his moral authority despite being beaten. In contrast, the neighbor who did the beating experienced breathlessness. The land dispute moved slowly through the courts, but the clouds had given their verdict. Prem Singh's steady breath signified the validity of his claim on the land and a moral self. When I asked my neighbors, they agreed with this assessment, Memibai added that she and Sundar had tended to him during the week he had been hospitalized and again at home.

Clouds' effects on people's moral classification suggest that they do not simply group people together in unpredictable ways. Instead, cloud collectivities center on correctitude and cloudly adjudication of individual actions and comportments. By doing so, cloud connectivity troubles established social distinctions and connections. They reorganize kin and caste-based flows of care and solidarity to direct the choreographies of abandonment that Shankar Singh experienced as breathlessness. At the intersection of individual and collective actions, clouds create new ways of understanding the socialities of illness and care that shape how people live together with disease and in time. They show that atmospheric connections are central frames of life and illness experience, which have the potential to precipitate unsettling social categories framed around correctness, mistakes, and the dangers posed by agency and action. The entanglement of clouds, bacteria, and discernment makes for a body that is as marked by caste and kinship as it is transformed by moral choices and clouds. It is this openness to biomoral atmospheres that Vardhe Singh knew well.

VARDHABA'S BODIES

Shantibai's brother-in-law, Vardhe Singh Rawat, is an expert on clouds and bodies. An energetic man in his late forties, Vardhe Singh's faded yellow turban, large intelligent eyes, and easy smile enliven a wide face and nearly bald head. Most people call him Vardhaba or Vardhe uncle. A farmer like his neighbors, Vardhaba is keenly interested in rain and the water level in his stone well, but his attention expands beyond an attunement to clouds as harbingers and porters of rain. Vardhaba manages the clouds' effect on bodies as a practitioner of branding [*daam lagano*].

Shantibai learned midwifery from Vardhaba's mother, and Vardhaba learned of bodily flows, clouds, and branding from his father and uncle. This ability to interpret and manage the rotating body's entanglement with clouds made Vardhaba, like Shantibai, one of Ambawati's most sought after experts in bodily matters. Women consulted Shantibai for assistance and advice concerning fertility, family planning, birthing, and children, and men and women called on Vardhaba in cases of pain, congestion, weakness, and breathlessness. Most often he recommended rest and dietary changes, but occasionally he prescribed and applied a brand or burn to the body. Though branding is painful, Vardhaba often suggested it for people dealing with TB's sentinel symptoms, like persistent cough, breathlessness, and chest pain, as well as for stomachaches or toothaches. Blockages like those Prem Singh and Shantibai described could cause gas, stomach pain, and breathlessness. Vardhaba's brands could break up bodily knots or clogs.

Because brands leave lifelong traces, they appeared omnipresent in the village. Most adults have one or two of these oval scars, often on their backs or bellies. Though some of the thumbprint-sized brands were applied outside Ambawati, or by his father and uncle, most of the fresh burn marks on Shankar Singh and others were Vardhaba's. The ubiquitous marks of his treatments encouraged me to seek him out earlier than most healers, and I visited Vardhaba's veranda long before I took Takhat Singh's tantra lessons or spent hours at the village health center with Suresh.

When I first told him that I would like to learn about his work, Vardhaba asked me to sit near the ashes of a now extinguished fire on the veranda. As soon as I was seated, he grabbed my arm. With a cheeky grin, he asked if I wanted to see how to make a brand, saying, "Raghuveer can hold you down if you need it. He usually does." His burly eldest son, Raghuveer Singh, who was leaning against one of the veranda's posts, took a jocular step in my direction. He chuckled with his father as they saw fear rise in my eyes. Vardhaba released my elbow to slap his thigh in laughter as I stammered about feeling very well and not needing a brand. With that, the whole house fell to laughing. Even Vardhaba's wife and daughter-in-law pulled their *lungda*s over their faces to laugh with abandon. As we steadied our chuckles and held our sides, Vardhaba continued, "All right, I'll just tell you about it then. Maybe when someone comes I will send a child to call for you. You'd be good for holding people down with Raghuveer," he joked again. After another round of laughter, he began to explain his work.

Adept at locating the body's multiple "veins," or energy flows, Vardhaba explained that burns dislodge knots to reestablish movement or rotation within the veins, or *nas*. He told me that when these veins are blocked, the body's air and serum cannot move. This causes breathlessness, cough, throbbing pain, and congestion. The blockages, he said, are troublesome all the time but when the clouds pull on them, they can be particularly painful, even deadly.

"The body has nine veins," Vardhaba said, leaning over to touch me again. This time he put two fingers on my Achilles tendon and said, "Look here," giving it a tug. From there he began to map my body's veins by following a web of tendons, ligaments, and sinews. He moved his hand behind my knee to tweak the tendon there, saying, "Here." He repeated the tweaks and the "here" at sinewy spots in my lower back and a knotted muscle under my shoulder blade to complete the flow. After finishing he said, "That's one of them." Astounded by this new way of imagining my own body, I felt a reverberating sensation move through my body. It was almost akin to the way the body of a guitar vibrates when a string is plucked.

"You have another vein in the other leg and one on the front of each leg," he said, before taking my arm and plucking the tendons at my wrist, elbow joint, and underarm. "These are in both arms, one on top and one on bottom," he said, as he gently tapped the tendon connecting my neck muscle and clavicle. With an air of summation, he said, "They all meet here," resting his hand on the long and stringy muscle at the nape of my neck, "before they connect with the ninth one, your brain." After creating this tactile map of a dynamic vascular body, Vardhaba said, "See, normally everything moves well in this, but sometimes they get jammed. Usually, it is when there is a change in temperature like when you work very hard and drink cold water, then there is a jam. Or when the clouds come out. They pull up on all the old wounds and people say, 'Ouch it hurts.'"

The body that Vardhaba mapped onto mine drew lines through an entanglement of flesh, function, and attention. Blockages could arise because of conflicts between body and environment or be activated by the passing of clouds. The same fleshy material that biomedicine imagines as discrete organ systems made of separated parts and walled cells, Vardhaba saw, touched, and healed as interconnected lines or veins moving within and across the body. From what biomedicine suggests are merely sinewy anchors for organ systems, Vardhaba visually and sensorially evidenced a body of flows that was open to the climatic world.[21]

Handling a short rod made from the same clay used for roof tiles, he continued, "I put this in the fire until it gets red hot. Then I hold it with a piece of cloth wrapped around my end and press the other onto the right spot [on the skin] above the vein." "Psshhhhh," he said, making the sound of sizzling flesh. It was no wonder that Raghuveer needed to hold people down; the procedure created serious burns. The silver-dollar-sized brands seep pus and scab over before leaving a large, often oval scar. "The seeping pus (*peep*) is important," Vardhaba told me. "It is the matter that created the blockage leaving the body. The brands should build a large scab, that is the blockage and the wound (*zakham*) coming out." Rather than using fire to seal the body, Vardhaba opened the knots that closed it off from air and allowed the clouds to cause trouble. Though Marina Peterson points out that a body open to the world is vulnerable to it, Vardhaba suggests that being closed off has its own liabilities.[22]

I asked Vardhaba if he put the brand where patients reported pain, and he explained that he did not. Clouds, it seems, move things within the body too, and a struggle to breathe may indicate far more than just the state of the lung. Vardhaba said, "The body is connected by veins, and so when something gets blocked in them, that might cause trouble in another part of the body. Like a toothache. Obviously, we do not brand the tooth during a toothache. Toothaches are caused by a blockage right here," he said pointing to the place on my right arm where the bicep and deltoid met. "We put a brand there to release the block, but for a toothache we don't use a rod. We use a needle." Indeed, I had seen thin straight scars across some of my friends' biceps before. Now I knew why. Like the unpredictable connection between a cloud and its bodily effect, Vardhaba's body abided by a different logic of correspondence, one less static than biomedical ones. For him the body was far more dynamic. Arms could cause toothaches. Backs could induce chest pain. Livers could cause stomachaches. The atmospherically entangled and relational body in Vardhaba's experience held fast to cause and effect, but it put a little more space and time between them.

Cloud connections seemed to work through deferral in space and time rather than direct and instant causation. Their pull did not just cause pain; it delayed and distributed the effects of the world on the body. In other words, connection between the locations of pain and pathology might not always be clear. Similarly, clouds may enter flows precisely because the body was no longer a set of discrete, nested containers designed to keep the world out. Pathology may also move through a body made of flows in ways that might be unimaginable for one of its membranes. Vardhaba's body, with its vocabulary of veins, could entangle with a biomedical definition and remain salient even for those who, like Shantibai, had learned about the body's internal organs under the tutelage of a local nongovernmental organization.

Though the flowing body might fit within a biomedical one, exhalation rather than inhalation made life within it possible. Cloudy connection mattered precisely because it could close the routes of bodily exhalations or take them out of rhythm with the world of wind. Clouds could pull up on and activate scars to block bodily congress with the wind, trapping heat and other accumulated gases to create pain and pathology. Air exiting the body is as necessary as air entering it. In fact, gas buildup, like air buildup, is a key bodily preoccupation across north India.[23] Among the middle classes, gas as an idiom of complaint and way of making sense of the body does far more work than that of the biomedical idea of indigestion.[24] It can refer to kinds of pains roving from stomach to head and swellings from feet to fingers. In Ambawati, to speak of *rolation*, veins, and brands is to speak of gas in another way, as air or breath.

These nine flows of air and serum could fit in the empty spaces left by a biomedical body, just as clouds and TB could be together in Shankar Singh's body and his eventual demise. No longer tethered only to organs but also made of the circuits connecting them, the body was open to the effects of clouds and their moral arbitration through breath. Though incredibly painful, Vardhaba's brands might be like pressure valves for air, pus, or gas pent up in once flowing bodies. They open the body and its veins to the world through new avenues and draw blockages out. In other words, they open a new connection between body and world through a painful festering wound and eventually a scar. They might even let a little pent-up self out. By opening the body's veiny systems to include clouds, weather, and air, Vardhaba and his red-hot brand move flesh into a set of relations characterized not by protective bounds or discrete individuals but by nebulous connections and entanglements. His is a body of indirect relations but relations nonetheless.

When Vardhaba's brands fail to open these flows, it gestures back to the moral messages of clouds. One day, after Siddharth Singh began TB treatment, but before his bacteria responded to it, I visited him to find his shirt unbuttoned. Three fresh and oozing burn marks on his sternum made buttoning it too painful. I asked him what happened, and he explained:

> A few days back I could not breathe. I had such bad *dam chalna* that we called for Vardhaba to give me a brand. He came with the ceramic and did it. For a while the breath movement stopped, everything became normal. The next day it started again so we called him again. He came again and said he would try again right near the first brand, so that it would perhaps be right on the vein. It hurt very badly, and things got better for a while, but then it started up again. We sent my son to fetch Vardhaba again, but this time he was not at home. So my father took a clay shingle and tried to

do it, but he got scared and I had to do it myself. That did not really work either, but now my breath is calmer. See that one with the raised burned flesh coming up.

I looked at my friend's sternum. Each wound had bits of burned flesh sticking out, but one was a bit larger. "That one is mine. I did it to myself like Pratap Singh [Vardhaba's uncle] used to do when he was sick." Pratap Singh was the first of Ambawati's TB sufferers I had ever known, and the disease had killed him about five years before. The two bedbound men had aimed to soothe an atmospherically entangled body with fire and more pain. For me they were connected.

In Siddharth Singh's case people spoke of two possible impertinences that might make branding less effective and his breath a message from the clouds. One was an action done without thinking and the other was made of untempered future-oriented desire. Siddharth pondered both of them and at times made sense of his breathlessness as failed bodily rotation due to thoughtlessly bathing in cold water, an action taken without thinking. At other times, he assumed that leaving his family to work in the factory where a stone fell and injured him was the cause of his breathlessness. He regretted leaving his parents alone to go work for money. He regretted even more how much he had enjoyed that freedom. Siddharth Singh worried that his work in the factory and the injury it caused might have been a result of selfishness and unbridled aspiration. In each case, cloudy entanglement and breathlessness was the impetus to moral reflection and consideration of unmediated desire's effect on the present and future. His scar seemed to manage or renew breath by reopening the body to the world through a burn. Both men had burns now. In the eyes of their neighbors, Shankar Singh failed the cloud's moral test because he acted toward his desired future through theft. Care for him was minimal. Siddharth Singh, however, who labored in service of his future, scraped by with troubled breath, but his momentary moral slip was worthy of forgiveness and care.

Vardhaba's veinous, rotating body, connected to and part of clouds, is an entanglement of nature and culture, or organ and environment, that cannot be parsed using biology's strategies of separation and purification. Instead, it is open to the multiplicity of clouds and states. As Sarah Pinto suggests of relations, clouds could be "means, not just objects, of under-standing."[25] They are means of understanding breathing as entangled body and self, just as much as they are entities to be known in themselves.

THE VERTIGINOUS VARIABILITY OF CLOUDS

The historian of science Lorraine Daston has shown that clouds subvert science and modernism's impetus to speciate, stabilize, organize, and ra-tionalize the natural world into universalizable taxonomic categories. They are rapidly recombinant. They trouble breathless ethnographic attempts to stabilize social structures from vibrant life. Clouds' virtuality and unpre-dictability raise questions about categorizing both clouds and people that neither my friends in Ambawati nor anthropologists can easily resolve. By suggesting that representation cannot keep up with the changing clouds, Daston presents a final example of the anxious lateral forms of cotemporal sociality that clouds can engender. In a vein similar to the challenges faced by those describing vibrant social forms, Daston writes of the challenge to describe and taxonomize clouds as virtuality's challenge to scientific stabilization and taxonomy: "Now imagine all of these ten million-odd species constantly metamorphosing into one another and into interme-diate forms—not just evolution speeded up to cinematic tempo but ev-erything changing into everything else, all at once, not just past forms to present forms but also present to past and this present form to another one, without regard to taxon or phylogeny. That is variability—the vertiginous variability of clouds."[26] It is this variability that an entanglement of clouds, TB bacteria, selves, and breath reveals and provokes people in Ambawati and me to describe.

Action, environment, and ethics are tangled with breath, which is more than simple air taken in. Rather, these stories about TB-related breath show that breath also takes collective environment and personal action into the body and self. It is no wonder we went soul-searching in our confusion. Inherited categories like bloodlines cannot keep up with unpredictable ev-eryday social life. Clouds and the social taxonomies their messages might create provide new categories for social life that reveals its variability. Their entanglement with TB in Ambawati offers an opportunity to think about how collectivities and atmospheres morph with each other.

To an attuned body, clouds can carry messages about the worlds and people over whom they pass. They might even reshape social connections through their motion and present a way of living in a world in which material forms of agency are just one of many. They prophesied the forms of care that Shankar Singh would receive by sending moral messages about him. These messages diminished the importance of other ways of relating or parsing one's obligation to people and created what public health might call TB stigma.

Biosociality with and in the shadow of clouds creates amorphous collectivities of people, and bodies affected by them shifted the meaning and salience of other relations like kinship and caste. They even transformed what the body could and could not be made of. In their revelatory function, the clouds that incite breathlessness show how seemingly static social connections are just as mobile and flexible. The obligations to care that some imagine track kinship and caste are overshadowed by clouds' capacity to reveal mistakes and incorrectness in bodies and selves through breath. They give responses, no matter how uncomfortable, to challenging questions of why some but not others sicken and die from an airborne infectious disease.

SEVEN

FORESTS

I am imbued with landscapes, it is the only retreat that I can have. Hidden beneath the river waters, shining on the pavements of the town, asleep in the green of grass and tree, sparkling in the salt and sands, secretly tormented, those that enhance their skies, those that reveal their depths.
—Édouard Glissant, *Treatise on the Whole-World*

A FARMER IN HIS fifties, Devi Singh was the first of Ambawati's residents to be diagnosed and treated for multiple-drug-resistant tuberculosis (MDR-TB). His diagnosis was both surprising and predictable. He had never coughed much but spent a year consulting physicians about shortness of breath and chest pain. Eventually, he began TB treatment, but his health did not improve. Suresh, the community nurse, sent a sample of Devi Singh's sputum for drug-resistance testing and the results of the laborious bacterial culture arrived months later. They reported that the mycobacteria in Devi Singh's sputum were resistant to two of the four standard TB drugs. A few days later Devi Singh began two years of MDR-TB treatment. This time he took six pharmaceuticals that could kill TB bacteria resistant to cheaper, less toxic drugs. I knew Devi Singh before his biopolitical status as an MDR-TB patient was thrust on him, but after he started treatment I wanted to learn more about his life with TB bacteria and his perspective on what would inevitably be a long entanglement with pharmaceuticals.

At the clinic I asked if he would tell me about his new treatment. In response he invited me to join him at home as he took his medicines. It was in the village's forested portion nearly one and a half kilometers from the nearest neighbor. Several days later I asked directions and set out to visit. I traversed familiar hamlets and wheat fields before entering a path through a thicket of scrubby teak saplings. Once an old growth forest, people had cut it in hopes of wresting fields from the tangle of trees, bushes, and plants. The forest, however, persisted. Though prospectors diligently cut trees and the grass that grew around them, new shoots sprouted from old stumps in clusters of threes or fours. As I continued onward, I heard a couple cutting dried grass somewhere behind the immense curtain of tattered teak leaves. Convinced that, as the adage goes, "the plow gains the right," they would spend years cutting trees, rooting out bushes, and adding manure to stake a claim on the land through cultivation.[1]

Soon I worried that I had lost my way. I considered turning back to ask the grass cutters for directions or veering southward toward Takhat Singh's house. Indecision, however, pushed me forward down the narrow dirt path. I walked up and down hills, crossing dry creek beds in search of a clearing or change in the brush that might indicate Devi Singh's house. Finally, a mahua[2] tree rose above the coppiced teaks in the distance. Someone had told me that Devi Singh's house was near a mahua tree, so I headed in its direction. Soon a low-slung mud house and six white cattle came into view on a hill just beyond a small patch of wheat. The cattle were sheen, and the wheat was well tended. Devi Singh and his family had cultivated several small parcels of land and made their home here amidst the forest for years.[3] He watched and waved as I climbed the hill.

When I finally arrived Devi Singh beckoned me to a small pavilion his family had fashioned from teak poles and leafy dhak[4] branches. There I sat on the cot next to his and we exchanged pleasantries before quietly looking down on the seemingly endless mass of trees. Devi Singh had spent much of his life in the forest cutting wood, claiming land, and grazing cattle. He knew intimately its resident panthers, people displaced by a hydroelectric dam project, flying squirrels, hidden liquor stills, grotto temples, trees, bushes, and plants. Now, in the third month of toxic drug-resistant TB treatments, however, he was often too dizzy to work. He spent most days resting and looking out over the forest.

Engrossed by the forest, I wondered how someone who lived on an airy hilltop twenty minutes from a neighbor could find himself sick with

a social disease like tuberculosis, let alone its iatrogenic, hyperencultur-
ated drug-resistant iteration. Of course, this was foolish. Romantic-era
metaphors of pristine or wild "nature" guided me to assume that the forest
insulated Devi Singh from social life and social illness, but this was a
misperception. Living in the forest did not mean being alone or away from
the many connections that social breath and life create. My walk should
have taught me that much.

Forests, like bodies, are not empty or inert. Their flora, fauna, and
atmospheric relations organize the coming and going of people, bacteria, and other susceptibilities across geographies. They blur categories
like domestic and wild, social and natural, individual and collective. As
we began to chat, I realized that Devi Singh knew this well. The bacteria inhabiting Devi Singh's lungs were, after all, accidently cultivated
by medicine and evolution into a forestlike tangle of social and natural
processes that made him both singular and multiple. He even used this
peopled forest as a guiding metaphor for his life and his entanglement with
drug-resistant TB.

Though Devi Singh found meaning in his connection to the forest,
Hindu epics often epitomize the jungle as a dangerous, unpredictable
realm outside hierarchical sociality.[5] In these texts, action that endangers
hierarchical and inherited social structures, such as intentional or accidental adultery, misrecognition, and kidnapping, often happens in the
forest.[6] The forest's danger, then, may lie not in its animals or its empti-
ness but in its contagious ability to rearrange the inherited and cultivated
but fragile structures of agrarian social life. Indeed, Devi Singh and his
neighbors often commented on the forest's proximity and explained that
its atmosphere could allow more evanescent ways of being with others.[7]
Ambawati's forest was host, my friends explained, to practices—theft,
adultery, hunting, friendship, and magic—that endanger property, caste,
and kinship relations but gave social life texture, nonetheless. People often
glossed lateral connections' known and unknown effects as the influence
of the jungle—and what might happen in it—on selves and social lives.
To describe their difference from the more decorous, they often called
themselves *jangali*, or "forested," and constituted by connections that were
ardhu, which means "lateral" or "lying down" rather than being "cultivated"

or "standing." Being *jangali*, with its hodgepodge of cultivated patches of self, lateral infiltrations of affect or desire, and rooted trees of inheritance, is the central trope organizing Devi Singh's account of illness and life with bacteria.[8]

In a history of antibiotic resistance, the historian Hannah Landecker borrows the term "reassortment" from microbiology to highlight lateral connections' potential to jostle linear history and clear narratives of cause and effect.[9] Landecker draws inspiration from bacteria's capacity to exchange genes generationally through reproduction and laterally through proximity and contemporality to suggest that things may not always be one after another. Reassortment foregrounds microbial potential to subvert linear history and industrially standardized antibiotics by moving genetic information among microbes whose relations are not inherited but forged through the shared time and space of proximity. Devi Singh's tubercular lungs embodied social reassortment too. They were host to lateral, accidental, uninherited, and uncultivated relations to a bacteria shaped by the human use of antibiotics, or antilife. TB bacteria makes his material body *jangali* and forest-like too. The reassortment and intrusion of forest and bacteria in his lungs subvert both social and scientific ways of knowing connection through time. It is this social and bodily capacity to evade and embrace chronology that provides an opening for the anthropological study of TB and of South Asia.

For Devi Singh, and perhaps for anthropology, the forest can provide a situated language to attend to reassortment's lateral relations and ways of thinking about the copresence of people and bacteria. This perspective must work alongside powerful genealogical metaphors of cultivation and progress. Anand Pandian has shown that cultivation metaphors and the imperative to "deliberately" cultivate one's economic life and moral self—drawn from colonialism's standardizing plantation biologics—is a central but fraught project of reflexive and intentional subject formation in precolonial, colonial, and postcolonial South Asia.[10] Pandian suggests subjects hoping to be modern must implement strategies that craft a singular treelike self that is rooted in a set of stable relations. This kind of linear "development is the promise of a gradual improvement of life, and the fulfillment of its potential for progressive growth through deliberate endeavors in transformation."[11] Life, Pandian shows, has been marked by development's metaphor of inevitable progression, people moving from backward to modern and bacteria from drug susceptible to drug resistant. For subjects who are caught up in these progressions, to host MDR-TB is to fail at self-cultivation or self-improvement and insist on the possibility of lateral relations. It is also to cultivate biopolitical and bacterial resistance.

Drug resistance is an eminently undesirable outcome of industrialized antibiotic production, haphazard treatment, microbial evolution, and inequality. It casts doubt on the very biopolitics that rely on pharmaceutical or technological cultivation and standardization to manage tuberculosis. Even more alarmingly, within public health, resistance is a political category made biological through its application to bacterial evolution and imputed back onto people afflicted by drug-resistant bacteria.[12] Public health's discourse on MDR-TB, which Heather Paxson calls microbiopolitics,[13] is a hybrid of politics and biology that imputes to MDR-TB patients and their bacteria a willful desire to subvert or evade cultivation.[14] Caught in this discursive tangle, public health imagines Devi Singh to have knowingly made unhealthy, frivolous, and self-centered decisions that privilege immediate comfort over his biological life and the population's future health.[15] In response, this chapter follows Devi Singh's account of the reassortments that happen in and around the forest to reveal a more-than-human politics of simultaneity, accommodation, and parody rather than cultivated resistance.

Quintessentially entangled, a forest hosts people and things that have individual histories and come together in the lateral proximity of simultaneity. This chapter follows Devi Singh's lead to argue that the forest is both site and analytic of sociality. Forest atmospherics and the social processes that occur in them can reveal relations of laterality, simultaneity, and plurality that occlude, supersede, complicate, and sometimes reinforce the cultivated relations of lineage and inheritance that dominate analyses of social and microbial life.[16] I argue that to understand the social life and experience of MDR-TB anthropology must think laterality and lineage together. The forest as atmosphere unifies moments of structure, moments of simultaneity, moments of intentionality, and moments of infiltration so that they all might be considered together. The chapter first engages Devi Singh's story of diagnosis to question TB science's idea that patients search for medical care progressively and show that overlapping simultaneity of care and pharmaceuticals make his body a forest. It follows how drugs, physicians, and bacteria come together in ways that overlap to elude biopolitics' inevitably progressing tree and path metaphors. After that, it sits with Devi Singh's evocation of "duty" to describe a budding lateral relation to the state that leaves room for accommodation and irony's capacity to reassort meaning and citizenship. Finally, the chapter engages thieves. Devi Singh, another resident of the forest and reassorter extraordinaire, embraces some forms of lateral exchange to manage problems posed by object-pilfering thieves, coercive care systems, and vitality-sapping bacteria. By imagining life and self with drug-resistant TB bacteria as a forest—in which a diversity of entities live next to and often in relationships to each other without inherited connection—Devi Singh might provide a method to subvert plantation logics' processes of crafting human and bacterial homogeneity through cultivation, mass reproduction, labor standardization or control, and chemical management.[17]

COHABITATION AND SIMULTANEITY
Breaking our reverie, I asked Devi Singh how he came to spend his days under the improvised pavilion. His response was a complex account replete with kinship's vertical relations and simultaneity's horizontal ones of spreading bacteria and pills. Beginning with an entanglement of more-than-human relations, he said, "I knew it was a medical problem because of that bull over there." He pointed to a long-horned bullock among the cattle and continued, "I was cultivating[18] the field with him, and he turned quickly and hit me with his horn in the side of the chest. It really hurt. It hurt even to breathe. When it did not get better, I started to look for medicine." Because the pain was due to injury incurred while using an ox-drawn implement to skim the weeds out of the spaces between rows of plants in his monocrop fields, Devi Singh sought biomedical treatment.

He visited qualified and unqualified physicians, nurses, and pharmacists, receiving advice and treatments from each.[19] He explained, "Eventually, I went to Govindlal in Sagwai. He gave me injections and some pills. They did not do much, so I went to Dr. Mathur, who gave me some more pills. I took those and the ones that Govindlal gave me for a while. I kept taking all the pills and everything, but my side still hurt. I didn't know how pills would help it, but I kept taking them. It's what the doctors suggested." I nodded and Devi Singh went on: "One day when I was in the village house, Mohit came by on his motorcycle, so I flagged him down and he gave me a bottle [of IV fluids] too. I did all this, and I kept taking pills."

Each of the three men were well-known sources of biomedical pharmaceuticals in the area. Govindlal was a nurse who had his own storefront practice in Sagwai. Dr. Mathur was an informally trained but state-certified Registered Medical Practitioner who practiced from his home clinic, and Mohit was informally trained and unregistered. Each gave Devi Singh a different mix of antibiotics, steroids, and other pharmaceuticals. Though he met these practitioners one at a time, Devi Singh took the pharmaceuticals they prescribed simultaneously and cumulatively. The three different treatments entered, overlapped, and marked Devi Singh's body and narrative.

Simultaneity makes disaggregating the effects of one drug or physician from the others nearly impossible. It foils the patient-pathway metaphors that global public health uses to document patient and microbial action. A horizontal unifying trope of progression, pathways help public health literature imagine patients as moving from one physician to the next. They progress in a sequence toward TB diagnosis and increasingly specialized care. Microbes follow, maturing from latent to active and, if things go wrong, to drug-resistant TB. This literature collects meandering and circuitous narratives like Devi Singh's and through much admirable and innovative interpretive labor arranges them into a sequence of symptom, diagnosis, treatment, occasionally drug resistance, and more treatment.[20] The trope's very structure elicits and crafts a progressing, self-knowing individual afflicted by a progressing disease.[21] That one might feel lost or in doubt while traveling this path, as I did on the way through the forest to Devi Singh's house, or even double back to ask directions, or take multiple

actions and pharmaceuticals at once, has no place in the progressive metaphor. Neither do initially acquired drug resistance or bodily immunity.

Devi Singh's narrative about medicine was not a path organized around
reflexive decisions in search of the truth about his ailment. Instead, he took
tentative and simultaneous steps to efface bodily pain that he expected to
diminish with time. Biomedical interventions did modulate some of Devi
Singh's pain, but he did not improve as quickly as he hoped: "My side still
hurt, and my brother-in-law said there was a very good doctor in Salumbar, so eventually we took the motorcycle to see him." A larger town in
the hilly parts of Mewar, Salumbar is one center of south Rajasthan's indigenous community and the source of the bus that connected Ambawati
to villages of relatives and market towns. There, Devi Singh visited the
doctor whom his brother-in-law recommended. The man was an uncertified biomedical practitioner too. "That Bengali doctor told me that I would
need to take a course for several months.[22] He sold us the medicines and
we came back. It went on like that for a couple of months. We would go,
get the medicines, and come home. I kept going to some of the doctors
in Sagwai and Sadri then too in the middle if I needed anything. Ouf, I
remember how it hurt with every bump in the road," Devi Singh recalled.
Devi Singh's body and bacteria were metabolizing and incorporating more
medicines.

TANGLED ROOTS AND TANGLED BACTERIA
I asked if the doctor in Salumbar said anything about TB, and Devi Singh
replied, "We spent almost 200,000 rupees at the time, but no one said
anything about TB until later. I did feel a little better from the course
in Salumbar, though." Though the doctor had not openly spoken of TB,
"course" is a common euphemism for TB treatment.[23] Devi Singh used
the English word twice in quick succession, and I began to wonder if the
physician had perhaps been gesturing to TB. Curious, I decided to borrow
a tactic I learned from physicians. Rifampicin, an essential part of TB
treatment, tends to color urine red. Even if caregivers never mention TB
in their consultation, many people remember this startling bodily change.
For this reason, physicians who meet a coughing patient for the first time
often ask about red urine. I asked Devi Singh about this too. He quickly

replied, "Yes, for a while it turned red. It was red on and off from then. I don't remember when the first time was, but I was startled. The doctor in Salumbar told me it was normal when I asked him about it." That his urine turned red "on and off" might suggest that Devi Singh had likely, on the guidance of the doctor in Salumbar, been taking at least one drug that could kill TB bacteria.[24] It was now one that his bacteria were resistant to.

When exposed to anti-TB drugs like rifampicin, many of the bacteria die, but those that do not continue to reproduce and spread resistant genes laterally. Then, as an accident of treatment by drugs that no longer kill some bacteria, the resistant bacteria slowly replace those that are not resistant as if an invasive species in a forest or field. Hannah Landecker calls this process of reassortment the biology of history and suggests that parallel changes to bacteria and their DNA might be a way to think of events as having both lateral and genealogical effects.[25] Landecker's is an invitation to think with sequentially progressing tree and simultaneously spreading forest metaphors to describe connected selves that are shaped by breath, bacteria, and pharmaceuticals as well as history. Rifampicin's possible role in this diversity of antibiotic resistance connects Devi Singh to the doctor in Salumbar long after he sought care elsewhere. Even more alarmingly, because he was never tested for resistance before being given rifampicin it is impossible to know whether the bacteria became resistant in Devi Singh's body or if it arrived there already so armored. The medicine may have cultivated resistance from susceptible bacteria or simply allowed it to flourish and spread. Or the bacteria in his lungs may have been a forest of resistant and susceptible microbes long before he sought care, connecting him to others in different times and places in a tangle of uncultivated and unintentional relations.[26]

After about a year of "running around everywhere," Devi Singh visited another physician in Udaipur. This physician was certified and practiced in a well-known private hospital. "He looked at my reports and asked me to do some more tests," Devi Singh told me. "They took another photograph of my chest and blood and all again." Though the doctor asked for more tests, the process of building a diagnosis did not start over. He used Devi Singh's pile of documents about earlier tests and treatments to learn what other physicians had thought could be the problem and how their treatments may have affected Devi Singh. Earlier physicians spread into his diagnosis and into Devi Singh's body. Rather than the outcome of an unfolding individual physician's process of discovery, diagnosis and treatment in Udaipur had roots in what came before. Diagnosis was a tangled knot of bodily signs, stories, and of course, paperwork that distorted the unfolding of time and disease.

Like many patients throughout India, Devi Singh carried with him a large plastic sack full of reports and notes made by some but not all of his physicians. These polyethene archives are common sights in clinics across India. The documents inside them often tell as much about a patient's journey as the patient does. When seeing a patient for the first time, physicians or their helpers often excavate these plastic sacks in an archeological process to know a body or bacteria that is now fully entangled with cultural pharmaceuticals.[27] Devi Singh's spreading account and the linear texts within the ad hoc file bled into each other. The papers fill in silences, add confusion, and support or refute claims to truth. In cases of discrepancy the text, by virtue of its capacity to create a line of progressing dates, is privileged over the patient's spreading narrative of simultaneity. A physician rarely notes that he viewed the file in his own reports, and though these files often inform the creation of patient pathways by social scientists, their organizing effect is seldom documented. Doing so could reveal the haphazard circuitous loops of actors and actions that go into knowing or even creating disease and drug resistance.

Devi Singh went on, "Until then I thought it was still the injury from the bull, but that doctor, he said it was also TB. The injury had been filled up with yogurt and the doctor explained that TB might be inside it."[28] Though it is likely that the previous physician suspected that Devi Singh's pain could have been due to TB and attempted to treat it surreptitiously, this was the first time anyone shared these concerns with Devi Singh.

Without a diagnosis, Devi Singh experienced illness as everyday aches and pains. Their source was a domestic bull, not a semiwild bacterium that one could cultivate a relation or resistance to. Through diagnosis Devi Singh's discomfort could emerge as its own bacterial entity with a history, name, and identity: TB. Devi Singh continued, "The doctor told us that I would need to take eight months of medicines, but I told him we had no money left." He had already mortgaged his fields to a liquor dealer and spent the money his sons sent back from their work as laborers in Gujarat to pay doctors. "The doctor said we could get the medicines from the government if we liked. He sent us to the government hospital in Udaipur and told us that they would give me another test for TB." Devi Singh was unsure about this course of action. He explained that he "did not much like having to go to the government hospital and never coughed up too much phlegm." He said, "I was never really as sick as people get with TB, I was just coughing, and it hurt to breathe." Nonetheless, Devi Singh submitted a sputum sample to the government hospital in Udaipur. Another microscopic inspection found TB bacteria in his sputum again: "The government result came back, and they said I would get the medicine here at home. We went back and showed it to the other doctor. He said it was good to take the government medicine and prescribed me some other things to help the pain go away and some powder to eat. I ate it until it was gone, but after that I have just eaten the eggs that hen over there lays for me." Devi Singh started, or perhaps restarted, TB treatment from the Ambawati health center when the medicines arrived a week later. He diligently took the pills, but after several more months of medicines the sputum samples he submitted to Suresh still contained TB bacteria.

Devi Singh continued to take his medicines, but Suresh worried that something was not quite right. Because national TB policy until 2012 required continuing an ineffective treatment to its end, their only option was to stay the standardized course.[29] This plan changed, however, when the district TB officer, a physician, visited Ambawati's clinic one evening for a village health fair. Responsible for district-wide TB control, the officer gave a broadly didactic lecture on TB, its symptoms, and the importance of accessing tests. Afterward, he and Suresh discussed Ambawati's high number of people in TB treatment. Inspired by the nascent expansion of MDR-TB testing and treatment that the merely months-old policy change made possible, the officer wondered if any residents were not improving despite regularly taking their medicine. Suresh suggested Devi Singh and Siddharth Singh. The TB officer gave Suresh two large specimen tubes in which to collect the men's sputum for drug-sensitivity testing.

"One day I went to the clinic and Suresh told me to spit into a big tube with a red cap and send it with Roshan Singh to the hospital in the city," Devi Singh explained. When the sample was ready, Devi Singh's son Roshan took it and Siddharth Singh's father with Siddharth Singh's sample by motorcycle to the district TB center. From there, the TB officer forwarded the samples to the Gujarat state TB laboratory for bacterial culturing and drug-resistance testing.[30] Several months later, Suresh got word that Devi Singh and his son would need to visit the district TB center for MDR-TB treatment initiation and counseling. Along with the bacteria grew uncultivated but binding relations between Devi Singh, his body, the state, and global health.

Like most narratives of TB in Ambawati, Devi Singh's story was one of simultaneity with circuitous paths, treelike causal events, and substories that makes pinpointing a critical event or single moment of cultivated resistance impossible. It moves through and between structures like kinship, the state, pharmaceutical reason, caste, and self, shifting each in its own way. This tangle of relations' new name, MDR-TB, reassorted relations of simultaneity and social breath into those of debt and duty.

DEBTS AND DUTIES

On another visit I found myself staring down at the forest again. This time, I asked Devi Singh if he could cut wood and graze cattle in the forest during the intensive new treatment. He explained that, though he frequented the forest during earlier treatments, his new medicines left him dizzy, thirsty, and exhausted. I lamented this state, but Devi Singh recalled his first encounter with the district TB officer. He explained that the technocrat connected MDR-TB treatment to a new relation of "duty" that kept him out of the forest. He said,

> I went to see the big doctor. He gave me a checkup, listened to my chest, and such. Then he explained to me that I had a big tuberculosis. He said that the government was going to be taking care of me from then on. That the government was providing me with a 200,000-rupee course of medication and that I should think of this as my new job, like I'm on government duty.
>
> He told me that the government was going to send a box of medicine every month to Suresh at the health center, and I should go there or send someone

there to get the medicines. This time I would have injections too. *Annadata*[31] said that probably I would have some side effects from the medicines and that I should just take my medicines and go to sleep. I remember I told him that I could not sleep all day, but he told me that sleeping and taking this medicine would be my most important job for the next two years.

He said that if anyone gave me any trouble, I should say that the government was paying me 200,000 rupees to rest, that resting was my job now and the government was paying me to do it. I became a government employee. It is my job to rest. So I work a little in the morning and then I take my medicine and have my lunch and rest. I liked the doctor and I said to him, "*Hukam*,[32] you have saved my life, I will do whatever you say," and he responded, "It is you and the medicine that are saving your life, not me. This is the government providing the medicine, so now you are being paid so much money just to rest and take these medicines. It is your work." So here I am lying down and on government duty.

With that, Devi Singh chuckled and reclined a little on his cot. He had finished this part of his story. It is a fascinating account of what happens when bacteria and Devi Singh are no longer susceptible to TB treatment's plantation logic of standardization and surveillance. Expensive publicly provided drugs and a new strategy of care were the only option left for Devi Singh and public health, but they required new duties from each.

As it began to treat drug-resistant TB, Indian public health also grew new relations to technocracy, individual pharmaceutical cultivation, and the emerging global humanitarian apparatus of MDR-TB control that centered patients rather than governance.[33] This was meaningful to both Devi Singh and his physician. For Devi Singh the new regimen meant avoiding agricultural work and meriting care by performing a docile surveilled self. For the physician it meant curing Devi Singh without insisting on subject cultivation. Both viewed preventing bacterial reproduction and spread as doing his duty as a citizen. These duties came with long histories for both.

For decades the government of India followed conventional TB wisdom and deprioritized treatment for people with MDR-TB.[34] This triaging of care left many to die and it resonated with strategies used to govern people like Devi Singh who lived in the forest. Soon after independence, the Indian state, caught up in its own romantic and biodeterminist project of categorization, deemed people like Devi Singh as in need of particular care or cultivation by the pastoral, *annadata* state. First it worked to protect indigenous people through isolation and separation from those deemed mainstream. To keep money lenders, liquor dealers, and others out of areas where indigenous people lived, the state made all sales of indigenous-owned land to nonindigenous buyers illegal and limited the number of roads constructed in areas where many indigenous people lived.[35] It also turned large tracts of forest land into preserves. When isolation failed, a neoliberal policy regime began to use care instead. It initiated health promotion and scholarship programs while harmonizing development with the market by implementing incentives for both state actors and service users. These positive inducements hope to guide indigenous people to cultivate themselves as citizens commensurable to everyone else. This new policy echoes early reformers who argued that fostering certain social forms would slowly phase out those deemed anathema or dangerous to Indian social life.[36]

Together these two policy decisions frame Ambawati today. They laid the historical foundations for its single paved road, its service by private Jungle Mail buses rather than public ones, its collective struggle for development, and the large wall around much of its forest. Withholding resources, fencing off forests, and connecting care to comportment is part of a long history of antagonism between the state and Ambawati's Rawats. A new government duty for Devi Singh might rework antagonisms around rights to health and the forest, as well as the debts and duties of citizenship.[37]

Framing Devi Singh's rest as a "government duty," the physician worked to repair the relations of mutual suspicion that characterized state care for TB and indigenous people. "Government duty" and 200,000-rupee payments contested older forms of TB care that framed Devi Singh as resistant subject, who had usurped public forest land and might create resistant bacteria, and developmental state politics that imagined neglect as care. Instead of making Devi Singh responsible for his illness and accusing him and those like him of being resistant biopolitical saboteurs, his doctor subverts ideas of a romantically reflexive, controlled, and cultivating self whose TB is a moral, political, and social failure. Instead, he brings Devi

Singh into connective relations of duty to the state. He frames subjection to the toxic pharmaceuticals as paid labor done on behalf of the state.

Devi Singh responds with a barrage of patronage words that index a new form of pastoral relationship, but the doctor resists them. In the narrative, he refers to the doctor as *annadata* and *hukam* to recognize the state and its actors as in positions of power over his life. Both terms are frequently used for people of substantially higher status, particularly patrons, landlords, and Rajputs. Using these words, he builds, or perhaps more precisely recognizes, his relations to the doctor as those of dependence, hierarchy, and patronage within the lateral connections made by TB bacteria, simultaneity, and duty. Nonetheless, by living within and between them, Devi Singh subverts their power. Connected by the new biopolitical relations of risk, responsibility, and patronage created by MDR-TB globally and in Devi Singh's body, both men reworked the relationship of mutual avoidance between rural farmer and state bureaucrat to one of reciprocal duty.

After forty years of illicit forest labor, Devi Singh was now a government employee. Paid in medicine but not money, he had an official duty to rest. His new government duty, the repetitive and regularized work of resting to make the most of state resources, was indeed a new way of organizing lateral relations of production between active state and docile cultivated citizen. The doctor gave Devi Singh a productive role that was not cultivating fields or managing cattle. From this new status, Devi Singh made himself a metaphor and a mockery of the productive, contributing, and reproducing state employee. Laughing at his own story of good but idle citizenship, he seems to have appreciated the ironic parallel between himself and a languid or corrupt state employee. Indeed, government duty's meanings were simultaneous and complicated. I often wonder if Devi Singh did not see it all as one big joke that he played on the state by staying alive in the forest. Perhaps *hukam* and *annadata* were as duplicitous as evocations of duty.

FOREST DUTY

Others often talked about working in the forest as their daily duty. They were poking fun at those who had regular, formal employment and allowing a possible sense of irony to make its way through Devi Singh's comment about being on government duty. Nanibai Rawat, Devi Singh's cousin and my neighbor, reminded me that Devi Singh's story of rest as government duty may have been a kind of ironic subjection to the state's ways of being connected. Like Devi Singh before his illness, Nanibai grazed animals and cut wood in the forest nearly every day. After finishing her daily housework, cooking a pot of vegetables, and nestling several balls of dough in the embers of the cooking fire for her family's lunch, Nanibai usually set out around ten. As she left, she often laughed to her neighbors that she was "going on duty."

In households aspiring to middle-class status, "duty" referred to formal-sector work done by people like bank tellers or public servants or teachers. These occupations' stable income, considerable comfort, and easy work (compared with the toil and uncertainty of agricultural labor) were all signs of social cultivation and economic success. "Duty" occupations were points of pride for those who commanded them and a target of sarcasm for those who did not. Nanibai and others jocularly borrowed the English word "duty," with its air of officialdom, to describe repetitive daily tasks like going to the forest. They parodied nine-to-five salaried "duty" by equating it with their informal but repetitive labor in the forest and fields. In her version Nanibai set her agricultural and forest labor as equal to that of the middle class's and mocked the fantasy of stability provided by regular but monotonous public and private service sector employment.[38] Devi Singh might have too.

Nanibai's duty consisted of walking to the forest amid a herd of goats and three water buffalo with a stick, an ax, and a burlap-covered water bottle. As they walked the four kilometers to the forest, Nanibai hustled to keep the animals out of fields and other people's pastures. Once through the break in the wall between forest and scrub, the animals fanned out to eat leaves and other forest plants. Nanibai often set to work chopping a headload of dead wood while the animals grazed. About an hour before evening, when the animals were fed and wood chopped, Nanibai wrapped the bundle of long branches in vines, balanced it on her head, and set off for home with the animals. When she reached her family's enclosure in the village, she stored the wood in the barnyard to use or sell. Each day, Nanibai brought something from the forest with her. In the drier months, she carried tree leaves to feed animals, and, when the time was right, she collected thousands of tendu leaves to be packed and sold to cigarette factories. Like those who went to regular employment, Nanibai collected a crop she had tended to but not sown, cultivated, or organized. Her "duty" was this daily work of making life from what was not wholly cultivated. Duty might suggest other ways of organizing life than cultivating it. Nanibai's and Devi Singh's previous duties were a particular kind of production by gathering what did not need cultivation but required work, knowledge, transformation, and tending, nonetheless.

For most people in Ambawati, stable service employment and the cultivated, refined self that it requires are both unattainable and boring. Some even preferred the forest's flexible, roving work of gathering to the agricultural labors of cultivation, which they often simply called weeding. When I asked Nanibai if she found it tiresome to come walking home every day with hips wobbling from the weight of the wood she had cut, she quipped with a smile, "I much prefer the forest to weeding the fields all day. I leave that to my daughters-in-law. They say they are afraid of the forest, but not me. I have my ax, and I can throw rocks [*batta tokno*] with the best of them. Besides, I never come back empty handed." Her task allowed her to leave the orderly and surveilled fields of the village and enter an atmosphere of risk and discovery.

Her *jangali* duty and its play on formally being "on duty" as an employee might suggest a bioethics of being with rather than guarding or managing life. Nanibai's sylvan "duty" was to produce what she gathered rather than what she reproduced or cultivated. For her, forest duty might have been a microcosm of a larger lateral web of relations of production that worked on the traffic between forest and village, wild and cultivated. She was, in her own words, "free in the forest's cool open air and able to make a bit of money by selling bundles of wood," and by doing so she made a mockery of Ambawati's formally employed residents' contractual duties and the idea that women, for their protection, should remain at home and eschew financial gains. Indeed, this uncultivated self was not backward or wild; it was simply unwilling to fall completely into the agricultural village's structures and cultivated fields.

The forest presented an alternative or double entendre of social, economic, and moral duty with its own aesthetics and morals of self for

Ambawatians. It also provided another way to imagine duty to the state and others in Devi Singh's forest of MDR-TB bacteria and toxic drugs. Now in debilitating treatment for MDR-TB that was both wild and cultivated, Devi Singh's "government duty" was similar to Nanibai's forested duty. It was a form of duty that meant contributing without privileging cultivation. Resting and dealing with the unintended and uncultivated effects of pharmaceuticals did not produce anything but sought rather to avoid the reproduction of bacteria. The doctor suggested that, by avoiding the hard reproductive work of cultivating living fields, attending to family relations, and even cultivating an aspiring economic self, Devi Singh was both preserving his own life and cultivating sanitary citizenship. Still, his duty to the state may have been one like Nanibai's work of subverting surveillance by accessing the forests' alternative ways of being and living through reassortment.

THEFT AND REASSORTED RELATIONS

The forest's atmospheric entanglement complicates one's duty to people or things, but "thievery" was the most frequent way of talking about *jangali* life's unruly capacity to reorganize relations. Devi Singh paralleled his life with bacteria and his life with thieves. Theft shifts relations of ownership and use between people and things. Like birth, death, marriage, debt, and friendship, theft's transformation of the connection between person and object can shift a whole raft of received relations. Within the remembered past, theft was a way of forming new relations to things and also kin. Even people were stolen to become community members. Two old men trace their presence in Ambawati to having been stolen from their homes on the other side of the forest as children. They worked in their captors' fields before eventually marrying young women in these families. Of similar caste but different lineage from their captors, they were ideal marriage partners. Perhaps part of stealing them away from their families and natal villages was to enable men without sons to give their land to daughters. This is precisely what happened in both cases. Today, the old men, their children, and their grandchildren are part of the community, knitted in by relations of marriage, inter-reliance, land, neighbor, maternal relations, and friendship, but they maintain their own lineages. Their theft brought to being a whole set of relations not described by anthropology's family tree metaphors or concepts like patrilocality or male-dominated land ownership. Just as adultery potentially subverts and strengthens family trees by secretly connecting people, theft also builds lateral relations to preserve vertical ones.[39] Spread and genealogy need each other.

In November 2012 Ambawati had been buzzed with rumors of rock-throwing thieves entering the village from the forest two nights earlier. Stones had been thrown at houses in the two hamlets closest to the thirty-kilometer-wide forest. Thieves almost always seemed to arrive in Ambawati from the forest and Devi Singh's was the first house they might pass. On my next visit I asked him, "Don't you worry about thieves, living so far away from others and so near the forest?" Everyone was on edge, but Devi Singh responded with a chuckle, "Why would I worry about thieves?" Before I could answer, he continued, "I like being up here far away from anyone bothering me. Imagine if thieves come here throwing rocks at my house at night, what do they want? They are probably just hungry and certainly they're not going to carry gunnysacks of wheat away on their backs. I'll give them the thing I have that's useful to them, food." As he spoke of thieves, Devi Singh slipped between the possible and the potential. He continued, explaining that it was more useful to think of these passersby as potential friends than as thieves by giving them what they might steal,

> I ask my wife to make them some food.[40] We feed them bread and buttermilk and whatever vegetables we have. We let them rest and have water. After all, having crossed the whole forest they are tired and hungry. With food, water, and rest, they go on their way. We can easily give that, and they'll find more interesting things [to steal] than wheat and our cows in other houses. Cows and wheat are much harder to get home than jewelry or other nice things. If we feed them, they become our guests and our friends. They'll leave us with our few things because we have given them what they really need at the moment. That's why they are thieves anyway, to fulfill a need. By feeding them, we're friends.

Devi Singh seemed to feel vaguely connected to pilfering sylvan strangers, and his response to thieves and behavior associated with the forest was to build relations. The visitors were neither family nor lineage mates, but they were often, many implied, of the same Rawat caste. As such, they were open to relations crafted by food and drink, the only thing Devi Singh had aplenty. Beyond caste, Devi Singh shared a familiarity with the forest and its potential to fulfill needs of food, care, and hospitality with potential and actual thieves. Thus, his most practical response, as a fellow denizen of the forest, was to offer the thieves hospitality. For Devi Singh, hospitality both preserved the self and changed it by building new layers of connection that did not reproduce existing structures.[41] It was a practice of living with rather than resisting.

By stealing and making an item their own or passing it along to another, thieves reassort existing relationships to remake webs of materiality, value, and significance within and among them. In his own turn and through hospitality, Devi Singh transformed thief from stranger to friend and remade networks just as he created a duty to the state from treatment. A forested relationship occurred as bonds of shared need, location, and friendship intertwined with caste.

Devi Singh's willingness to build temporary relations with thieves by recognizing their simultaneity as self and other does not suggest that he was willing to accommodate the TB bacteria in his body. Instead, he used the same moral and practical strategies of relational reassortment with the forests' thieves as he did with the people and things that MDR-TB brought him. Biomedicine, the technocrat, pharmaceuticals, and side effects were just a few examples. Indeed, creating a relationship with TB treatment rather than resisting it was, much like his work to build friendship with the thieves, an attempt to avoid a negative outcome through giving of what he had. Devi Singh's recourse to commensality and complicity with thief and antimicrobial state alike made for relations other than the hierarchically organized connections of aggressor and aggressed, thief and victim, host and guest, body and bacteria, culture and nature, and self and other. He took what the world offered him and brought it back to his home, in this case not wood or tendu leaves, but pharmaceuticals. These reassortments of objects and relations made Devi Singh part of a forest of relations that were both genealogical and lateral. So was the illness that kept him in bed. It was part of him, something that he had made, and yet also wholly other. Breath, it seemed, like theft, the forest, and bacterial DNA, was powerful in its capacity to reassort relations and lives of bacteria and people.

FIBRILLOUS BODIES AND BACTERIA

Postcolonial science studies have shown that science, like the lateral relations that I have suggested occur in the atmospheric forest, builds spreading multiplex networks of individuals and alter their constituent parts in the process. As Banu Subramaniam writes,

> Like the thigmotropic tendrils of plants, the fibrils of science seek support structures, and thus come to scale political and social scaffolding in different contexts. I use the term fibril, from botany, to highlight the organic, living natures of knowledge as it travels and takes different shapes in different contexts. As science's thigmotropic tendrils build infrastructures in varied contexts, they build on the local terrains and scaffolding and organically generate dense knots and thickets of social meanings. Hence, while we interpret these knots as social categories—sex, gender, class, caste, sexuality—they are never the same across the world.[42]

Perhaps the *jangali* and science-y are not that different after all. Devi Singh's forest body and subjectivity is similarly replete with fibrillous relationality that, like science, reassorts cultivated arboreal structures such as caste, kinship, and marriage. In his account, these fibrils are the lateral forestlike socialities of simultaneity such as breath, thievery, simultaneity, and duty. By avoiding forest metaphors, biological and social science risk missing the forms of relational life and causation that might not so easily enter paradigms of linear cause and effect, sexual reproduction, and inheritance but move through them nonetheless. These lateral, lying down relations provide new lenses for interpreting how diseases, meanings, and materials bring people together.

While Subramaniam uses tendrils to think through connections, Devi Singh and I draw inspiration from the forest that we gazed at with its trees, bushes, and vines to interpret the tangles that make him or MDR-TB *jangali*. The forest might provide Devi Singh with an atmosphere in which TB can move between his biography and his microbiome. Perhaps it gives him a way to imagine the debility he suffers as a result of the toxic pharmaceuticals given to him by the state and the need to continue making himself available to intervention without subjection. His narration of simultaneity with bacteria and government duty is a reassorted act of simultaneous submission and usurpation. The jumble of the breathy forest was not without cultivated patches, but time and again it reveals not a biopolitics of resistance but a biologic of tenacity. Life and breath, it seems, has a tenacity even beyond the death of the body.

To interpret Devi Singh's life with drug-resistant TB bacteria through public health science's progress-oriented arboreal or pathway metaphors makes Devi Singh responsible for his care and its outcome.[43] It also hides other possible relations built through reassortment, simultaneity, and history. It asks him to search for a cause or tipping point for drug resistance and resistance to the state in his personal behavior, subjectivity, or decision-making self. Such a cause cannot, however, be found there. Instead, when listening to his story of sickness it becomes clear that pain, care, resistance, and treatment are made possible and interpreted with a forest of relations that inform and supersede Devi Singh's affliction. His illness was shaped by his sons, his brother-in-law, his wife, the hen pecking at the ground whose eggs were part of this treatment regimen, a nationwide initiative to treat resistant forms of TB, trained and untrained physicians through the southeastern finger of Rajasthan, and the fresh air that he and I both thought would do him good. His life, too, remained entangled with TB and its effects even after two more years of pharmaceuticals and tests that finally revealed that he was cured. Cure, as Bharat Venkat reminds us, is a complicated matter with MDR-TB, and though Devi Singh's bacteria are gone for now, he may never be totally out of the woods.[44]

Just as forested relations and the contagious influence of the forest show that relations can and do change, a change in the texture of one relation rustles through others. Devi Singh's relations to the state's MDR-TB treatment initiative changed the way he lived and imagined relations to his children, who no longer needed to send as much money; to his wife and brothers, who could not scold him for resting instead of plowing their fields; and to Suresh, for whom Devi Singh's affection grew. The substance and quality of kinship relations or duties were changed by reassorting relations of friendship and theft.

Spreading bacterial, pharmaceutical, and care relations connect what might otherwise seem like linear genealogy of treelike events. These connections make separating an original bacterium from those adjusted or made local by these medicines impossible. This also means that Devi

Singh's resistance was not cultivated by an intentional, biopolitically resistant self but by a forest of factors in which biopolitics and its ways of seeing and acting on the world are several among many ways of dealing with the intersection of futurity and health. The reassortment and simultaneity of human and bacterial life is like a mixed-up forest in which homogeneity forms just a small part within in a larger landscape of heterogeneity. It reveals a tenaciously hodgepodge world that the cultivation of future pharmaceutical stability cannot organize through science and its commitment to privilege reproduction as the meaning of life.

EIGHT

AFTERLIFE

Kahan se aaya?
Kahan jaonge?
Khabar karo apne tan ki.

Where did you come from?
Where will you go?
Take stock of your embodied soul.

—Kabiri Bhajan

MY FRIEND RAI SINGH Rawat died at home in October of 2011. He was twenty-four and had been sick with TB for months, perhaps years. He eventually began treatment, but the disease was unrelenting. It consumed his tall lanky body and he died. His uncle and cousins organized a small funeral. His mother, Mangibai, and his young wife observed forty days of mourning. They wailed laments from inside the house when any new visitor arrived. "O Raiyo, my Raiyo, why have you left me so quickly? Where did you go?" they sobbed.[1] His two-year-old son Prasad sat with them. When Mangibai emerged from the small house, she walked with a newly acquired limp. It was as if both Mangibai's heart and body had been irreparably injured by the death of her only son. The limp also seemed to address Mangibai's question "Where did you go?" It suggested that Rai Singh did not go anywhere. He remained present in her body and in Ambawati's breathed atmosphere. Later we would learn that he was even present as a ghost who could cause pain and occasionally enter living bodies to usurp their voice and pant for breath. Death had transformed him from having breath to being breath.

169

Rai Singh's abiding, if occasionally mischievous, presence as ghost and ancestor did not surprise those who knew him. Even in life he was a trickster. He loved to ensnare bystanders in pranks or riddles. I do not enjoy riddles but was often a target of his Wagri double entendres, especially after a drink or two. In these moments I, like others whom he called friend, usually took the bait before demanding that he speak simply. To such exasperation, Rai Singh often gleefully responded, "Don't worry, we will all die." This never seemed like much of an answer to me, and he continues to test the limits of my brain and patience even in death. Indeed, his simultaneous departure and presence is perhaps his final riddle: What of life when the human and nonhuman dead abide in atmospheres?

In the years following his death, neighbors and I have slowly worked through Rai Singh's conundrum. I have been struck by the questions our conversations raise. Is one dead if one's breath, agency, and story abide? Can no-longer-embodied selves inhabit or animate atmospheres? What do we, the embodied, owe spectral neighbors and kin? Can we care for one another and the dead by reading signs in clouds, fanning air, sweeping dust, or managing mud? Does atmospheric care for bodies and locations itself have an afterlife? Though we rarely posed such questions directly, their themes wove through conversations about how to live and breathe in an atmosphere permeated by TB. Together they center on an existential and ethnographic concern for what immaterial beings, who abide in affective and climatic environments, can teach the living.

At the entangled thresholds of death, language, and unending bereavement, this chapter theorizes an atmosphere of afterlife, a *bios* without *zoë*.[2] Each preceding chapter has narrated a story, or a *bios*, of atmospherically entangled TB through the ways that people care for breath's ephemeral vitality. Each narrative was an entanglement of material and immaterial influences or agencies that gave TB and atmospheric care its shape and form. Along the way, life and troubled breath have evaded biomedicine's story of TB infection as the chance meeting of discrete antagonistic human and bacterial lives. TB and life in Ambawati have merged as material, affective, and more-than-human entanglements or atmospheres. This chapter suggests that atmospheric care and contagion along with breath might have atmospheric afterlives that effect airborne infectious disease. Inspired by

Veena Das's treatment of language, lamentation, and the body, the chapter is an ethnographic account of how everyday and breathy "transactions between body and language lead to an articulation of the world in which the strangeness of the world revealed by death, by its non-inhabitability, can be transformed into a world in which one can dwell again, in full awareness of a life that has to be lived in loss."[3]

Atmospheres, I have argued, shape logics of care and bacteria in the face of a TB epidemic. Still, death as the dissolution of a material body—human, bacterial, cloud, dust mote, or otherwise—might be the limit of an entity's entanglement in a living atmosphere. In Ambawati, however, this does not seem to be the case, at least not for Rai Singh and others. There, the dead retain a capacity to act on and entangle with breaths, bodies, or bacteria regardless of materiality. Engaging them requires an atmospheric liveliness that can unhitch *bios* from the material, *zoë*. They open the possibility of an atmosphere entangled with the living and the dead. It is as atmospherically entangled with the dead that TB moves between lives and afterlives to afflict breaths, environments, and people who experience death without disappearance.

Despite an absence of material form, the postmaterial dead, like Rai Singh, might act or even live in material and immaterial atmospheres of care and vulnerability. Perhaps Rai Singh's riddle is an invitation to consider social worlds of breath and TB suffering that emerge when the dead can or must remain alive and active in an atmosphere. Agency, relations, the self, and even cause and effect seem to extend past the body's death to abide in an atmospheric afterlife in which the bodily and the disembodied might live together. Like other atmospheres, atmospheres of afterlife demand care and attention. They also facilitate a reconsideration of biomedicine's epistemological limits.

Many of the people I met while researching TB in Ambawati have died. Within biomedical stories of TB, they are statistics and endings. The dead represent failed programs and failed adherence, but sometimes, even more alarmingly, they are a solution to the biomedical problem of contagion. The dead's breath cannot spread bacteria or their lungs play host to resistance. As biomedically dead, Ambawati's TB dead have reached the end of contagion and biopolitics. In her ethnography of brain death,

Margaret Lock shows that biomedical and medicolegal preoccupations with fixing death as a point of no return have roots in Victorian-era anxieties about medical liability and being buried alive.[4] The dead needed to be very and truly dead. Lock argues that even in the highly technical milieu of organ donation, biomedical concerns for separating the death from the living are social questions. They concern "the location of the essence of the person, and when and under what conditions person and body cease to exist."[5] In short, biomedically discerning death is about discerning an end to personhood with its relationships and potentials. Requiring no more care or mourning, the biomedically dead cease to exist. In biomedicine then, the TB dead can leave no traces except in body counts, like the statistics of TB dead for 2021: 1.6 million people globally of which 480,000 are Indian, or over 1,300 Indians per day.[6]

Though biomedical frames interpret TB death as a cessation of body and person, concerns in Ambawati about the TB dead's persistence locate what Lock has called "the essence of the person" differently. People who have died from TB there, and perhaps anywhere, are more open ended.[7] Most are mourned and some have afterlives irreducible to datafication and dispersal. Neighbors have carried their bodies to the cremation ground and reduced them to ashes before sweeping the ashes into repurposed sixteen-liter oil tins. Male relatives have taken the ashes on a long trek to the Ganges or twenty kilometers north to a spring-fed pond that begins one of Rajasthan's great rivers. There, men have dispersed the ashes into the water, tin urns and all, before returning home to a collective meal and settling of debts. Mourning continues for forty days after the death and then in a modulated state for a year. Death rituals like these distribute material bodies and their accrued or absorbed dirt into the world and water outside Ambawati. They speed the disconnection of body from soul, but occasionally rituals fail, and the entanglement of breath, self, and personhood's rights and responsibilities remain.[8] In some cases, perhaps most, mourning has no end point. These dead receive ritual and everyday attention as ancestors, ghosts, or both for decades and generations to come. They are deeply, persistently social.

Ethnographic accounts of death and personhood across South Asia have shown that the dead can live social lives with demands, responsibilities, and voices of their own.[9] In these social worlds with ghosts, agency and subjectivity persist beyond the vital body's embodied personhood. Persons can breathe and speak through the bodies of others. Margaret Trawick and Amy Allocco have both written of women who took on afterlives of care, becoming ancestor spirits and family deities after premature deaths in Tamil Nadu,[10] and Lindsay Harlan and Brighupati Singh write of men killed by violence entering the Rajasthani pantheon as healing and mischievous deities.[11] In each case, however, the social and moral status of such persistent persons is ambiguous. The afterliving can be comforting presences and givers of care as well as troublemakers who demand attention and social action. Rai Singh and others in Ambawati persist in this same way, borrowing bodies, making claims when necessary, and unpredictably abiding in atmospheres. Perhaps they even imbue an atmosphere with afterlife's affects of mourning and levity by murmuring, "Don't worry, we will all die."

Robert Desjarlais suggests that, though everyone dies, just as everyone breathes, death is shaped by aesthetics and concerns for lives, deaths, and afterlives.[12] Death as the reorganization of an entanglement of body, breath, and soul in Ambawati and across the subcontinent is often discussed with the vocabulary of "good" death or "bad" death.[13] When understood in moralizing terms such as good and bad, the quality of a death might reveal and even shape the quality of one's moral life and afterlife. A good death, indicative of goodness overall, is placid. It facilitates a departure of the soul at an old age. As comfort in death might affect the soul, the stakes of atmospheric care for the living extend to the facilitation of a good or placid death. When death from TB occurs, however, it is often the result of failed medical, cosmological, and atmospheric care. It leaves debts unpaid and breath out of joint.

Most of those killed by TB in Ambawati were young or middle-aged men who experienced intense pain at the end of their lives. Theirs were deemed bad deaths. Like Rai Singh and Shankar Singh, they struggled to breathe and even move during the final days of bodily life. Painful, unexpected, or violent bad death is alarming, constantly possible, and somehow lurking despite the utmost caution. In the wake of a bad death passed in a gasping struggle to breathe and vomiting of blood, breath and perhaps by extension the soul might retain the trappings of the body and social life even as it leaves the vital body to mingle with the atmosphere. In this sense Rai Singh's death stuck with Mangibai as a persistent sign of failed atmospheric care and a reminder to provide more. Death shapes a disembodied but atmospheric social and political self and a living atmosphere of afterlife.

Even without a body, the need to breathe follows those killed by TB in Ambawati, and atmospheric care for the self and others continues. When those killed by TB speak through mediums they often wheeze and struggle for breath as if breath is still afflicted by TB. When the dead and their disembodied breath are marked by TB, they might point to a continued entanglement and anxiously suggest that the breathing body's connections, politics, and burdens on the soul could have an afterlife too. Afterliving entities like ghosts and ancestors can and do enter the bodies of mediums to make claims on relatives and neighbors. The wheezing tubercular ghosts of afterlife could reveal the traces of a moral and physical body with its exposures and infections on transcendent life-breath, or *praan*.

Some Ambawatians argued that Rai Singh's TB clung to him. Despite ritual work to free him, he and his troubled breath abides in Ambawati's social and climatic atmosphere. A person's body may be killed by TB, but his or her breath abides to afflict afterlives and hang in the village air and clouds, maybe even sticking in the mud or kicked up with dust. Atmospheric persistence in a context of bodily death suggests that TB's moral and social life seeps into an atmosphere in which the dead can and do act. Deaths, good or bad, might integrate individuals into affective and breathed atmospheres rather than achieve total disillusion in ways that shape the affective and physical lives of those still living in bodies. The ghosts of TB and its biopolitics of breath suggest that the end of troubled bodily breath owing to TB death is only one part in a larger process of atmospheric attunement and living alongside death in a TB epidemic.[14]

In her ethnographic account of one death in an atmosphere of death, Clara Han writes of a mother's unyielding mourning for her son. Han suggests that "despite the pervasiveness of death, death—from the perspective of the singular one—does not become normal. Learning to live grief is learning it anew, for each and every death."[15] In Ambawati, just as an individual breath is a singular experience of a broader cumulative and repetitive relationship between individual and atmosphere, each TB death is a new and particular event that mingles with a larger climatic and affective atmosphere imbued with the traces of death and those who have died.[16] One death, like Rai Singh's is not reducible to a statistic or a trend. Instead, it shifts a whole atmosphere of life and afterlife, reverberating through relations to the living and the dead in which grief is learned anew. Perhaps we all limp if Mangibai does.

Following Han's suggestion that the affective experience of death recurs with each death but always in the context of others, this chapter considers how a material and affective atmosphere of mourning might coalesce at the intersection of breath, TB-related death, and quotidian acts of grief. It extends an atmospheric approach by suggesting that social and affective atmospheres in which death is pervasive, like Ambawati's, are inflected not just by persistent ambient grief but by the ways that death's "experiential significance," as Han calls it, "arises with regard to each and every death."[17] In a context where death is common, an attention to atmospheric afterlives may help interpret forms of atmospheric care and atmospheric injury that persist as mourning and reassurance that all will die.

To engage living in an atmosphere of afterlife, this chapter follows ghosts, particularly Rai Singh, and their acts and invocations of care. First, it considers a taxonomic story of breaths that seamlessly becomes a ghost story in which tubercular ghosts struggle to breathe and reveal an afterlife of infection. Second, it hears of ghosts before and after Rai Singh's death from TB and how they haunt the story of his material body and access to care. Finally, it takes on a material view of persistent haunting by thinking with Rai Singh's mother, Mangibai, and the limp that pursued her after Rai Singh's death from tuberculosis. Together these three parts reveal that even death, it seems, cannot be imagined through a wholly materialist, universalist lens. When viewed from a breathy perspective the separation between life and afterlife is one defined by *bios* and its complicated embrace of material and metaphor. Tubercular breath's persistence within an atmosphere of afterlife and grief highlights how practices around bodily death in Ambawati and South Asia subvert a binary opposition between life and death. Breathy life extends beyond the ontological limits of a re-spiring body to renegotiate being and unbeing.

MEMIBAI'S GHOST STORY
Memibai Meghwal's taxonomical story of three breaths, with which many of this book's reflections began, draws connections between forms of breath and forms of being. It also attends to death. As we sat packing tendu leaves, she told me that breath could be divided into physical *sans*, vital *dam*, and cosmological *praan*. As she finished, Memibai added that life did not end with a cessation of the body's mechanical *sans* or powerful *dam* breaths. Instead, life was tangled up with breath's soulful, or *praanik*, persistence. *Praan*, Memibai explained, is a breath that abides with the soul. "When someone dies, we say respiration-breath (*sans*) is broken," she explained. "We can also say that he broke his strength-breath (*dam*)," she continued, this time giving the body agency over vital breath. "But about *praan*, we say life-breath (*praan*) went out." When I asked what she meant, she said, "Life-breath continues. It goes with the soul." Memibai is not alone in this idea of a connected breath and soul that can persist after bodily cessation. Jonathan Parry and others have written of death ritual among Hindus in north India as a thirteen-day process of separating the numinous soul from the polluted body and its effects.[18] He, like Memibai, explains that the body becomes inert as *praan* leaves. The soul, however, remains to depart via the skull later during cremation. The soul and *praan* breath then abide near the relatives of the deceased before leaving on the tenth or thirteenth day. Death is a process and one in which bodily air as life-breath "goes out and your soul goes out," departing as the soul loosens its entanglement with the world and its imprints. Without a single event, death's threshold is ambiguous. Even breath can have an afterlife.

As we sat together binding tendu, Memibai's story turned from breath among respiring human bodies to wheezing ghosts. Anthropologists have begun to think about such liveliness beyond the body in a move toward ghosts and "hauntology." Examining the ontological reconfigura-tions that happen when material rationalism's boundaries are pried open long enough to let in ghosts, anthropologists interested in hauntology have attempted to take the social lives of the dead and those who live with

them seriously.[19] They question ocular-centric reason and material rationality, reframe the self's connections between the body and mind, think
about languages of suffering and trauma across space and time, and attend
to ways social life is made and persists across generations.[20] Ghosts, they
show, are consummately political subjects, wrapped up in political struggles with interests and affinities that seek redress and repair by making
claims on and through the living as anxieties, hauntings, and what rational empiricism cannot explain or oppress.[21] Jacques Derrida links ghosts
to the neoliberal condition, evoking the ghostly voice of Hamlet's father
to say that sequential or genealogical time is out of joint and was never
really going that smoothly.[22] Others have written of ghosts who haunt
institutional spaces like hospitals or roads to make claims on those who
pass them by too quickly and without notice.[23] Thinking with ghosts has
made room for other ways of being that scientific rationalism's categories
of living and dead, active and inert cannot capture and cannot imagine.
Could ghosts in Ambawati extend TB's biopolitics into the afterlife and
afterlives into atmospheres?

In Ambawati, one need not pry open the ontological stakes of life to
make space for ghosts or social practices having to do with them. Ghosts
and ancestors abound and, invited or not, take part in social life because
they breathe.

With the entry of ghosts, Memi's story about the stuff of life became
a story of afterlife. It questioned the meaning of death, the end of bodily
affliction, and the necessity of an individualized body for participation
in social life. Yet the three breaths that her explanation deftly separated
became entangled. "If life-breath (*praan*) goes with the soul," I asked
her, "then what about ghosts and other things without bodies. Do they
have breath (*praan*)?" She replied in a thoughtful tone, "Of course they
have life-breath. When the mediums [*bhopas*] bring god out[24] don't their
respiration-breaths (*sans*) move?" Our friend Sundar jumped in, saying,
"It's like a double breath (double *sans*). When the deity or ghost comes out,
the medium has double breath. Ha, ha, ha, he pants." Laughing, Sundar
re-created Memi's earlier pantomime but with consternation. Sundar, who
was occasionally a medium for the family goddess Amba Mata and other
spirits, continued, "Remember when Buralal used to be a medium? He

would breathe so hard. And when it was the goddess, he would go hee, hee, hee," making what seemed a more feminine breath sound.

"It is the deity breathing in the medium?" I asked. "Yes," Sundar concluded. Memi picked up her thread: "It is the god and the medium. The medium's soul (*atma*) is not gone. It is just not present. So the medium must breathe [*hans kare*] very hard, breathing for two souls. Who knows, maybe a ghost had not been able to breathe for a long time without a body. So, he is struggling to breathe more.²⁵ He is still a *praani* even though he has no body now. He has a soul and life-breath, and as soon as he gets a body, he must breathe (*sans lena*)." At death it had left the body, along with the soul, to parts unknown, possibly to stay near its home or wander further afield. Who knows what could have happened to it on these journeys? Respiration-breath returned, however, to the ghost's soul and life-breath when it wished to take social life. Breath as *sans* and *praan*, Sundar and Memi conclude, intersect in the body. Together they make physical respiration an index of cosmological and vital life, but life-breath can persist in atmospheres after the body is gone.

*Praani*s, or creatures with breath, continued but needed bodily breath to speak and take on social voice in an atmosphere of afterlife. I thought about the mediums I had seen in action. To animate or enliven the ghost's social voice in a living body, the medium needed to respirate for both of the life-breaths now in his or her body. This was not always easy. The voices coming from a medium's body often gasp and wheeze as their inhabitant makes demands on embodied people, act as intermediaries, mortify the medium's fleshy body, and give advice about emotional and physical suffering. My mind had wandered to an occasion several months earlier and a tingle went up my spine. A stranger ghost had been visiting a friend in his dreams, and I had been invited to a ritual to appease it. We would seat this ghost in an uncarved stone body after conversing with it through Ambawati's most powerful medium.²⁶ The ghost finally entered the medium's body at two or three in the morning. It snarled, cursed, and hissed angrily. The medium's body, usually home to a kindly middle-aged man, panted and crouched like a caged animal ready to pounce. I was terrified and unable to sleep for days, wondering what kind of being this might have been. It was no wonder that my friend had hoped to end its appearance in his dreams. It too had a troubled life-breath and a troubled soul.

As Memi explained them, ghosts have both soul and breath. They are part of the world and as such are susceptible to it and capable of acting on it. They are even sometimes called winds. In an atmosphere of after-life, ghosts have *bios* and biography despite their lack of living materiality. They are narrated as alive because the worldly strata on which liveliness, or ontological being, depends is the atmospheric ephemeral breath, not the fleshy *zoë* body. A *bios*, or meaningful life, here needs no living material form, or *zoë*, to act and to be cared for. It does, however, need material to transform breath into speech. If breathing is being, then ghosts too should breathe, and they do. Indeed the ghosts of the TB dead gasp and wheeze, Memi told us. Her husband, who had been killed by TB, did when he was ritually invoked a few months later. The tubercular body takes on a tubercular afterlife as wheezing ghosts and maybe even tubercular souls.

BREATH WITHOUT BODY

Rai Singh's afterlife was connected to but not limited to what would happen to his mother or his body if he had died. It was also linked to what kind of ancestor or ghost he might become—in other words, the biomoral status of his soul and life-breath. Indeed, an afterlife for Rai Singh was not an ideal life and it would make things harder for Mangibai, for his wife, and for Prasad, but it was a life. It was a life without a body but one with breath and thus still somehow a part of the *bios* and the living meaningful world of action. Life after death was breathy, aerial, ephemeral, *praan*-y. It too needed to be cared for and attended to.

Not long after Rai Singh's death, I asked Roshan if he thought our friend would become one of the meddlesome ancestor spirits. He replied, "Of course he will. He died too young, and he was like that in life. Why would his soul be any different after death? It is just a matter of time, I think. Maybe not, but it's likely. Actually, I think he is already doing things. When Prasad is older, he will have to take care of all of this; until then Raiya will just linger, watching and making his mischief when he gets bored." Somehow Rai Singh's identity remained attached to his soul despite the rituals to disconnect it, and it stayed connected in part because TB troubled not just his body but his breath.

Before and after Prasad installs his father as an ancestor, Rai Singh might speak wheezily through mediums to pronounce his desires and the motivations of his trickery. Until installed as an ancestor his spirit and breath would wander as part of the atmosphere, doing unpredictable and meddlesome things. Though without a breathing body, Rai Singh has agency and biography, causing mischief, popping up to scare and spook in dreams, and wheeze desires through mediums' bodies, but he no longer has the capacity of autobiography, to speak and breath and live for himself with his own body. Occasionally, Rai Singh, as his *bhaav* (being, existence, characteristic, mind, heart, soul, or emotion), comes to willing mediums, called *bhopa*s, and sometimes unwilling ones. When he does he breathes and speaks to the collective from a borrowed body. As Memi explained, the medium's is a double breath, one for the ghost and one for himself. Another form of collective atmospheric biopolitics emerges.

Whereas respiration-breath and strength-breath end with the body, life-breath is transformed. In this sense, TB bacteria can trouble the link between body and breath as well as life itself. Struggles to breathe bring a restlessness to the soul in death, regardless of whether it is a placid one like Moti Singh's or a turbulent one like Rai Singh's. In that sense, Rai Singh and the many others who died from TB retain a *bios*, a narrative about agency and liveliness, after the end of material or killable life as *zoë*. The decisions Rai Singh made about life and death were framed by breathy biologics of afterlife that suggested a greater concern with the soul and life-breath than with the body and respiration-breath. The story we tell about what life is relies on breath to enter the world, and life continues with the stories told about it. Rai Singh's worry about being alone was about a lack of breaths to tell his story and to distribute his life-breath among. *Praan*, after all, goes on with the soul to take up new bodies or to become a ghost, but the life-breath of men, and sometimes women, killed by TB remains in less ghostly, more material ways too.[27]

Life-breath, as ephemeral and aerial life that persists beyond the material, made TB and its capacity to trouble the breathing body all the more concerning. Tuberculosis destabilizes breathy life and brings wheezing and trouble to durable *praan*. Indeed, breathlessness in Ambawati was an existential problem with atmospheres of care and contagion extending far beyond the limits of life evoked by the body. Instead, breathlessness might continue pestering life even after death. Haunted by a material illness, ghosts like the one Rai Singh might have become wheeze. In fact, one of the most alarming parts of TB for my friends and neighborhood was its effect on afterlives, thus raising the stakes of atmospheric care and contagion. Troubled or disordered *praan* moves through the world even after the body's death. Those killed by the disease often shape the lives of still-embodied relatives by making claims on them through mediums but also by interacting with their bodies as illness, misfortune, and mischief, not to mention the future new bodies the soul might bring tubercular breathlessness to. In short, both breath and TB have lives, politics, and socialities after bodily death. Thus, a TB epidemic in Ambawati moves beyond the limits of the material body's death toward a biopolitical and atmospheric afterlife for Rai Singh and for the many spectral others killed by TB.

THE RISK OF AFTERLIVING
For the four years I knew him as a living person Rai Singh coughed. Rai Singh's ghost, though less terrifying than the stranger ghost, coughed and wheezed too. Both ghosts and TB pursued him in life and in death. In life his cough was not incessant; it was just as meddlesome as the ghosts were. Occasionally, he went to doctors and other healers. Once he took the rickety country bus from Ambawati three hours northeast to a shrine his father once frequented. He fell asleep on the way home and missed Ambawati. He had to walk the eight kilometers back from Sagwai in the dark. The next morning, he recounted the day's events to Roshan and me: "I didn't mind the walk. It was the dreams that I had on the bus that scared me. They were about the ghost deity that I had gone to visit. Those dreams were on my mind the whole walk home. Maybe that's what's wrong with me. I guess I will have to go back and try again." Indeed, Rai Singh began to visit the shrine more regularly, and even began to avoid alcohol, but the cough continued. He also found himself haunted by thoughts of what life with his father might have been like and by other ghosts of the past. After a while he began to drink country liquor again.

A few months later, Rai Singh's wife became pregnant, and their son Prasad soon arrived. Rai Singh's view of the future seemed to brighten with Prasad, and he grew into his role as patriarch of the small family. "I'm not so alone anymore," he told me when he introduced me to the infant. He seemed less haunted by coughs and death. Things began looking up, and Rai Singh stood for election to the village panchayat, or governing committee, when his ward's seat was reserved for the Rawat category. He won his neighbors' votes, besting the hereditary headman's eldest son. Now he had a job to attend to. He liked being useful. He talked of finishing high school and began working to fix the road leading from the bus stand to his neighborhood. He even dug the foundation for a new stone house in front of his and Mangibai's mud and shingle one. The cough, however, persisted. He had been treated as a teenager for TB but no one thought he could get it again. Eventually, he and Mangibai decided that they had to go to the TB hospital. Rai Singh and Mangibai stayed in the same ward as Daulat Singh, just a few beds away but at different times.

Mangibai told me the story one day as we rested while doing our laundry at the neighborhood handpump. Rai Singh had been dead for about a year.

> Eventually, Raiya said to me, "Ma, let's go to Udaipur. We have to go. It's time." So I packed some things and got some money, and we went. Raiya knew the way. He managed things and I followed. We got admitted. They did an X-ray and all. We waited for the results. The first night went fine, but then on the second night we were sleeping and the man next to us, his breath broke, he died. Before he died, he really struggled, vomiting blood and foam all over. They tried to put him on a tank [of oxygen], but it did not help. He kept throwing up blood and then he went quiet, but his wife, she let out a bellow,[28] "He is gone. He has gone away." I lost my mind. I wanted to get out of there. I said, "Raiyo, let's go right now. This is a bad, dangerous place. We cannot live here. People are dying all around." But Raiyo, he said no. He said, "No, Ma, we came all this way. We have to stay just a bit longer. It is night. Where will we go? We must stay here." So we stayed, and the woman next to us, she continued to wail, and in the morning the Harijan orderlies came and took the dead man away. It was not long after they came that Riaya said to me, "Ma, get the things, let's go." So we came back here; Raiya was sick at home after that, until the end.

Potential death at the hospital and the materiality of the breathless body there were problems. Mangibai could neither read nor write nor dial a telephone. Rai Singh worried no one would come to help her if he was incapacitated. Worse yet, Mangibai and his body might be lost and unable to get home. The body, without breath, had little agency, and without others around to tend it, it would be left to the hospital's orderlies to manage.[29] He was, as he so often said, alone without a father or brother. This made even the material afterlife of his body a concern.

There seemed to be more she had left unsaid. Though caste pollution and the lifeless body's materiality posed problems, they were not the only reasons for the pair's hasty departure. The presence of death in the hospital was alarming, and the ghosts that had pursued him seemed to be there too waiting to afflict his afterlife. Years before, Ambawati's drummer, Sitaram Bhatt, had told me a story like Mangibai's. Months after doing laundry with Mangibai, I found it buried in the notes I had taken during one of my first summer visits to Ambawati. Sitaram had been sick with TB in 2009, before dying of the disease at home in 2010. Before he died, he told me about his visit to the TB hospital. The imagery he used is both haunting and replete with technoscientific anxiety about the body after breath:

> I went to the TB hospital. It's not so bad in the daytime, but at nighttime there are all kinds of things around. I had terrible dreams about ghosts when I was sleeping there. People don't die there in the daytime. They die at night, and in the morning the Harijans come and take them away to a shed. I saw it, that shed, once. There is a pool behind it. It is an alarming green pool and at night a steam comes off it. It's a green steam. Who knows what they do in that shed? Some people never even come to pick up the dead bodies. I did not want them to touch me, not the ghosts, not the orderlies. I saw that green pool, and I came back right away. I would rather die from sickness here than die from whatever happens there.

Mangibai was subtle about what alarmed the pair about the hospital, leaving the ghosts unspoken of but present. Sitaram's dreamlike narrative, however, makes the ghostly reason for both flights back to Ambawati clear. The hospital, this most rationalist of spaces, was marked by death, ghosts, caste, and fear of mismanagement after death. Little care seemed to be taken for afterlife and death's potential contagion to the soul. A chartreuse lake and its technicolor steam may have been a dream or a hallucination or poetic license. Still, it highlights the idea that at this rationalized institution where death is common there are more technological and cosmological events than meet the eye.

Atmospheric care for an afterlife and fear of dying among the ghosts in hospitals are often linked. The anthropologist Jean Langford has shown that Southeast Asian refugees living in the United States too evoke concerns for the soul and its existence beyond the material body when talking of death in the hospital.[30] Better for the body, the breath, and the family to hurry home even if that meant leaving care and risking another, perhaps only incrementally better, death. "Rai Singh did not even ask to leave the hospital. We just came home. The nurse tried to stop us, but he told her we could not stay there," Mangibai remembered.

Death rituals in Ambawati consider the moment when breath leaves the body as just part of what it means to die. Breath's separation from the body far from home complicates the continued presence of the breath and soul as it lets go of the body. Undergoing this process in the midst of stranger ghosts, perhaps like the terrifying one I met, is a danger for that soul. Dying among them risks a haunted afterlife of enslavement. For both Rai Singh and Sitaram, dying alone in the hospital meant being encircled by the place's many ghosts and possibly becoming one among them.

TB and TB death was troublesome; its occurrence in a hospital where the body would be handled by strangers, who might sink it to the bottom of a lake of neon green chemicals, was even more concerning. The copresence of death, caste, and ghosts in the hospital coupled with the possibility of dying there made it a place of bodily and extrabodily risk. Death in the haunted hospital could pose problems for an afterlife of disconnected body and soul. It could risk increasing the weight of the polluted, casted body on the soul. Here, the TB hospital atmosphere juxtaposed bacteria, the breathing body, caste, and ghosts in a way that could affect both Rai Singh's bodily life and breathy social afterlife.

In short, though ghosts shaped the form of death that Rai Singh and his persistent breath was subject to, so did the hospital. No one should die of TB, certainly not a bright and ambitious young man. Indeed, it was the hospital's inattention to an atmosphere of afterlife that complicated Rai Singh's treatment and perhaps led to his death at home. The institution's infrastructures of suspicion and pharmaceuticalized care shaped the tempo of his bodily death. It avoided the atmospheric either because of a limitation on consideration or an inability to see it. Rai Singh is right—we all die, but Rai Singh died from an entirely treatable disease and a form of care that reduces the dignity of the person to what can be exposed to death both literally and figuratively. Like nearly a half million others in India each year, he died from a painful but treatable infectious disease and a broken health infrastructure that his mother spoke of with a powerful vocabulary of fear and haunting.

LIVING IN ATMOSPHERES OF AFTERLIFE

TB structures life in Ambawati as mourning something that somehow remains present. Even if the bacteria that caused the infection disappear from the air, lungs, and atmospheres, TB will have an afterlife in the people who live there. TB troubling the soul-y life-breath means that it haunts both ghosts and souls. It also haunts the future, acquiring an afterlife among living bodies from which biomedicine has removed it but whose social lives were shifted by TB deaths.

Rai Singh lives on as a breath-filled, but not breathing, ghost, and in his mother's body. A few days after telling the story of their trip to the hospital, Mangibai stopped by my veranda to tell another story of TB-related suffering, this time her own. Mangibai had limped for months after Rai Singh's death. When she began to talk about her leg pain, Roshan, who was with me at the time, began to ask questions. He knew that Mangibai would tell a story about Rai Singh.

She replied to him, "Oh, Father, my foot has hurt for months. I have tried to heal it all over. I went to the doctor and even to the Chauth Mata temple in Eklingpura, and she said she'd take care of it, but nothing has changed.[31] It has been like this since the day Rai Singh died."

"How did it happen?" Roshan asked. Mangibai answered,

You remember the morning that he died, Roshana? He did not sleep well, and he was uneasy. He kept saying he was too hot and too nauseous, until he stopped speaking. We had a large tin wash pan near his bed, and he vomited blood into it. He vomited and vomited. Someone had to take the pan and dump it into the rubbish pit. I told his wife to stay with him while I went to dump it. It is a big heavy wash pan, the one I wash clothes in, and I carried it to the pit. Along the way Sonibai called out to me to ask what was happening, and I was alarmed and said, "My Raiya is very sick. I must dump this shit and hurry back to him." So I went to the pit and took the pan off my head, and as I lifted it off my head it slipped and came crashing down and hit me on the shin. It hit me and I fell down and the dirtiness in the pan went everywhere. I nearly fell down into the rubbish pit. I could not really walk, but Rai Singh was sick at home. I could not leave him, so I pulled myself up and dragged myself home. I was not there very long then before Rai Singh left. He vomited more blood and then his breath went out and it was all over. . . . Now it has been months, and I still limp. Before, I had Raiya, my son, but he has been replaced by a limp and this stick to support me. I will carry them both until I die.

One of Rai Singh's afterlives was immaterial, that of a ghost meddling in others' business. The other was material, taken into Mangibai's own body as the limp. Though she was never afflicted by TB, the illness entered her body as pain and melancholy, nonetheless. Jason Throop might call this a mood or sentiment, but for Mangibai it was more than just an affective atmosphere of afterlife.[32] It was bodily. She memorialized Rai Singh in each step, not because she wanted to, but because of what happened on the day that his breath left his body. Their lives, always and already entangled, remained so long after. His body had entered her own. His absence was made material in the bamboo stick and the limp. His biography and that of Mangibai could not be separated. He lived on with her.

As Margaret Trawick has written of grief, "No amount of fire or water can drive certain memories away."[33] Rai Singh's life marked the material of his mother's body long after the end of his own. This effect is like the hundreds of TB-related deaths in Ambawati that have marked the bodies of their survivors through deprivations incurred during their care and in the loss of their presence as economic actors, intimate partners, dispute resolvers, caste mates, parents, and children. Indeed, TB as a social disease can and will live on in breath, bodies, and narration long after it stops afflicting people here.

Despite Rai Singh's potential for social interaction after bodily death, there can be no doubt that Mangibai mourns Rai Singh and that, as Prasad grows up, he keenly feels the lack of his father. Indeed, the persistence of troubled breath troubled Mangibai as much as it had troubled Rai Singh. She worried that Rai Singh had not found peace, or *shanti*, because the body and its desires were still plaguing him. Rai's afterlife was that of a limp, a presence, a stumble, a bodily entanglement, and a wheezing ghost checking in on his infant son.

BROKEN BREATH AND ENTANGLED ATMOSPHERES
In Ambawati, breath is enculturated and made atmospheric through situated practice and a TB epidemic. So is death. At the intersection of individual and shared physical practice, meanings frame breath and death as intertwined immaterial yet necessary aspects of bodily existence. They both shape the socially defined limits of bodily possibility and lively exchange with the world and, as antipodes, give each other meaning, and yet both are simultaneously individual and continuous. Breath in Ambawati guides narration, practices of the body, and life away from biomedicine's universalized skinbound fleshy body and its death as a total social end. Enculturated, living breath shakes death from the materialist and universalist anchors that locate breath's absence as the end of the body's material autonomy or potential autonomy. If at death breath leaves the body and life-breath "goes with the soul," as Memibai tells us, life understood through breath extends beyond the disintegration of the worldly material body in fire, water, and ritual. Breath and TB have afterlives far beyond what biomedicine's pharmaceutical interventions can address.

Death in Ambawati and much of South Asia is one of Rai Singh's riddles. The departure of breath from the body makes for a radical shift in the politics of possible breathy life, not its end. Indeed, breath and *praan* guide the stories of atmospheric life in Ambawati. They make afterlife a part of TB-related care and concern. To care for atmospheres and manage contagion, then, is to enact grief and radical hope. It attends to the person, the body, and something more numinous or abiding. In an atmosphere of afterlife, small acts of fanning air, discerning clouds, clearing mud, sweeping dust, engaging forests, and breathing itself are radical acts that spread from present to past and future bodies and places. These gestures have their own afterlives just as bacteria do. They are affective and material but can never be reduced to simple presence or absence. They are always up in the air.

Analyzing TB-related deaths as atmospheric phenomena with atmospheric effects and language thus offers an ethnographic opportunity to think about the sociality of the dead who, as ghosts or grief or new infections, live on as social actors and even material presences. Rai Singh's death from TB and what happens to him after it reveal that death is a pervasive yet individual experience that shapes breathed atmospheres. It creates an atmosphere in which the dead can be subjects and objects of both atmospheric care and contagion. Atmospheres where the more than human and once human can live, I argue, highlight the ethereal and material presence of selves no longer in their own body's breaths that are entangled with both sick and well, living and other dead. Taking this persistence seriously reveals relational practices that center on mourning, bodily disillusion, and the atmospheric continuity of a self. As an atmospheric phenomenon, death and the socialities entangled within it subvert materiality's boundaries and move atmospheric care across forms of existence. This time an atmosphere and its ethnography straddle ontological frontiers separating being from nothingness and body from breath and language.

NINE

ENTANGLEMENT AGAIN

After all, as with cures, there are always endings—there is no ending to
endings.

—Bharat Venkat, *At the Limits of Cure*

IN MAY OF 2021 Tiger sent me a worried message on WhatsApp. Ambawati had reported its first case of the COVID-19 Delta variant. The
COVID-19 virus had been disrupting life in Asia and across the planet for
nearly sixteen months. Now after entangling with humans and ecologies
at a planetary scale, the virus's Delta variant had emerged as a particularly
virulent and deadly iteration of the airborne infectious pathogen. Though
nationwide shutdowns, curfews, quarantines, and restrictions on mobility
had devastating effects on the lives of the poor, India had largely dodged
earlier waves of the virus. In May of 2021, however, it was sweeping the
country. From late March to June of 2021, COVID-19's Delta variant sickened millions, killed hundreds of thousands, and brought the health care
system to its breaking point. By July 2021, as the spring wave of COVID-
19 began to wane, the India Council of Medical Research reported that
two out three Indians had been infected by the virus, which had been
unknown to science just two years earlier.[1]

Since my fieldwork in Ambawati, the years had been good to Tiger.
He had finished college and gotten excellent grades. He had even passed
the competitive public service exam and become a teacher in a school near
Ambawati. He had built his mother, Memibai, a new brick house and
was slowly applying its finishing touches. When public schools closed in
March of 2020, Tiger was assigned to what he called COVID duty. This

meant that for almost a year he surveyed homes in his school's village, distributing information and monitoring the many residents who returned from cities. In March of 2020 when fear and economic shutdowns made life in crowded and comparatively expensive informal urban settlements very difficult, millions of Indians returned to rural communities under great duress, often traveling a thousand kilometers by bus, motorcycle, and even on foot. Many worried that the exhausted returnees would bring COVID-19 with them. Tiger was indeed concerned that this work would expose him to the virus, but he wore a mask and got on with it. Things were steady for months, and we kept in touch. He and his wife welcomed their first child, and he used time out of school to study for another competitive public service exam. Life went on amid a pandemic.

Now he was worried. An atmospheric entanglement had snapped together again as COVID-19 suddenly seemed everywhere. Anticipating a high number of deaths and a lack of media attention to Ambawati and other rural Dalit communities, Tiger began keeping a journal. We hoped to publish the text online, and he sent me photos of his daily entries. Weeks later, when voices critical of the government's COVID-19 response met strong opposition, Tiger grew concerned that publishing his journal might endanger his livelihood. We decided to shelve the project. As I finished this book about a year later, his entries haunted me. They revealed a novel infectious disease working through the same atmospheres and anxieties that TB had traveled for decades. "People are acting like it is TB," he wrote.[2]

> They are not getting tests. They think about what the government will do to them. They lie when they are surveyed because they are worried that if they are sick, they will be taken away to a hospital and who knows what will happen to their bodies. They just stay home and hope to get better. The government says that the country is shining, but until there is development and social equality this will happen again and again.

The similarities are startling. Atmospheric entanglements of TB and now COVID-19 are ephemeral, contingent, and environmental, but they are also durable. As COVID-19 moved among people in shared time and space it mixed with and reshaped social structures, atmospheres, and even microbial DNA, just as TB does. In Tiger's view these entanglements were created by disease, political economy, inequality, and even climate change. He believed they would happen again. I agree with him. COVID-19 in Tiger's journal, like TB in this book, is wrapped up in concerns for governance, public health, development, and care. This enmeshment shapes infectious agents themselves, how they move, and how people deal with them. Even more clearly this time, atmospheric entanglements with pathogens were related to proximity and the question of what it means to live together with disease.

Proximity in this book and throughout the COVID-19 pandemic was, and remains, a proximity of atmospheric entanglements established by breath and the social, ethical, and political relationships it transects. We cannot, I have argued, think about disease without considering how its politics and circulation are mediated by social and climatic atmospheres. Anthropology cannot remain breathless.

The analytic strength of considering shared atmospheres abides in social vulnerability and proximity's disregard for clear separations between the world, the body, the subject, and the ethical. Writing of ways that COVID-19 confinement attempted to limit shared breath in New Zealand/Aotearoa, which recombined and reassorted sociality and citizenship, Susanna Trnka notes, "Proximity's (ethical) significance was thrown into relief during lockdown through the *effort* required to uphold new legal regulations."[3] Indeed, as this book has shown, airborne infectious disease and political injunctions to simultaneously care for oneself and others has a tendency to throw inequality into relief. Individual and distributed forms of care require effort, but inequalities frame the experience, meaning, and outcome of that effort. Trnka elaborates on the lived complexity, which Ambawatians knew well, of New Zealanders being interpolated as individual subjects of collective public health, arguing that "abilities to make choices (about proximity and regulations) were shaped by long-standing axes of disadvantage, notably class and ethnicity, alongside new variables such as occupation (e.g., essential service work) and household and family composition."[4] Here too COVID-19 rehearses the entanglements that I have traced in this book. Trnka and Tiger even seem to share my concerns about overlooking breath's entanglement with social atmospheres. Like me, they worry that severing breath's connections to the social can simultaneously naturalize inequality as disease risk factors and reduce health outcomes to the effects of cultural difference or individual choice.

Breath, now more than ever, is individual and collective. As infectious diseases jostle existing biopolitical constellations, one's political life enters one's material life through exposure to microbes, vaccines, and pharmaceuticals, as well as one's response to them. If lines between state and self ever really existed in India, they are especially blurred where public health responses to both TB and COVID-19 were, and remain, simultaneously lax, pastoral, and draconian.[5] As Ambawatians entangled with TB have known for more than a decade, individuals are left to seek diagnosis and to enact personal preventive measures toward the public good. Those who do not or cannot often face challenges associated with being resistant subjects and citizens. Sometimes these challenges abide even unto death.

In response to the interdependence of social and biological existence that social diseases like TB and COVID-19 reveal, in this book I have focused on atmospheric entanglements' proclivity to enmesh ethical and social life with climatic and biological life. Both public health and anthropology often risk overemphasizing one factor or the other. I have argued that constructing atmospheric entanglement as an ethnographic object requires considering how biological and social frames enrich and endanger each.[6] Atmospheric entanglements in this book contest the biopolitical impulse to simultaneously naturalize and politicize social difference as biological difference and life chances. Yet atmospheric entanglements also allow us to track how bacteria and atmospheres play vital roles in more-than-human social worlds. Neither biological life nor social life can wholly determine the other.

Breathy entanglements also draw our attention to material and social phenomena that matter for life with tuberculosis even when they seem only loosely connected to bodies or bacteria. Material entities like dust and mud take on deeply charged meanings about development and history. These substances and their meanings enter bodies and shape life chances. Similarly, meanings associated with less obviously material atmospheres like air, clouds, and the afterlife have real material effects on bodily life and raise questions about how atmospheres might be alive too. Atmospheric entanglements allow for an expanded view on what is alive, as well as how material and social life coalesce within worlds of shared air and infectious disease. By focusing on atmospheric entanglements this book has shown how clouds can be social actors, mud and dust can be political, and breath can traverse boundaries of human and world, life and afterlife.

Ideas that extend agency to atmospheric phenomena might seem to radically contest biomedical ways of knowing, but for Ambawatians they are an inherent part of living. Indeed, biomedical and atmospheric ways of knowing are not mutually exclusive in Ambawati. Their entanglement might even foster life itself. They intersect and often enrich each other in ideas and practices concerning how to live with disease and how to live well. Throughout this book, Ambawati's epistemic entanglement has been a source of insight and of alternative ways to understand biological and social interconnections.

By examining where biomedicine's materialist and Ambawatians' atmospheric perspectives on disease diverge and converge in bodies and bacteria, I have identified a new analytic for public health and anthropology that is particularly useful when interpreting social diseases like TB and COVID-19. For public health, atmospheric entanglements suggest a less individualized and reflexive frame on human action with which to study stigma, social support, patient pathways, patient history, and disease etiology. For anthropology, atmospheric entanglements provide material to rethink our frames on the potential for material bodies and disease to shape atmospheres, subjectivity, kinship, biosociality, caste, and social inequality. In what follows I briefly outline what an atmospherically entangled perspective might imply for both fields.

AN ATMOSPHERICALLY ENTANGLED PUBLIC HEALTH

For public health and those interested in eliminating TB, atmospheric entanglements give context and nuance to critical medical anthropology's claim that TB must be addressed through social and infrastructural intervention. As global public health works to develop a patient-centered care paradigm for TB, the presence of atmospheric entanglements suggests that providing accessible and accompanied pharmaceutical treatment might not be enough. Recognizing the atmospherically entangled condition of infectious diseases that concern global health might highlight the world's atmospheric effects on the individual. They trouble the frames that ethically oblige a sick person to take sole responsibility for the social impact of her disease. They also require global public health to develop approaches that are simultaneously centered on the patient and address the significant challenges of infrastructure and inequality that TB's atmospheric entanglement poses.

Breath is no longer context or mere air; it is social and political just as clearly as it is intimate and individual. By encouraging public health to seriously engage Ambawatian perspectives on TB as an atmospheric disease, my hope is that public health might begin to consider the necessity of building systems of atmospheric care. Attention to the atmospheres where TB exists and how people manage them, often without help, highlights the importance of building safe breathing spaces for patients and clinicians in hospitals, clinics, and public spaces. Infrastructural improvements to health systems and everyday life in rural and urban India, like electrification and ventilation, sanitation, paved roads, as well as antimicrobial lights and ventilation in hospitals, clinics, and other places where people share air, will be integral to eliminating the disease. New sciences of air circulation, personal protection, and infection control bring new biomedical logics of life with which to imagine the power, risk, and contagion of breath and its relations. By focusing on TB's atmospheric entanglements, these technologies might resist the impetus to further lay the burden of disease control on those already fighting for their lives.

Atmospheric care may even highlight the importance of caring for spaces through a broader public health attention to climate change and its unequal effect on the environments in which we live. As calls for care as an alternative to late-capitalist logics of production and expansion gain momentum, it is crucial that we add precision about what kinds of atmospheric care and caregivers this new public health vision might include.[7] This book has shown that Ambawatian forms of atmospheric care such as creating a comfortable breathing space, scrambling for cash, seeking out a healer, accompanying another at a hospital, and even being complicit in a lie must be considered care. Atmospheric care, however, cannot be left only to families and communities. It must be supported and even provided by a public health system. Caring for breath and for TB must mean caring for relationships and rotations between body and world in ways that seem far from the bedside and that go beyond simple solutions to bridge the gaps created by inequality. Instead, public health practices must attend to air and its entanglements as much as to its breathers.

Ambawati provides a glimpse at the need for a public health paradigm that relies less on distributing pharmaceuticals and conducting surveillance and more on understanding the complex interplay between inequality and health outcomes. Most of all, these approaches must abandon the idea that patients with antimicrobial-resistant bacteria resist health care intervention and pose a danger to us all. Understanding affected people's stories and the bacteria that afflict them as atmospherically entangled with development, social lives, and histories of exclusion will be a first step to better understanding the problem of antimicrobial resistance as a collective struggle rather than simply an individual one.

A BREATHING ANTHROPOLOGY AND AN ATMOSPHERICALLY ENTANGLED ETHICS

For anthropology, atmospheric entanglement provides a lens on the predicaments of living together in an unequal world. Atmospheric entanglements require anthropological attention to breath. They ask anthropologists to consider how the constant iterative intertwining of climate, bacteria, bodies, and social worlds stirs up social action. They take our discipline back to Gajanandibai's tea stand to sit and breathe deeply. Indeed, I have asked us to breathe in a few Ambawatian ideas about how to live and die in an epidemic and to let them mingle with our own. Now, at the end of this book, we might emit them, entangled with other perspectives and logics of life, back into the world to shape new ideas and perhaps inform action.

For anthropology to breathe and think with Ambawati we must turn our attention to atmospheric aspects of the social. Until now anthropological accounts of atmospheres have considered them either as affective atmospheres of shared meanings and rippling, but often unstated, sensations or as climatic assemblages in which politics, science, and exposures take flight and mingle with air. I have argued that these two perspectives cannot be separated. Anthropological attention to atmospheres must think material and meaning together. To do so is to see how atmospheres connect bodies and selves to each other and to spaces. It is also to see how atmospheres—as affective and material climates—have lives of their own. They too are vital parts of a world in which human life is conditioned by social and planetary life.

When understood as vital and affective biomoral ecologies, atmospheres might present anthropology with a new way to think about ethics. Atmospheric entanglements of affects and objects, this book has shown, inflect everyday responses to the moral and ethical quandaries posed by shared breath and infectious disease. Recall Gajanandibai's tea stand and the sparks that engulfed us as a gust of wind unexpectedly passed through. This atmosphere of wind, smoke, sparks, technology, gender, and bacteria suddenly coalesced and required a response. Though immaterial, the ethical and affective conditions of possibility for our collective and individual reaction were also entangled within it. Though my neighbor likely spent little time in reflection before he admonished Gajanandibai for carelessness, his unique position within the entanglement made it feel like the right, or an acceptable, thing to do. Similarly, chiding Kalyan Singh for coughing bacteria into the shared air seemed—despite its potential public and person health benefits—unneighborly, unkind, and perhaps unhelpful. Indeed, these are the atmospherically entangled ethics that this book has attempted to bring to anthropology's attention. Viewing ethical action as atmospherically entangled requires us to pay attention to the split-second ways that people chart a moral course through our human condition of being both entangled with others and an individual.[8]

The feel and texture of simultaneously affective and climatic atmospheres give seemingly internal processes of human ethical discernment a more-than-human shape. Atmospheres, I have argued, often guide decisions about when it is acceptable to lie to a doctor, or leave TB treatment, or skip out of caring for a cousin. They even shape decisions to ask a grandson to leave school to care for his father or to set work aside and rest through the dizzying side effects of toxic drugs. By attending to the ways that affects and climates mingle, we might begin to imagine an atmospherically entangled ethics. With it, anthropologists might better describe how people make meaningful, if rarely reflexive, decisions to care for oneself and others at once, or not. Essentially, an ethics of atmospheric entanglement can help us better understand what it is to be human.

Throughout this book I have traced TB's connections, as I traced the sparks and smoke from Gajanandibai's bellows, as they interacted with different bodies and atmospheres. This has posed many challenges. Occasionally atmospheric connections have, like sparks, been gleamingly obvious trajectories from cause to effect. In most cases, however, they are more like smoke. They diffuse and spread in bodies and worlds to make fleeting immaterial connections of various kinds. These diffuse atmospheric connections move amphibiously among ways of knowing too. Again, much like smoke, they can sometimes be seen, sometimes be smelled, sometimes be felt as irritation in the lungs, and sometimes be all three. Because public health and anthropology, like other academic disciplines, are oriented toward order, classification, and causality, they often lack the tools and language to observe and describe such atmospheric entanglements. Atmospheric entanglements of TB and life are dynamic and often nonlinear. They frequently lack clear beginnings or endings. Their effects too are messy. This is because the multiple co-constitutive relationships that build atmospheric entanglements often happen simultaneously and alter all factors involved. It is not surprising that atmospheric entanglements are often overlooked in favor of the more stable forms of linear connection and social structure that anthropological methodical and analytic tools are best suited to understand. Nonetheless, I have tried to outline several strategies so that anthropology can rise to the challenge and better understand how people live entangled lives. These include thinking across ways of knowing, attending to affect, listening for multiple meanings associated with material things, and focusing on where bodies, worlds, and ideas overlap.

I have listened to people as they accounted for the cause and effects of relations among disease, environments, and people. Sometimes these stories—like those that people told about moral connections between clouds and selves authorizing a withdrawal of care or about clinicians threatening to deny patients treatment after missing a dose of TB medication—had me nearly as dazed as the parrot that fell of out Prem Singh's peepal tree. Thinking with entanglements, it seems, asks anthropologists to take multiple simultaneous ways of knowing seriously, even when they shake us or create what feels like aporia.[9] In this book that other way of thinking has as often been public health as it has been an Ambawatian conceptualization of atmospheric vitality. This, I hope, has provided a lens with which to see how non-Western and vitalist perspectives substantiate and even work on atmospheres. Though much of anthropology's atmospheric turn has revealed how experts and technology measure and substantiate atmospheres, Ambawati has provided an opportunity to imagine alternative languages to describe the power atmospheres and their politics have on particular bodies and shared social worlds.

As I listened to my neighbors in Ambawati, it was clear that biomedical rationality and atmospheric vitality could and did enmesh with each other as people engaged with public health intervention and the world. Sometimes the cause of life's connection and vulnerability was the wind, at other times it was Gajanandibai's mechanical cranking, and at still others it was delicate, easily irritated lung tissue. Sometimes danger was our proximity as neighbors, and at other times it was the bacilli on Kalyan Singh's breath. Life even in Ambawati's most vitalist of formulations— in which airs can have and move caste, mud can cause disease, clouds can reveal moral qualities, and the dead live among us—is entangled with the rationalized world of industrialization, biopolitics, development, and of course, pharmaceuticals. To imagine ways of living and knowing the world in Ambawati as all vitalist or all rationalist is to miss the point.[10] Vital and rational can and do coexist in the everyday and even more obviously in illness experience. Life is a jumble of breaths and selves that make for risk and for love, rationality, and vitality together.

Human action and social structures have a powerful role to play in this jumble, but humans are only some of the many living entities within an atmospheric entanglement. Indeed, entanglement is, I have argued, life. As anthropology begins to grapple with what it means to live with the entangled effects of lively infectious disease, climate change, and social inequality, this book has offered an analytic language to describe entangled social and biological atmospheres. Breath is a good place to start because it blurs the enlightenment lines separating body and world, nature and culture, human and nonhuman that anthropology once relied on.

Similarly, atmospheric entanglements reveal that there is no breath outside of culture, but there is no culture outside of breath. This simple argument gives our anthropological tools new purpose and new objects of analysis. Breaths are dynamic and looping iterations. As simultaneously parts and processes, they are of immense use to an anthropology of entanglement that aims to chart a course in which social phenomena are both their own unique entity or event and part of much larger processes. As both unique iteration and process itself, breath can provide a nuanced theory of human life. I have argued that by studying breath we might create a new template for understanding both life itself and life as inseparable from its planetary and historical context. Breath and its entanglements also exit the material and social body changed. Perhaps this is a small moment of the human shaping the planetary. It is in this entanglement and exchange that an amalgam of air, body, and ideas shape and enliven social structures and worlds. By focusing on life with TB as an atmospheric entanglement, I have begun to show how bacterial, biological, and social life cannot be separated as human experiences and as ethnographic objects.

I have argued that to miss the atmospheric entanglements of life and subjectivity is perhaps to misrepresent the self. Anthropologists struggle to suspend atmospheric life for long enough to render them into language. The same is true for the subject. I have shown how people like Tiger and Gajanandibai might be both agents and effects of entanglement. This has not been to reduce them to examples of abject sufferers or to exaggerate them as omnipotent and omniscient makers of reflexive choices. The atmospherically entangled subject that this book sketches might even provide a more subtle lens on subjectivity for a new anthropology of atmospheric entanglements and ethics. This subject is both an individual person and a member of collective muddling through the constraints on knowledge and power that social life, as epistemology and social inequality, puts on them. Perhaps this knowing that our place in a larger entanglement shapes us and what we know is the best we can ask for, but there is hope too in being an actor entangled with many.

After I bade goodbye to Gajanandibai and others at the tea stall, I walked down the dirt road toward my home across the street from Ramba, Bhanwaribai, Chainram, and Meeradevi Meghwal. When I arrived, I greeted them before opening the door to my house. I was hungry and the power was out, so I sat on the threshold to knead flour and water together to make chapatis. I had been exposed to TB that day, but life went on. As I struck a match to light my stove and began rolling out the soft dough, Meeradevi sent her daughter Tara across the street with a small bowl of lentils. "Mumi knows you like these," she said as she placed the bowl near the stove. I thanked her. Sweat began to collect on my forehead as I flipped my second chapati. The heat had exhausted me, but the smell of hot chapatis and Meeradevi's lentils helped me go on. Nearly ready, the chapati swelled with air before sending out a puff of steam as I tamped it down again. Atmospheric and ethical relations of give and take, inhalation and exhalation, effort and exhaustion were the stuff of life indeed. So was TB. With each of them, social worlds of care, sustenance, and danger entangled themselves anew, "almost as hardly killed as easily wounded: sustaining for a while, without defense, the enormous assaults of the universe."[11]

NOTES

Chapter One

1. Throughout this book I have adopted pseudonyms for everyone. I chose names that seemed to best fit the person's social identity and age. Similarly, Ambawati, Sagwai, and Sadri are pseudonyms for real places. I do this to protect people's identities, particularly health workers who might be easily associated with a particular health institution.

2. "Indigeneity" is a complicated term in South Asia, and I use it here with considerable caution. I follow André Béteille in using "indigeneity" to indicate marginality (2006). Béteille and many others—like Baviskar (2006); Chakrabarty (2006); Gooch (2006); Hardiman (2007); and Moodie (2015)—argue that "indigeneity" in South Asia indicates a political form with a set of fantasies about connection to the environment, history, and mobility. For me it is a way of talking about economic and social marginalization and a particular position of social, economic, and environmental difference in the eyes of the broader Indian society and the state.

3. Michael Hathaway has shown that wind is a particularly meaningful metaphor for development and ideological change when considering environmentalist movements in China (2013). I wish to show that other materials and their metaphors do similar work in Ambawati too.

4. For histories of the programmatic management of TB globally, see McMillen (2015). For India, see Amrith (2006) and Brimnes (2016).

5. TB often enters ethnography as an aside or as contextual information. A surprising number of ethnographies of South Asia report interlocutors sick or dying from TB. See Das (2015); Trawick (2017); Piliavsky (2021); and Saria (2021) for a few recent examples. In literature, Aman Sethi's *A Free Man* (2011) profiles the life of a TB-afflicted laborer in Delhi, and TB appears in Katherine Boo's *Behind the Beautiful Forevers* (2012).

6. For more on the development of this perspective in South Asia, see Brimnes (2016); Harper (2014); Seeberg (2014); and Ecks and Harper (2013). For a important critique of this transition in India, see Banerji (1999).

7. I am particularly inspired here by Nancy (2002); Paxson (2008); Bubandt (2014); Nading (2014); Tsing (2015); Kirksey (2015); Tsing, Mathews, and Bubandt (2019); and many others.

8. According to Margaret Lock and Vinh-Kim Nguyen, "Local biologies refers to the way in which biological and social processes are inseparably entangled over time, resulting in human biological difference" that become "artifacts—snapshots frozen in time of ceaseless biosocial differentiation [in which] individual bodies represent a

microcosm of these ceaseless interactions" (2018, 90). The concept of local biology has been fruitfully extended to many facets of medical anthropology (Nading 2017). In conversations about TB, it has been used to understand multiple-drug-resistant TB (Lock and Nguyen 2018), to study the situated laboratory practices that fit TB into categories and localize them (Koch 2011), and to engage the epistemic entanglement of HIV and TB (Engelmann and Kehr 2015).

9. For ethnographies that engage some of these aspects of life in Rajasthan, see Snodgrass (2006); Gold and Gujar (2002); Piliavsky (2021); and Carstairs (1958, 1983).

10. For more on India's poverty line and the public distribution system, see Béteille (2003); Gupta and Sharma (2006); and U. Rao (2018). For a detailed study on the politics of development interventions in India, see Sharma (2008).

11. In this sense Ambawati is representative of Dipankar Gupta's Indian village of small landholdings and circulation to and from the city (2005b).

12. Charles Metcalfe is reported, though perhaps erroneously, to have first termed Indian villages "little republics" in a report to the United Kingdom's House of Commons in 1832. Regardless of origin, the term has been intellectually powerful. For a brief account on these perspectives among colonial administrators, see Srinivas and Shah (1960) For classical studies on these forms of village life, see Wiser, Wiser, and Wadley (2000); Marriott (1955); and Srinivas (1976). One might also consult Marx (1853) on the Indian village or M. K. Gandhi's *Village Swaraj* (1962).

13. For other accounts of life in scattered villages like these, see Unnithan-Kumar (1997) and Kumar (1984), among others.

14. Many have become loosely associated with a political movement called the Kshatriya Rawat Rajput Parishad that is affiliated with the Hindu right-wing Bharatiya Janata Party (BJP; Indian People's Party). This has often led to an alignment with Hindutva values concerning kinship and cosmology, as well as a more neoliberalized view of citizenship. It inflects forms of subjectivity that privilege ritual hierarchy over indigeneity as a source of identity and social value. This is ironic, given that investment in asserting Hinduism indigeneity in India. For more on this, see Sundar (2002). For more on flexible identities in southeast Rajasthan, see Unnithan-Kumar (1997).

15. Srinivas (1959). For a longitudinal view of a similar process occurring a few hundred kilometers north, see Carstairs (1983).

16. There is a massive literature on contestation around caste hierarchy. For some examples, see Srinivas (1952); Cohn (1987); Bandyopadhyay (2004); Chatterjee (2004); and Lee (2021a).

17. New movements like the Meghvansh Andolan have encouraged or remembered solidarities between Meghwal and Salvi groups. For a longer narrative about the complexity of a larger Chamar community to which Meghwals and Salvis in Ambawati once belonged, see Rawat (2011). See also Snodgrass (2006) for a nuanced ethnography of the shifts in social identity in south Rajasthan over the last forty years. The Dalit author and activist Kusum Meghwal has also written of her experience in this community (2019).

18. For more on the successes and failures of these reservation politics, see Jaffrelot (2003); Moodie (2015); and Ciotti (2010).

19. For more, see A. Rao (2009) and Teltumbde (2017).

20. RNTCP 2013.

21. For an important anthropological critique of biomedicine's categorization of latent and active TB, see Koch (2011).

22. Indeed, the theme for the International Union Against TB and Lung Disease's 2013 annual conference (the largest annual gathering of TB scientists) was Shared Air, Safe Air. Despite the theme and presentation titles related to it, there was little talk of shared air at the event. There was much concern for pharmaceuticals, though (International Union Against TB and Lung Disease 2013).

23. Feldberg 1995.

24. Koch 2013, 310.

25. For more on public health narratives of social determinants and health seeking, see Craig, Joly, and Zumla (2014); Craig et al. (2017); and Chikovore et al. (2015). For more on social determinants and TB treatment, see Munro et al. (2007) for a systematic review. See Jaggarajamma (2007) and Deshmukh et al. (2018) for Indian examples. For more on stigma, see Daftary (2012); Sommerland et al. (2017); or Craig et al. (2017). For examples of anthropologists who have engaged this conversation, see Rubel and Garro (1992) and Nichter (1994).

26. Farmer 1999.

27. McDonald and Harper 2019; Gandy and Zumla 2003; Kehr 2016.

28. WHO 2022.

29. Packard 1989. For more on TB's epistemological entanglements, see Engelmann and Kehr (2015) and Farmer (1999).

30. McMillen 2015.

31. Harper 2014; Hunleth 2017; Stevenson 2014.

32. See Porter and Ogden (1997); Engel (2015); and McMillen (2015).

33. Venkat 2021.

34. Keshavjee 2014.

35. For more on subjectivity, see Foucault (1982, 1990, 2009); Aretxaga (1997); Fischer (2003); Biehl, Good, and Kleinman (2007); Good et al. (2008); and Pandolfo (2018).

36. For an analysis of "belief" or "cultural belief" as set up in opposition to biomedicine, see Good (1993) and Farmer (1997).

37. Anthropology has not been alone in its atmospheric turn. Those interested in atmospheric turns within other humanities and social science disciplines may look to the philosophers Peter Sloterdijk (2011), Luce Irigaray (1999), and Gaston Bachelard (1988); the cultural geographers Derek McCormack (2018) and Gernot Böhme (1998); the labor historian Janet Greenlees (2019); and the science and technology scholars Steven Connor (2010) and Michelle Murphy (2006) for examples.

38. For pathbreaking anthropological work on atmospheres related to pollution and toxin exposure, see Choy (2012); Fortun et al. (2014); and Shapiro (2015). For an account of the effects of climate change on breathing and space-making practices among Americans afflicted by asthma, see Kenner (2018) and Vine (2019).

39. Stewart 2011, 452.

40. Choy and Zee 2015. For more on the challenges of representation posed by atmospheres, see Ingold (2007).

41. Choy 2011, 2012; Zee 2021.

42. M. Peterson 2021.

43. Howe 2015, 2019.

44. Harris 2021; Ahmann 2020.

45. Haraway 1991, 178.

46. For more on anthropological conversations around resistance, see Scott (1985); Comaroff (1985); Ong (1987); Graeber (2009); Mahmood (2011); Ortner (2016); and Alexandrakis (2016). For reflections on refusal, see Shange (2019) and Prasse-Freeman (2022), and for a philosophical take, see Gros (2020).

47. Stewart 2011, 452.

48. Stewart 445.

49. For more on the moral aspects of biological entities in South Asia, see Marriott and Inden (1977) for a general introduction and attention to food or Berger for an update (2013). Copeman (2009) provides excellent accounts of blood's biomoral qualities. Joseph Alter's study of semen (1992a, 1992b, 2000, 2011) as a biomoral substance recounts an entanglement of cosmology, masculinity, sexuality, and the body that Vaibhav Saria (2021) extends. Lawrence Cohen's attention to care for the elderly discusses the biomoral considerations of food (1998), and in other places he has considered biomedicine's reformulation of biomorality as bioavailability (2007a). Sarah Pinto's account of placenta, particularly the biomoral effects of cutting the umbilical cord, also cannot be missed (2008).

50. For more on biomoral ecologies, see Gold (1998) and Gold and Gujar (2002).

51. For more on caste and the communicability of caste as a bodily substance, see Holdrege (1998).

52. Lee 2021b.

53. Barad 2007.

54. For more on the challenges breathing poses to theories of embodiment and representation, see Ingold (2020).

55. Mauss (1935) 2006.

56. Solomon 2021, 105.

57. Solomon 2022.

58. Solomon 2021, 105.

59. Entanglement as a concept in anthropology and in science and technology studies has been exceedingly fruitful. It has led to a nuanced consideration of life with animals (Nading 2014; Tsing 2015; Haraway 2016), ecology (Kirksey 2015; Lamoreaux 2016), relationality (Strathern 2020), queered anthropology (Eriksen and Jacobsen 2019), subjectivity (Pandolfo 2018), medicine (Engelmann and Kehr 2015; Niewöhner and Lock 2018; Stonington 2022), and ethnographic methods (Laszczkowski and Reeves 2018; Candea 2019; Weiss 2020).

60. Veena Das suggests that this formulation of the subject reduces noncontemplative action to "mere behavior" (2012, 139).

61. Butler 2005; Stewart 2007.

62. Affliction, as Veena Das argues, is always distributed through those proximate in spatial and social life because it comes to be normal and frame the everyday (2015). Perhaps, in other words, it is atmospheric.

63. For examples of caste as an effect of cosmological systems, see Dumont (1974) and Moffat (1979). For insight on caste as effect of political systems, see S. Bayly (2001);

Dirks (2001); and D. Gupta (2005a). For more on the *jajmani* system and other forms of caste practice in exchange, see Gould (1964); Wiser (1988); Snodgrass (2001, 2006); and Raheja (1988).

64. Ambedkar 1946, 2014.

65. Pinto 2008.

66. For more on the entanglement of kinship, caste, and indigeneity in south Rajasthan, see Unnithan-Kumar (1997).

67. Biopolitics has been an exceedingly fruitful concept for anthropology. Anthropologists inspired by Foucault (1990, 2009, 2010) and Nicholas Rose (2007) have written about the intersection of biological and political life in pharmaceuticals (Biehl 2005; Petryna, Lakoff, and Kleinman 2006; Sunder Rajan 2006), forms of citizenship (Petryna 2002; Nguyen 2010), psychic worlds (Stevenson 2014), asylum (Fassin 2001; Ticktin 2011), and genetics (Rabinow 2002; Fullwiley 2011; Witmarsh 2011).

68. Foucault 1990, 2010.

69. Chatterjee 2004.

70. Foucault 1990, 1991, 2009.

71. Vine 2019, 27.

72. Felicity Aulino defines care as "habituated ways people provide for one another" (2019, 3). Care has been an essential methodological and analytic concept in anthropology. It has been an effective lens on gender and kinship (Tronto 1993; Garcia 2010; Sue 2019; Mody 2020; Banerjee 2020), politics (Aulino 2019; Mol 2008), bricolage (Caduff 2019; Mol, Moser, and Pols 2010), ethics (Kleinman 2019; Black 2018), social change (Allison 2013, 2023), and future making (Mattingly 1998).

73. Vine 2019, 22.

74. For more on responsibilization, see Trnka and Trundle (2017).

75. Scheduled Areas and Tribes Commission 1961, 6.

76. See Scheduled Areas and Tribes Commission (1961); Jaffrelot (2003); Moodie (2015); Hooja (2004); Sharma (2008); and Gupta and Sharma (2006).

77. Mathew 2000; Chatterjee 2004; Mazzarella 2006.

78. Sarin and Dey 1995; Khatri and Frieden 2002; Gangolli, Duggal, and Shukla 2005.

79. *Ficus religiosa.*

Chapter Two

Excerpt from *The Gay Science* by Friedrich Nietzsche, translated by Walter Kaufmann, copyright © 1974 by Penguin Random House LLC. Used by permission of Random House, an imprint and division of Penguin Random House LLC. All rights reserved.

1. Though all names in this book are pseudonyms, I have maintained local naming conventions that mark caste, age, and gender. On first mention I give each interlocutor's full name. This means I have included the person's given name and caste-based surname. After the first mention, I use the name each is called in Ambawati. Even men's given names still mark caste, as all Rawat men append Singh, or "lion," to their given name. All Meghwal men (at least those over twenty-five) end their given name in either Ram or Lal. In this, both groups follow broader trends across rural north India. For the purposes of clarity, readers can assume that any male name ending in Singh will have the

surname Rawat and any male name ending without it will have the surname Meghwal. For women I use the suffix *-bai*, or "sister," for married women, as happens in Ambawati. I also use *-devi* for a few more cosmopolitan married women who use this as their suffix. In Ambawati *bai* is often written as *bhai*, but this means "brother" in standard Hindi, so I avoid that spelling here.

2. Anand Taneja has written extensively on the meaning and sociality of Islamicate grave sites and saintly shrines called *peer babas*, which Siddharth Singh and his family attended (2012, 2017). Carla Bellamy has also written of a large Islamicate site just over two hundred kilometers south of Ambawati in Jabua, Madhya Pradesh (2011). Both authors note that Hindus frequently access these Islamicate sites

3. Satyanarayana et al. 2011; Kapoor et al. 2012; Shewade et al. 2019.

4. Subbaraman et al. 2016.

5. Chadha et al. 2011; Thomas et al. 2018.

6. Green 2008, 284.

7. Ambawati is at a linguistic intersection. Mewari (a plains dialect of Rajasthani), Wagri (a dialect of Bhili spoken in southeast Rajasthan), and Hindi all overlap in everyday speech and even in the same sentence. Speakers oscillate between languages on the basis of convenience and caste, calling their linguistic mélange either "hill language" or "lying down dialect," an ironic inversion of formal Hindi's "standing dialect." Many Rawats draw on vocabulary and grammatical structures linked to Wagri, and Meghwals create the same sentence using words and grammatical rules from Mewari. This of course is not uniform. Technical terms and occasional conversations between men occurred in Hindi. Some people likely added more Hindi words for my benefit. This makes the inclusion and identification of emic terms a bit more complicated and reveals the analytic work necessary even to identify a term or concept as emic or local. It seems that *local* terms, as is the case with many other things, are a construction of the anthropological gaze.

8. *Diospyros melanoxylon*.

9. Memibai's *praani* reminds of Tim Choy's (2011) analytic and methodological insistence that anthropologists think of "breathers" as a category that encompasses all those exposed to and reliant on air through a need to breathe.

10. Hindi speakers will likely note that reducing the immense semantic work of *praan* to "breath" in this instance is a potential error in translation. I do not wish to impute that Memibai was not referring to something far more numinous than simply breath. She was getting at a breathy substance of life far closer to the soul than simple respiration. Please allow me one page to further develop my argument, before complicating what *praan* might indicate.

11. As most Hindi speakers will know, these three words have multiple meanings. *Dam*, for example, can mean breath and strength, an instant, to boil, or famously, to take hit off a chillum. As breath and strength's best fit, I used strength-breath to indicate *dam*. *Praan* is equally tricky. Most Hindi speakers might translate *praani* simply as a being rather than a breather. This is correct, but it loses some of the cosmological ephemerality of *praan* that I hope to retain. Others might translate *praan* as a soul, but Memibai did not. She uses the word *atma* for soul. Thus, I translate *praan* as soul-breath wherever possible.

12. Pronounced like the English word "dumb."

13. If a word is shared by Hindi and Mewari or Wagri and retains the same sense, I enclose it in parentheses to mark it as Hindi, though I do not mean to assert that Hindi is more standard or original than the other two. It is simply better documented.

14. Here, she used the Hindi word *takhat*. It is noteworthy that she chose *takhat* and its connection to force rather than *himmat* or *fursath*, which are words for strength but have connotations less about force than courage and opportunity, respectively.

15. *Dam* can mean both "breath" and "strength" or "endurance."

16. Mol 2003.

17. This suggests that breath, as a bodily material with moral and even ontological meanings, is a biomoral substance multiple.

18. I am particularly inspired by Stefania Pandolfo's (2018) idea of a knot of the soul and the ways that multiple meanings and moral stakes come to be entangled in meanings that make conscious and unconscious connections of psychological and ethnographic anxiety. Meaning, Pandolfo shows, always evades singularity and a unified ethical code.

19. Solomon 2021, 105.

20. Solomon, 104.

21. When I asked what Hindi or Mewari word people might use to describe this, they most often chose *lay*, which describes a tempo, as in music.

22. Martin 1987.

23. Brighupati Singh has written of these kinds of balanced social relationships as being constituted by an ethic of give and take. Singh has asserted a need for "a more delicate string theory of relations" in order to represent ephemeral and less than causal connection between people and between people and things (2015, 386). My point here is that there exist far more than conscious relations of give and take that stretch the strings, or in my case breaths, between people. This is not particularly new; Marilyn Strathern has written extensively of what an anthropology of relations as practice might look like (2020). This work has inspired Lucinda Ramberg's argument that kinship makes persons (2014) and Aidan Seale-Feldman's point that both inherited and lateral everyday relations of being can be important ways to think about contagion (2019). Finally, it is worth noting that I take seriously Michael. W. Scott's statement that anthropologists often assert an individual self to Western subjects and a relational one to the ethnographic other (2016). One of the key stakes in this book is to find a path between these two poles and argue for a self that is both individual and reflexive, on one hand, and inextricably entangled in relations, on the other. Breath is my strategy to do so.

24. Overt intimacy and vulnerability between spouses would have raised a scandal, and Siddharth Singh's children were not strong enough to create the rigorous pressure Nabudi considered essential.

25. Many anthropologists of care attend to these sites of intimacy methodologically. Kleinman (2019) and Yates-Doerr (2020) are fine examples. Others, such as Aulino (2019) and Mol (2008), however, have pointed out that care is often a set of physical acts that one does for those to whom one has relations. I have focused more on the second stream because of the atmospheric nature of the care and relations I wish to consider. These relations intersect with other forms of sociality too (Ahmann 2020).

26. For more on the challenges of *seva* as intergenerational care, see L. Cohen (1998); Lamb (2000); and Banerjee (2020).

27. Connections between breath and internal fire or hotness have been well documented in classical Ayurveda (Cerulli 2012) and Greek philosophy (Aristotle 1986) Similarly, folk and Ayurvedic ideas of hot and cold are common in Ambawati, as they are in much of South Asia (Langford 2002). That kerosine burns so insistently might have made it an excellent fit into the hot side of the paradigm and thus an appropriate way to heat up a body with too little heat.

28. I draw on Harris Solomon's "moral economy of breathing" and "breath's relational affordances" (2022, 172–173).

29. Solomon 2021; Vine 2019, 22.

30. I find Derrida's exhortation that "if the nonphonetic moment menaces the history and the life of the spirit as self-presence in breath, it is because it menaces substantiality" (1998, 26) to be particularly helpful when thinking about breath, language, and logic.

31. The connection between transformations in labor, bodily attunement, and self-creation have been well documented by anthropologists and others from Marx (1971) until today. Excellent examples include Kondo (1990); Ong (1987); and Comaroff (1985). In South Asia, historians like Dipesh Chakrabarty (1989) and anthropologists like Jefferey Snodgrass (2006) have also documented this connection.

32. Solomon (2022, 172). Similarly, Joseph Alter has written extensively about interdigitation of bodily substance, masculinity, and vitality as strength, both inner and outer, physical and political in South Asia (1992, 2000, 2011).

33. Lawrence Cohen has called this confluence of vital interchangeability and intimacy "bioavailability" (2007a).

34. Appadurai 2004.

35. This breathy conundrum echoes Jacob Copeman's point that blood's biomoral status can and does shift over time as its vitality takes on less and more characteristics of the individual or collective (2009). He shows how blood became a national, transferable substance in practice, but here breath comes to be shared by a family as vital capacity to act.

36. Barbara Holdrege has written of the Hindu body and the heritability of karma (1998). At work here is another example of the divisible body shared among grandfather, father, and son.

37. For more on the interaction between HIV and TB, see Engelmann and Kehr (2015). For more on HIV in India, see Van Hollen (2013).

38. Wagad is the Banswara and Dungarpur region in the extreme southeast of Rajasthan.

39. For more on tantra in India, see Urban (2003, 2009) or Ramberg (2016).

40. Urban 2003, 3.

41. Saria 2021; Alter 1992.

42. Like many occult practitioners, Takhat Singh styled himself a benevolent helper akin to Jeanne Favret-Saada's (1980) *désorcelers*. The malefactor in tantra, like witchcraft in rural France, is always another whose body and words had been prepared differently.

43. See Veena Das on asceticism and power (1977).

44. Like many Hindus, families in Ambawati each have their own lineage deity of *khuldevta*. In Ambawati, there are several. They include Ghora Bhairav, Chauth Mata, Amba Mata, and Narsinghi Mata. Siddharth Singh's family deity was Ghora Bhairav, an avatar of Shiva.

45. Harlan 2003.

46. Death by violence while herding cattle is a common trope in stories of Rajasthani deities like Gogaji or Tejaji, and Nathubaoji is a local iteration of these stories (Singh 2012).

47. Siddharth Singh is a somewhat well-known singer of possession songs, or *Dhak-Thali Geet*. As such, he is active in the family and the region's devotional community. For more on *Dhak-Thali* and possession songs in southeastern Rajasthan, see Kumar (1984); Hardiman (1987); Roche (2000); and Harlan (2003).

48. R. S. Khare has called this practiced medicine. His point that medicine in India is far more concerned with the pragmatic alleviation of suffering than ideological issues like diagnosis or fidelity to a particular healing system or even source of suffering is very clearly on display here (1996).

49. Seeberg 2020; Meinert and Seeberg 2022.

50. Here, I am inspired by Gina Ulysse's postcolonial reparative and creative collective work of *rasanblaj*, or putting back together collectively in order to question the scope of segregated and colonialist frameworks (2016).

51. Lock 2002; Povinelli 2016.

52. Choy 2011.

Chapter Three

1. Ambawati's clinic is a primary health subcenter, or *prathmik upswasth kendra*. This is the smallest unit of the large network of hospitals and clinics run by India's National Rural Health Mission. If no other health infrastructure exists in a panchayat, the smallest unit of governance, it will have an *upswasth kendra*, which serves about five thousand people.

2. No engagement with postcolonial pastoral governance can miss out on Akhil Gupta's point that development in India has long been about forms of sovereignty and citizenship for both the state and the subject (1998). Partha Chatterjee's *The Politics of the Governed* extends this idea by arguing that a liberal pastoral state, constituted by poverty alleviation programs and schemes of all sorts, is the hallmark of political action and governance among most Indians rather than participation in policy, discipline, or control (2004). William Mazzarella (2006) and Ursula Rao (2018, 2019) have also shown how technology is part of the aspiration for a break with unequal or corrupt forms of governance often characterized as both in the past and a reason for unfulfilled development promises.

3. Amin and Chakrabarty 1997; Guha 1997; Hardiman 1987.

4. Jerry Zee's account of dust storms and Chinese development better explains what I would like to say here about dust and postcolonialism. He writes, "Weather events and aerosols in particular—a mounting crisis in particulate air pollution and catastrophic seasonal dust storms that was quickly becoming a signature of Chinese cities—appeared as shadow-histories of the present, a meteorological aspect of a time most often narrated through rapid development" (2021, 8). Multiple shadow histories swirl in dust.

5. Stoler 2013; Chabrol 2018.

6. Stoler 2013, 10.

7. Stoler, 10.

8. For important work on philanthrocapitalism and its new forms of extraction and imperialism, see Birn (2014) and McGoey (2015, 2021).

9. The multistory hospitals built in Bhopal to deal with the long-term effects of the 1984 gas disaster that use only one or two floors and block off the others because of insufficient staff or equipment are particularly poignant examples of this. I thank Bridget Hanna for this compelling example of newly constructed pastoral infrastructures covered in dust.

10. Marder 2016; Parikka 2015.

11. Rosin 2000; Zee 2021.

12. Ehrlich et al. 2021.

13. Trawick 2017, 188.

14. Here I am inspired by the work done among Black anthropologists and Black studies scholars engaging life in the wake of slavery. Their work, particularly that of Deborah Thomas, highlights the centrality of the plantation with its attempts to standardize labor, plants, land, and people in the colonial project (2019). My aim here is to reveal that same kind of plantation logic within global TB medicine as it works to standardize TB care and treatment, patient subjectivity, and TB bacteria. For more on the interplay between standardization and massification in medicine and bacterial life, see Landecker (2016).

15. Das 1995.

16. Ranajit Guha (1997), Sandra Freitag (1985, 1992), Christopher Bayly (1996), and Bernard Cohn (1996) have written beautifully of this process of bureaucratization, census taking, and surveillance in general, and David Arnold (1993), Jordanna Bailkin (2006), and Bharat Venkat (2021) have extensively documented and analyzed health's colonial forms in the Madras and Bombay Presidencies. Waltraud Ernst's (2010) work on the asylum and the use of India as a testing ground for forms of psychological care and control is also particularly insightful. Finally, David Hardiman (2006, 2007), Anand Pandian (2009), Megan Moodie (2015), and Anastasia Piliavsky (2021) have written important texts on colonial processes by which localizing and policing came to organize governance of those deemed constitutionally criminal.

17. Jerry Zee's *Continent in Dust* is a pathbreaking and moving account of the political life of dust in and above China (2021).

18. McMillen 2015.

19. Heather Paxson has called this politics and aesthetics of microbial life a microbiopolitics (2008), and Hannah Landecker shows how the processes and politics of resistance are entangled with standardization and industrialization in ways that put history into microbial biology (2016).

20. See Landecker (2016) and Helmreich (2009) for more on antibiotics and antibiotic resistance.

21. Lyle Fearnley (2020) expands an idea from Bruno Latour (1987) to show how movement between laboratory and field sciences is rife with these kinds of displacements. In fact, Georges Canguilhem's scientific ideologies prefigure what scientists find in the field (1994). In this formula, resistance is scientific ideology that slips between the microbiology lab and the community. It is wrapped up with ideas about who patients are and how a good political and biopolitical subject behaves.

22. Latour 1987, 1988; Fearnley 2020. When considering TB specifically Brimnes (2016), McMillen (2015), and Venkat (2021) have written stunningly beautiful and horrifyingly tragic histories of this confluence. I draw heavily from them when telling the twentieth-century story of TB throughout this book.

23. Gradmann 2019.

24. I am grateful to Christoph Gradmann for sharing Karel Styblo's personal letters with me. These letters are a valuable insight on how Styblo imagined his program and his patients.

25. Murray, Styblo, and Rouillon 1990; World Bank 1993.

26. Ogden, Gill, and Lush 2003.

27. The anthropologist Jens Seeberg was part of this transition and has written extensively about the implementation of the program and its values in Odisha, India (2013, 2014, 2020). Similarly, Ian Harper has provided a detailed account of DOTS implementation in Nepal (2006, 2014).

28. Until very recently clinical terms used to describe TB patients drew heavily from penal metaphors. In addition to being suspects, those unable to take their medicine or who were lost to follow-up were "noncompliant" and occasionally "absconders." India-based activists like Blessina Kumar have been influential in removing much of this language, but the system's inbuilt counterinsurgency logics continue. For more on this, see Zachariah et al. (2012) and Ditiu and Kumar (2012).

29. Thomas Frieden was the World Health Organization consultant in charge of implementing the program in India from 1996 to 2001, before becoming the New York City Health Commissioner and then director of the US Centers for Disease Control and Prevention in 2009. He was influential in the creation of guidelines prohibiting DOTS administration by family members (Khatri and Frieden 2002). The tuberculosis files for India (T9:ind) in the WHO archives at Geneva are an eye-opening source in this regard.

30. Sarin and Dey 1995; Arora and Sarin 2000; Khatri and Frieden 2002.

31. Emma Tarlo's account of the ways New Delhi bureaucrats were pulled into mass sterilization campaigns and often resorted to sterilizing themselves and their families when quotas were not met is a compelling case of this in another heath bureaucracy (2001). Similarly, Veena Das's man wearing a police uniform during an anti-Sikh riot is another example of the ways that the state interpolates and is interpolated in everyday acts of inhabitation (2007).

32. Freitag 1991; Radhakrishna 2001; Moodie 2015; Pandian 2009; Piliavsky 2021.

33. Kumar 1984.

34. Chatterjee 2004.

35. Guha 1997.

36. Garcia 2010, 20.

37. Unlike the South African TB patients who Randall Packard suggests return home from urban and industrial work to seek and receive care for TB among family members, Kesarlal was obliged to return home to a web of fractured and fractious social relations (1989).

38. This is not necessarily true. Kesarlal could have asked to transfer his medicines to another clinic, but he, like many others, worried that transferring the medicines would

mean missing doses and risking the possibility of arriving at a new clinic only to be told that the staff knew nothing of their transfer.

39. "He who owns the mill never goes hungry," my neighbors often said. This was both a commentary on the power of those who could access the means of production in a small way and a veiled critique suggesting that mill owners dipped the flour for their own daily bread out of the wheat that others had entrusted them to process.

40. Shah 2012, 1173–1174.

41. Liisa Malkki has called this a sedentarist metaphysics (1992) and suggests it is constitutive of humanitarianism's view on refugees and the global south more generally. Johanna Crane has shown ontological sedentism at work in global health as well (2013). Health system assumptions about patients like Kesarlal are another example.

42. A. Gupta 2012.

43. Gaudilliere et al. 2022.

44. Porter and Ogden 1997; Venkat 2021.

45. Balasubramanian, Oommen, and Samuel 2000.

46. WHO 2014.

47. For more on pharmaceutical futures, see Petryna, Lakoff, and Kleinman (2006); K. Peterson (2014); Dixon and Chandler (2019); and Venkat (2021).

48. In a similar vein, Ed Cohen's work shows how the political concept of immunity came to be mapped on bodily responses to pathogens through the metaphors scientists drew from their broader political economic atmosphere as they interpreted the cellular phenomena they observed (2009).

49. For more on the ways that pharmaceuticals transform practices of treatment and policy limits the work of community health workers to nonpharmaceutical forms of care, see McKay (2018).

50. Stevenson 2014, 85.

51. For more on bureaucratization and standardization in biomedicine, particularly triage, see Lachenal, Lefevre, and Nguyen (2014) and Nguyen (2010).

52. Sisodia et al. 2006.

53. Engel 2015.

54. D'souza et al. 2009.

55. RNTCP 2012.

56. For more on the conflation of culture and drug resistance, see Farmer (2003).

57. For more on antibiotic stewardship and shortage, see Brhlikova et al. (2011); Street (2014); and Harper and Rawal (2015).

58. Bhanwaribai's instruction to burn the dust resonates with C. Ryan Jobson's provocation to consider letting anthropology burn (2020). Both seem to be ways of thinking about ridding spaces and conversations of unruly residues. Of course, my neighbor knew that even if one did burn dust, new particles were kicked up all the time to settle again.

59. WHO 2011a, 2011b.

60. Pai and Pai 2012; Engel et al. 2015.

61. Creswell et al. 2014.

62. Raizada et al. 2014.

63. Farmer 1999.
64. Stoler 2013, 10.
65. Zee 2021, 11.
66. Brimnes 2016.
67. A. Rao 2009; Ambedkar 2014; Chakrabarty 2018.
68. Chatterjee 2004; Moodie 2015.

Chapter Four

1. Each year during the goddess Durga's Navratri festival, Ambawati's village goddess Narsinghi Mata frequents the bodies of community mediums for nine days and nights. On the tenth day she leaves. Just before her departure, she gives advice about the coming year. I and about two hundred people heard her give this and other advice on October 24, 2012.
2. Vine 2019.
3. Stewart 2011, 3.
4. Choy 2011, 146, 162.
5. Choy, 143.
6. Sylvie Fainzang's account of alcoholism as a contagious illness highlights the way that smell transfers the effects of alcohol use from one spouse to another, though these embodied effects are not the same (1996).
7. Choy 2011, 161.
8. Ahmann 2020.
9. M. Peterson 2021.
10. Harris 2021.
11. Kuriyama 1999.
12. Jouanna 2012.
13. Johann von Herder (2004) and American cultural anthropologists of the Columbia school who were steeped in German philosophy follow his lead to link climes with social forms. Franz Boas's famous descriptions of Inuit relations to snow and ice as a lens on social relations is one example. So is his attention to the effect of American "environment" on the children of immigrants' bodies (1912). Margaret Mead's study of Arapesh temperament is another example (Mead 1963). Similarly, in the Romantic era and the biologics of its inheritors, social life and meaning was shaped by a dialogical relationship between the weather and the people who lived there (Cohn 1996; Cunningham and Jardine 1990; Sontag 1990). Romantic authors write of crusty ship captains whose language, hands, and behavior are made rough by the sea's salty air. The phlegmatic characters of Brontë novels and the poetry of Tennyson and Browning take on the gray tones of foggy English moors.
14. Greenlees 2019. See also Cymene Howe, who shows that wind in some twenty-first-century contexts undergoes a further transformation as energetic material with a power of its own to be technologically tamed (2019).
15. Ghertner 2021.
16. Phenomenologists have explored the boundaries of air, primarily in relation to our ability to perceive its presence. Peter Sloterdijk understands air as something that

can be sensed, arguing that air must enter the body's sensory ambit to matter (2011). That the wind can be seen, felt, and heard only when it is moving across space to the body is unimportant for Sloterdijk. In this model, air and wind stagnate, suggesting that atmospheres are affective, sensory conditions of social possibility but writing out their climatic agency. In fact, when air is allowed to move, it might shape atmospheres of affect through heat or cold, among other things (Stewart 2007; Ingold 2007). However, it can do so, according to phenomenology, only when it moves and enters human bodies through breath and other means. By accounting for the mobile agency of air the experience of TB and breathing more generally extend to concerns with contagion, hygiene, modernity, and development, making it a phenomenology of political ecology. For more on this, see E. P. Thompson (1964).

17. Ideas of caste as subtle substance (Holdrege 1998) accumulated and sloughed off by the body as nexus between material and immaterial substances marked by action as well as inheritance means that caste's subtle substances too might move in the air.

18. For more on children providing care, see Jean Hunleth (2017). Veena Das also considers the ways that a child comes to learn death when his mother is slowly killed by TB despite much care seeking in Delhi (2015).

19. Another neighbor, who had farmed poppies for much of her adult life, was unable to access morphine and palliative care when diagnosed with end-stage uterine cancer. The inability of those who grow the raw materials for palliative care to access it is yet another example of extractive economics at work in Ambawati. For more on cancer in India, see D. Banerjee (2020) and Van Hollen (2018).

20. South Rajasthan and western Madhya Pradesh are some of India's largest producers of the raw materials necessary to make morphine. Farmers like Dhan Singh once even held the rights to grow this controlled substance but lost them over time. They continue to work as day laborers in the fields of those, mostly middle-caste farmers, who have the rights today. His comment about the poppy fumes is a reminder of similar concerns for airborne poppy fumes in *The Wizard of Oz* (1939).

21. B. Venkat reports similar complaints among twentieth-century British and Indian TB patients who searched for healing atmospheres and in the process posed a considerable problem for travel between colony and metropole (2021).

22. For more on sociotechnical forms on breath, see Harris Solomon's work on the socialization of breath in relation to respirators in Mumbai (2021) and Margaret Lock's discussion of the iron lung and the effects of respirators on the definition of life (2002).

23. Sloterdijk has commented on bubbles as a condition of phenomenological life in and writing of atmospheres (2011).

24. Solomon 2021.

25. Labor migration across India often works through kinship and fictive kin practices through which people do not move to an unknown city alone but in collectives that must also be worked on. For more, see Uday Chandra (2021) and Namita Dharia (2022).

26. *Azadirachta indica.*

27. Women often avoided the women's public toilet altogether and waited to return to the open field in Ambawati that served as the toilet there. Unsurprisingly, rates of urinary tract infection in Rajasthan are some of the highest in India. For more, see Bhasin (2004).

28. Cymene Howe (2019) writes of this transformation of wind into a resource. Potential energy is a central part of twenty-first-century environmental capital and brings air into a world of speculation.

29. *Vayara* can affect livestock too. Dhoni's father was well known for his expertise in putting air on animals and humans. Only weeks before, the mother of a neighbor had called Dhoni's father over to put some air on one of their goats, which had a runny nose and was sneezing.

30. Kalika Mata is an avatar of the goddess Kali whose temple is in Chittorgarh's famous hill fort. Indeed, Sajjan Singh would later face the direction of Chittor when ritually managing my air. Kali is an important part of tantric and Shakta religious practice throughout India and Ambawati.

31. Kuriyama 1994, 1999.

32. Helen Lambert (1992, 1997, 2017) has written of similar healing actions aimed at moving sickness through the body, often out the head or feet.

33. For more on air and wind within the classical Ayurvedic corpus, see Filliozat (1964).

34. For more on this, see the SAFE (shared air fraction estimate) study in South Africa (Nathavitharana et al. 2022), as well as Nathavitharana et al. (2021) and Mistry, Tolani, and Osrin (2012).

35. For example, my mother was horrified by my acquired tendency to wipe my wet hands on my pants after using public restrooms after returning from Ambawati, where public towels were rarely available and to be avoided at all cost. Similarly, a Hindi professor once affectionately asked what had happened to my "good" Hindi after returning from a summer in Ambawati.

36. L. Cohen 2007b.

37. Anastasia Piliavsky has shown how habitudes are often seen to adhere to caste and that theft has been associated with or even been used as a sign of caste in southeast Rajasthan (2021).

38. Lee 2021b; Guru 2009; Sarukkai 2009.

39. Omprakash Valmiki's autobiographical and other work has similarly marked this book. Valmiki was part of the Dalit literary movement in Hindi and influenced the forms of self-assertion and denunciation that have shaped Dalit politics both in his native Uttar Pradesh and more broadly. His autobiography *Joothan* and poem "Kua Thakkur Ka" strongly resonate with life in Ambawati (2003).

40. Lee 2021a, 9.

41. Gold 2009, 371.

42. Gold 1998, 178.

43. Ambawatians like Dhan Singh would likely appreciate Kathleen Stewart's idea that affects can crackle through an atmosphere like lightning (2007).

44. Ramanujan 1989, 51.

45. People also often spoke of water in this way. If someone enjoyed or thrived in a place, onlookers said that the place's water suited the person. The same went for misery and sickness in a place. Then people would say that the place's water did not suit the person.

46. Here again I refer chiefly to Sloterdijk (2011).

Chapter Five

Excerpt from *Death, Beauty, Struggle: Untouchable Women Create the World* by Margaret Trawick copyright © 2017 University of Pennsylvania Press, p. 67. Reprinted with permission of the University of Pennsylvania Press.

1. Alkire and Seth 2015; Kunnath 2017.

2. McDowell 2012; Moodie 2015; Ramberg 2016.

3. Some even joked that Ambawati's everyday mélange of Hindi, Mewari, and Wagri was a *khichari boli*, or *khichari* language. *Khichari boli* is a play on words. *Khichari* can slide between a word for the popular somewhat casserole-like dish of rice or lentils that is often used to stand in for confusion and mixed-up-ness in general and the Mewari *kheech ri*, or muds. It thus highlights the mixed-up-ness of Ambawati's language and its status as a language of muck.

4. Douglas 1966; Masquelier 2005.

5. Tuberculosis Chemotherapy Center 1959; Amrith 2004, 2006; Brimnes 2016; Venkat 2021.

6. See McMillen (2016) for a general discussion. For a consideration of cost efficacy and the World Bank critique of hospitals, see World Bank (1993). For more on the move away from hospitals by India's TB-control program, see Sarin and Dey (1995).

7. Within the ethnographic study of TB there similarly is little attention to contemporary TB hospitals or TB hospitalization outside Europe. See Kehr 2021 and Gaudillière et al. 2022.

8. Kaufman 2005; Hannig 2017; Solomon 2022.

9. Livingston 2012; Street 2014; Banerjee 2020.

10. Chabrol 2018; Kehr 2018; Ruddock 2021.

11. Street 2014, 12.

12. Marx and Engels 1998, 53.

13. The National Rural Health Mission has established a norm that one thirty- to fifty-bed hospital should be set up for every hundred thousand people. These hospitals, called community health centers, or *saamudaayik swasthya kendra*, are often located in subdistrict headquarter towns such as Sadri. These hospitals are equipped to manage most health issues, from broken bones to surgery and prenatal care. TB can be diagnosed and treated in these hospitals.

14. Omkarlal Meghwal once told me that his son was a member of a new generation because he showed his children affection in public. "I never picked my children up in public, I would do it privately but in the street like this, never. My father scolded me, telling me I should not do so else others would see loving my children," he told me with an air of regret. Daulat Singh was among those who rarely showed affection, but it was clear to all who knew him that he loved his family deeply.

15. Unlike single-building hospitals, this one was a campus with each ward and activity in its own small building arranged along a hillside.

16. Anupama Rao has argued that Dalit status is always and already embodied through direct and structural violence, making the Dalit body the central site of self-making and vulnerability across India (2009).

17. Pinto 2008.

18. Lee 2017, 2021b.

19. Prasad 2015; Ghertner 2012.

20. Donzelot 1979; Sarkar 1992; Prasad 2015.

21. The majority of Ambawati's families hold Below Poverty Line (BPL) cards. These cards served, before India's biometric turn, as proof of identity and right to access resources like subsidized foodstuffs, heavily discounted health care, and scholarships. The poverty rate in India is hotly contested; see Béteille (2003).

22. For more on lies and omission in the clinic and their role, see Sylvie Fainzang's *An Anthropology of Lying* (2015) and Cecilia Van Hollen's "Handle with Care" (2018).

23. If he had known about Daulat Singh's two previous treatments, he might have ordered a sputum culture to test for antibiotic resistance, but in 2012 sputum cultures were rare and reserved only for those patients who clearly seemed to both exhibit drug resistance and have the ability to comply with the two-year course of treatment. The policy to expand MDR-TB treatment and use a faster molecular diagnostic tool, though written in 2012, would not be fully implemented until 2013 and 2014.

24. A large body of literature concerns the state's projects to document caste and religious identities as building frames on subjectivity. Bernard Cohn (1987) and Joel Lee (2021a) have both documented the fraught nature of this process and revealed similar instances of people expressing flexible or ambiguous identities in these frames. Katyani Seth has also revealed how processes of data collection are often moments when enumerators must act as data interpreters and translators (2018).

25. Chatterjee 2004.

26. Advisory Committee on the Revision of the Lists of Scheduled Castes and Scheduled Tribes 1965, 7; Scheduled Areas and Tribes Commission 1961; Moodie 2015.

27. For more on caste hierarchy and politics, see D. Gupta (2005a).

28. Hospital ethnographies are replete with this kind of information collection. See Livingston (2012); Street (2014); Chabrol (2018); and Ruddock (2021); among others.

29. Unnithan-Kumar 1997.

30. For more on debates about the status of indigeneity in India, see Karlsson and Subba (2013), particularly the essays by Baviskar, Béteille, and Chakrabarty in that volume.

31. Street 2014; Hannig 2017.

32. For more on hospitals as thresholds of modernity, see Kaufman (2005); Street (2014); and Abadía-Barrero (2022). Similarly, hospital exposure seems to place not just Daulat Singh but the whole family in the role of an expendable *Homo sacer* (Agamben 2017), Foucault's deviants (1975), or A. Gupta's citizens of a fickle bureaucracy (2012).

33. Latour 1988; Petryna 2002; Paxson 2008; Stevenson 2014.

34. Much has been written about India's poverty line, but in the years after our hospital visit these cards have been made biometric in hopes of preventing the theft that Mukesh worried about. For more on the pastoral biometric state and the ways that BPL cards create a particular embodied relationship to the neoliberal state, see Ursula Rao's excellent work (2018, 2019)

35. Judith Justice's now classic ethnography of a clinic in Nepal shows that attendants do an immense amount of infrastructural work in hospitals (1986). Some even provide medical care.

36. Sarukkai 2009.

37. Lee 2021b.

38. Parry 1994, 182, 216–217.

39. All this is particularly ironic given that X-ray was not part of the Revised National Tuberculosis Control Program standard of care. The policy required physicians to diagnose TB on the basis of sputum smear alone. X-ray had been a common diagnostic modality since the 1920s, but in an attempt to curb overtreatment in the 1990s, the World Health Organization discouraged X-ray as a diagnostic tool. This changed in the late 2010s when X-ray gained popularity as a screening tool before the Xpert testing machine was developed (Gaudillière et al. 2022).

40. For more on family members and others providing care in a Mumbai hospital, see Solomon (2022).

41. Comaroff and Comaroff 2003; Mazzarella 2006.

42. Rothman 1995; Condrau 2001.

Chapter Six

1. For more on Bengali doctors and their medical practices, see McDowell 2017.

2. "Vadare enero jaan le n go" in Wagri.

3. Amrita Daftary has written extensively on stigma and TB (2012).

4. Rabinow 1996, 99.

5. Rabinow, 103.

6. For clarity I have elected to use only *gawada* in this text. Some speakers in Ambawati use *gawada* exclusively. Others use *gawada* as singular and *gawadiya* as its plural form. Still others use only *gawadiya*. Language in Ambawati, like much of Rajasthan, is a continuum, and the choice of form here says much about the speaker's caste, location of the speaker's maternal village, and involvement in caste-based aspiration.

7. Clouds and TB were "double trouble," as Lukas Engelmann and Janina Kehr have termed co-occurrences that change their constitutive parts (2015).

8. Kalidasa 1868.

9. Kalidasa, 1.

10. Daniel 1987.

11. Susan Sontag has written much about the individualizing force of TB's intersection within romanticism and modernism in literature. She points to the interpretive work done to answer questions about why a particular person suffers from TB (1990).

12. Strathern 2005, 25–26.

13. Pinto 2011, 392.

14. Cody 2013.

15. Here Tiger is referring to the 2011 hit song "Dinka Chinka" from Salmaan Khan's hit *Ready*. The song's dance is full of shoulder shaking, pelvic thrusting, and other exaggerated movements.

16. Lowe 2010.

17. Lowe 2010, 627.

18. Theirs was not the imaginative cloud work that Gaston Bachelard suggests allows thinking about virtual and otherworldly possibilities, nor was it a metaphor of the dematerialized circulating information of cloud computing (1988; see also Hu 2015 and Amoore 2020). It was moral, ecological, and social work.

19. Here Prem Singh used the Hindi verb *phoolna*, often translated as "to bloom" in English. I have chosen to use "swell" rather than "bloom" because the sense in which he used it connoted expansion or unfurling but not fruition or ripening.

20. Prem Singh used Hindi *sahi admi* in one iteration of the phrase "correct man" and Wagri's *how manak* in the second. Though I am not sure why he switched languages for this phrase, both *sahi* and *how* indicate correctness in a moral or factual sense as well as a functional sense. I have translated both as "correct" rather than "good" or "functional" to retain the word's slipperiness as it moves between a functional body, ethical uprightness, and a proper example of masculinity. R. S. McGregor translates *sahi* as "1. adj. sound, right, correct; real, actual. 2. whole (a number w. following fraction). 3. Adv. (it is) quite right, or correct; really; exactly. 4. Very well, alight. 5. F. colloq. Confirmation, corroboration; signature" (McGregor 1993, 998).

21. Good 1993.

22. M. Peterson 2021.

23. Ecks 2014; Solomon 2016.

24. Solomon 2016.

25. Pinto 2011, 384.

26. Daston 2016, 47.

Chapter Seven

1. *Haak hai haq* asserts this maxim. It rhymes nicely while underlining how, in most land-related court cases, the one who cultivates the land often wins.

2. *Mahudica longifolica.*

3. These practices remind one of Anna Tsing's call for a patchy anthropology. This chapter aims to find out how small patches of practice are connected to broader global economies and concerns (2015).

4. *Butea monosperma.*

5. Mines 2005.

6. For instance, the accumulation and reproduction of knowledge and objects outside the bounds of caste occurs in the forest. In one story, the indigenous Eklavya learns archery from Brahman Dhronacharya in the forest before cutting off his finger to resolve the disorder his possession of elite knowledge portends (S. Rao 1968). The failures of paternal and lineage care that organize relations between men sends Rama to the forest, and his own sons Lav and Kush are misrecognized until they leave the forest (Tulsidas 2018; Mani 2008). Similarly, disputes around ownership and the misappropriation of objects in the Rajasthani epics of Tejaji, Devnarayana, Pabuji, and Nathubavji all occur in the forest or junglelike scrub. Finally, complex stories that question the credibility of paternity and female devotion, like those of Radha, Sita, Shakuntala, and Ahalya, are all set in forest (Pinto 2020).

7. Unnithan-Kumar 1997.

8. Much work has been done to show that Indian forests are not romantic and purely sylvan spaces but zones of sociality and governance. See Sundar (1997); Agrawal (2005); Rangarajan and Sivaramakrishnan (2014); and Sivaramakrishnan (2015).

9. Landecker 2016.

10. Pandian 2009, 39.

11. Pandian, 6.

12. See Farmer (1999). For more on biomedicine's biologization of political metaphors, see Ed Cohen (2009).

13. Paxson 2008.

14. For more on the imputation of resistance, see Farmer (1999). For instances when people do work to evade incarceration through positive TB tests, see Koch (2008). Erin Koch has shown that prisoners traffic in dried sputum in hopes of producing a TB-positive sample that might provide access to better conditions within the prison (2008).

15. Landecker 2016; Kehr 2021; Venkat 2021.

16. For more on this, see Gold and Gujar (2002).

17. For a robust literature on monocropping and the plantationocene, see Haraway et al. (2016); Thomas (2019); Tsing et al. (2019); and Wolford (2021).

18. A cultivator is a farm implement used to remove weeds by scratching just below the surface of the soil between rows of crops. In Rajasthan this tool is called *kalpana* and is an essential part of agriculture.

19. I hesitate in using "unqualified" here. Uncertified practitioners of biomedicine across India have various degrees of training and experience. Nonetheless, they often used pharmaceuticals in ways that diverge from biomedical best practices. For more, see Pinto (2004); McDowell and Pai (2016); and McDowell (2017).

20. For excellent examples of this work, see Bhattacharya Chakravarty et al. (2019).

21. In *Illness as Metaphor and AIDS and Its Metaphors*, Susan Sontag warns of the potential moral and epistemological dangers of associating diseases with metaphors of inevitable and segmented progress (1990).

22. "Bengali" is a common term for an unlicensed and often only cursorily trained provider of biomedicine. For more on Bengali doctors, see McDowell 2017.

23. It is drawn from the state's TB messaging, which borrows the English word to promise that "a full course is a sure cure" (pura course, pakka illaj). For more, see Venkat 2021.

24. Physicians often avoid disclosing stigmatized illness like cancer and TB to patients across India. This physician may have never given Devi Singh a TB diagnosis despite treating him for it. See Banerjee (2020) and Van Hollen (2018).

25. Landecker 2016.

26. For more on the technological production of disease categories and ontologies, see Koch (2011); Livingston (2012); and Crane (2013, particularly chap. 2).

27. For a fascinating analysis of patient files in north India, see seth (2022).

28. Devi Singh's yogurt (*dahi*) metaphor likely refers to the large white space on the X-ray created by a pleural effusion. Perhaps the bull-related injury did cause a buildup of fluid in which TB bacteria could activate, an entanglement and forest of causation indeed.

29. RNTCP 2012.

30. Rajasthan's state TB laboratory in Ajmer was undergoing renovation at the time, so samples were sent to the nearest state laboratory, in Gujarat.

31. *Annadata* is a common honorific attached to a feudal-era Rajput landlord that is directly translated as "giver of food." Devi Singh uses it here to refer to the doctor.

32. "Law giver" or "commander."

33. For an in-depth analysis of this tension between innovation and TB control in India, see Engel 2015.

34. RNTCP 2012.

35. See Unnithan-Kumar 1997; Hooja 2004; Hardiman 2007.

36. Pandian 2009; Moodie 2015; Piliavsky 2021.

37. Ambawati residents were similarly excluded from the 2006 Forest Rights Act, on which Anand Vaidya has written, because they did not live within the official bounds of the forest (2022). Once when a man was caught and arrested for cutting wood from the forest by a forest service guard, Ganga Singh yelled out to the guard as he passed by, "You'll have to go now and take a bath [*hampadna*] after the sin you've committed." The guard needing to bathe after endangering the life of another highlights how Ambawatians saw their separation from the forest as a lost source of livelihood akin to death.

38. Laura-Zoe Humphreys's work on film and television in Cuba highlights the political potential of irony and satire to create public space and debate despite marginality (2019). James Scott, of course, might call this a weapon of the weak (1985).

39. For more on the ways adultery can strengthen and subvert social structures through lateral relations, see Meiu (2016).

40. Here Devi Singh oscillates between speaking about a hypothetical and giving an account of what has happened. This ambiguity was present as he told the story, but I did not press him about whether it could have happened or did happen. The hypothetical and event are entangled. I did not see a value in asking Devi Singh to admit to associating with thieves. It seems a poignant example of the entanglement of a narrating and acting self.

41. Derrida and Dufourmantelle 2000.

42. Subramaniam 2020, 36.

43. For more on health care, responsibilization, and the state as a form of subject cultivation, see Trnka and Trundle (2017).

44. Venkat 2016, 2021.

Chapter Eight

1. Veena Das has poignantly written of women's lamentation in India. She notes that "the experience of loss in the flow of everyday life makes the voices of women 'public' in the process of mourning. In the genre of lamentation, women have control both through their bodies and through their language—grief is articulated through the body, for instance, by infliction of grievous hurt on oneself, 'objectifying' and making present the inner state, and is finally given a home in language" (Das 1996, 68). This well describes Mangibai's lamentation here and throughout the chapter.

2. For a nuanced discussion of *zoë* and *bios*, see Hannah Arendt (1958) and of course Giorgio Agamben (2017). I draw more heavily from Arendt here.

3. Das 1996, 68–69.

4. Lock 2002.

5. Lock, 73.

6. WHO 2022.

7. Lock 2002, 73.

8. Parry 1994.

9. Laidlaw 2005; Trawick 2017; Allocco 2020, 2021.

10. Trawick 2017; Allocco 2021.

11. Harlan 2003; Singh 2012.

12. Desjarlais 2016.

13. Lamb 2000; Solomon 2021.

14. Stevenson 2014.

15. Han 2015, 494.

16. Angela Garcia makes a similar argument about landscapes' effect on people, describing spaces and things in them as elegiac instantiations of trauma. Whereas for Garcia death abides in a landscape through discarded syringes, abandoned homes, and memorials at sites of death, here I am particularly interested in the ways that death and grief abide despite practices of dispersal rather than memorialization (2012).

17. Han 2015, 506.

18. Parry 1994.

19. Good 2019.

20. Rahimi 2021.

21. Gordon 1997.

22. Derrida 1994.

23. Masquelier 2002; Johnson 2013; Street 2018.

24. *Uttarna* was the word used here.

25. I have personified the ghost here as male. Sundar used masculine singular. She could have been using the masculine singular as a singular neuter, but it is grammatically unclear.

26. Many such black granite stones smeared with vermillion can be seen in Ambawati along paths and under trees. These have been set up by people troubled by ghosts in hopes that by giving the ghosts a body and ritual attention they would cease to trouble the person to whom they had been attached.

27. In Ambawati, women become ghosts and ancestor deities, but this happens far less frequently than for men. Sometimes these women are associated with and installed in their natal village rather than their marital one.

28. She said in Wagri, "Wah gaah kare." *Gaah* is the word most often used to describe the sound calves make when bleating for their mothers. It's somewhere between a moan, a bellow, and a shriek.

29. Parry (1994) has shown how Harijan ritual workers are an integral part of death rituals in Baneras and among high-caste Hindu communities. In Ambawati, families manage all aspects of death, from the preparation of the body to cremation and the sweeping up of the ashes. Only rarely is a priest involved, and Harijans are never present. Though Ambawati's historical Harijan jajmans live in Sagwai and do occasionally visit Ambawati, their labor is associated only with the removal of small animals' carcasses like dogs or cats, not death. Amy Allocco (2020) has shown that Dalit and Adivasi death practices across India diverge considerably from textual and Brahmanical practices.

30. Langford 2013.

31. Chauth Mata, or Chaur Mata, is the family, or *kul*, goddess for some of Ambawati's Rawat families. Rai Singh and Mangibai's family was one of them. The goddess in Eklingpura is famous for healing foot and leg issues.

32. Throop 2010.

33. Trawick 2017, 6.

Chapter Nine

1. Murhekar et al. 2021.

2. Tiger and I have worked in collaboration to select this short quote, and I include it here under a pseudonym. I use it with his permission.

3. Trnka 2021, 369; emphasis in original.

4. Trnka, 369.

5. For more on India's response to COVID-19, see Ghosh 2020; Caduff 2021; Banerjea, Boyce, and Dasgupta 2022; Caduff 2020.

6. Jasanoff 2007.

7. Care Collective 2021.

8. For more on quotidian moral worlds, see Arthur Kleinman's *What Really Matters* (2007) and his Tanner Lectures (1998).

9. Steven Epstein has called this the politics of knowledge (1998).

10. Dipesh Chakrabarty suggests that the wounded and vulnerable Dalit body and Adivasi vitalist ontologies might provide an exemplary mode of being that facilitates climate and social justice (2018). This might be the case, but neither "the Dalit body" nor Adivasi ontologies can be separated from the developmentalism and rationalism that has in part coproduced them, inequality, and the objectification of the planet.

11. Agee and Evans 2001, 51.

REFERENCES

Abadía-Barrero, César. 2022. *Health in Ruins: The Capitalist Destruction of Medical Care at a Colombian Maternity Hospital.* Durham, NC: Duke University Press.

Advisory Committee on the Revision of the Lists of Scheduled Castes and Scheduled Tribes. 1965. *The Report of the Advisory Committee on the Revision of the Lists of Scheduled Castes and Scheduled Tribes.* New Delhi: Government of India, Department of Social Security.

Agamben, Giorgio. 2017. *The Omnibus Homo Sacer.* Stanford, CA: Stanford University Press.

Agee, James, and Walker Evans. 2001 (1941). *Let Us Now Praise Famous Men: Three Tenant Families.* Boston: Houghton Mifflin.

Agrawal, Arun. 2005. *Environmentality: Technologies of Government and the Making of Subjects.* Durham, NC: Duke University Press.

Ahmann, Chloe. 2020. "Atmospheric Coalitions: Shifting the Middle in Late Industrial Baltimore." *Engaging Science, Technology, and Society* 6: 462–485.

Alexandrakis, Othon, ed. 2016. *Impulse to Act: A New Anthropology of Resistance and Social Justice.* Bloomington: Indiana University Press.

Alkire, Sabina, and Suman Seth. 2015. "Multidimensional Poverty Reduction in India between 1999 and 2006: Where and How?" *World Development* 72: 93–108.

Allison, Anne. 2013. *Precarious Japan.* Durham, NC: Duke University Press.

———. 2023. *Being Dead Otherwise.* Durham, NC: Duke University Press.

Allocco, Amy L. 2020. "Vernacular Practice, Gendered Tensions, and Interpretive Ambivalence in Hindu Death, Deification, and Domestication Narratives." *Journal of Hindu Studies* 13 (2): 144–171.

———. 2021. "Bringing the Dead Home: Hindu Invitation Rituals in Tamil South India." *Journal of the American Academy of Religion* 89 (1): 103–142.

Alter, Joseph S. 1992a. "The Sannyasi and the Indian Wrestler: The Anatomy of a Relationship." *American Ethnologist* 19 (2): 317–336.

———. 1992b. *The Wrestler's Body: Identity and Ideology in North India.* Berkeley: University of California Press.

———. 2000. *Gandhi's Body: Sex, Diet, and the Politics of Nationalism.* Philadelphia: University of Pennsylvania Press.

———. 2011. *Moral Materialism: Sex and Masculinity in Modern India.* New Delhi: Penguin Books.

Ambedkar, B. R. 1946. *What Congress and Gandhi Have Done to the Untouchables.* 2nd ed. Bombay: Thacker.

———. 2014. *Annihilation of Caste.* Annotated critical edition. London: Verso.

Amin, Shahid, and Dipesh Chakrabarty. 1997. *Subaltern Studies: Writings on South Asian History and Society.* Vol. 9. Oxford: Oxford University Press.

Amoore, Louise. 2020. *Cloud Ethics: Algorithms and the Attributes of Ourselves and Others.* Durham, NC: Duke University Press.

Amrith, Sunil S. 2004. "In Search of a 'Magic Bullet' for Tuberculosis: South India and Beyond, 1955–1965." *Social History of Medicine* 17 (1): 113–130.

———. 2006. *Decolonizing International Health: India and Southeast Asia, 1930–65.* New York: Palgrave Macmillan.

Appadurai, Arjun. 2004. "The Capacity to Aspire: Culture and the Terms of Recognition." In *Culture and Public Action,* edited by Vijayendra Rao and Michael Walton, 59–84. Stanford, CA: Stanford University Press.

Arendt, Hannah. 1958. *The Human Condition.* Charles R. Walgreen Foundation Lectures. Chicago: University of Chicago Press.

Aretxaga, Begoña. 1997. *Shattering Silence: Women, Nationalism, and Political Subjectivity in Northern Ireland.* Princeton, NJ: Princeton University Press.

Aristotle. 1986. *De Anima* [On the soul]. London: Penguin.

Arnold, David. 1993. *Colonizing the Body: State Medicine and Epidemic Disease in Nineteenth-Century India.* Berkeley: University of California Press.

Arora, V. K., and R. Sarin. 2000. "Revised National Tuberculosis Control Programme: Indian Perspective." *Indian Journal of Chest Diseases and Allied Sciences* 42 (1): 21–26.

Aulino, Felicity. 2019. *Rituals of Care: Karmic Politics in an Aging Thailand.* Ithaca, NY: Cornell University Press,.

Bachelard, Gaston. 1988. *Air and Dreams: An Essay on the Imagination of Movement.* Bachelard Translation Series. Dallas, TX: Dallas Institute.

Bailkin, Jordanna. 2006. "The Boot and the Spleen: When Was Murder Possible in British India?" *Comparative Studies in Society and History* 48 (2): 462–493.

Balasubramanian, V. N., K. Oommen, and R. Samuel. 2000. "DOT or Not? Direct Observation of Anti-Tuberculosis Treatment and Patient Outcomes, Kerala State, India." *International Journal of Tuberculosis and Lung Disease* 4 (5): 409–413.

Bandyopadhyay, Shekhar. 2004. *Caste, Culture and Hegemony: Social Dominance in Colonial Bengal.* New Delhi: Sage.

Banerjea, Niharika, Paul Boyce, and Rohit K. Dasgupta. 2022. *COVID-19 Assemblages: Queer and Feminist Ethnographies from South Asia.* New York: Routledge.

Banerjee, Dwaipayan. 2020. *Enduring Cancer: Life, Death, and Diagnosis in Delhi.* Durham, NC: Duke University Press.

Banerji, Debabar. 1999. "A Fundamental Shift in the Approach to International Health by WHO, UNICEF, and the World Bank: Instances of the Practice of 'Intellectual Fascism' and Totalitarianism in Some Asian Countries." *International Journal of Health Services* 29 (2): 227–259.

Barad, Karen. 2007. *Meeting the Universe Halfway: Quantum Physics and the Entanglement of Matter and Meaning.* Durham, NC: Duke University Press.

Baviskar, Amita. 2006. "The Politics of Being "Indigenous"." In *Indigeneity in India,* edited by Bengt T. Karlsson and Tanka Bahadur Subba, 33–50. London: Kegan Paul.

Bayly, Christopher A. 1996. *Empire and Information: Intelligence Gathering and Social Communication in India, 1780–1870*. Cambridge: Cambridge University Press.

Bayly, Susan. 2001. *Caste Society and Politics in India from the Eighteenth Century to the Modern Age*. Cambridge: Cambridge University Press.

Bellamy, Carla. 2011. *The Powerful Ephemeral: Everyday Healing in an Ambiguously Islamic Place*. Berkeley: University of California Press.

Berger, Rachel. 2013. "From the Biomoral to the Biopolitical: Ayurveda's Political Histories." *South Asian History and Culture* 4 (1): 48–64.

Béteille, André. 2003. "Poverty and Inequality." *Economic and Political Weekly* 38 (42): 4455–4463.

———. 2006. "What Should We Mean by 'Indigenous People.'" In *Indigeneity in India*, edited by Bengt Karlsson and Tanka Bahadur Subba, 19–32. London: Kegan Paul.

Bhasin, Veena. 2004. "Sexual Illnesses and Underutilization of Biomedicine among Tribal Women in Rajasthan." *The Anthropologist* 6 (1): 1–12.

Bhattacharya Chakravarty, Aruna, Sheela Rangan, Yatin Dholakia, Sonu Rai, Swaran Kamble, Tejaswi Raste, Sanchi Shah, Shimoni Shah, and Nerges Mistry. 2019. "Such a Long Journey: What Health Seeking Pathways of Patients with Drug Resistant Tuberculosis in Mumbai Tell Us." *PloS One* 14 (1): e0209924.

Biehl, João. 2005. *Vita: Life in a Zone of Social Abandonment*. Berkeley: University of California Press.

Biehl, João, Byron Good, and Arthur Kleinman. 2007. *Subjectivity: Ethnographic Investigations*. Berkeley: University of California Press.

Birn, Anne-Emanuelle. 2014. "Philanthrocapitalism, Past and Present: The Rockefeller Foundation, the Gates Foundation, and the Setting(s) of the International/Global Health Agenda." *Hypothesis* 12 (1): e8.

Black, Steven. 2018. "The Ethics and Aesthetics of Care." *Annual Review of Anthropology* 47: 79–95.

Boas, Franz. 1912. "Changes in the Bodily Form of Descendants of Immigrants." *American Anthropologist* 14 (3): 530–562.

Böhme, Gernot. 1998. "The Atmosphere of a City." *Issues in Contemporary Culture and Aesthetics* 7: 5–13.

Boo, Katherine. 2012. *Behind the Beautiful Forevers*. New York: Random House.

Brhlikova, Petra, Ian Harper, Roger Jeffery, Nabin Rawal, Madhusudhan Subedi, and M. R. Santhosh. 2011. "Trust and the Regulation of Pharmaceuticals: South Asia in a Globalised World." *Globalization and Health* 7 (1): 1–13.

Brimnes, Niels. 2016. *Languished Hopes: Tuberculosis, the State, and International Assistance in Twentieth-Century India*. New Delhi: Orient BlackSwan.

Bubandt, Nils. 2014. *The Empty Seashell: Witchcraft and Doubt on an Indonesian Island*. Ithaca, NY: Cornell University Press.

Butler, Judith. 2005. *Giving an Account of Oneself*. New York: Fordham University Press.

Caduff, Carlo. 2019. "Hot Chocolate." *Critical Inquiry* 45 (3): 787–803.

———. 2020. "What Went Wrong: Corona and the World after the Full Stop." *Medical Anthropology Quarterly* 34 (4): 467–487.

————. 2021. "Crisis and Critique: On Preparedness, Authoritarianism and the Regulatory State." *Political Anthropological Research on International Social Sciences (PARISS)* 2 (1): 5–15.

Candea, Matei. 2019. *Comparison in Anthropology: The Impossible Method*. Cambridge: Cambridge University Press.

Canguilhem, Georges 1994. *A Vital Rationalist: Selected Writings from Georges Canguilhem*. Edited by Francois Delaporte. New York: Zone Books.

Care Collective. 2021. *The Care Manifesto: The Politics of Interdependence*. London: Verso.

Carstairs, G. M. 1958. *The Twice-Born: A Study of a Community of High-Caste Hindus*. Bloomington: Indiana University Press.

————. 1983. *Death of a Witch: A Village in North India, 1950–1981*. London: Hutchinson.

Cerulli, Anthony Michael. 2012. *Somatic Lessons: Narrating Patienthood and Illness in Indian Medical Literature*. Albany: State University of New York Press.

Chabrol, Fanny. 2018. "Viral Hepatitis and a Hospital Infrastructure in Ruins in Cameroon." *Medical Anthropology* 37 (8): 645–658.

Chadha, Sarabjit S., Sharath B. N., Kishore Reddy, Jyothi Jaju, Vishnu P. H., Sreenivas Rao, Malik Parmar, Srinath Satyanarayana, Kuldeep Singh Sachdeva, and Nevin Wilson. 2011. "Operational Challenges in Diagnosing Multi-drug Resistant TB and Initiating Treatment in Andhra Pradesh, India." *PloS One* 6 (11): e26659.

Chakrabarty, Dipesh. 1989. *Rethinking Working-Class History: Bengal, 1890–1940*. Princeton, NJ: Princeton University Press.

————. 2006. "Politics Unlimited: The Global Adivasi and the Debate about the Political." In *Indigeneity In India*, edited by Bengt Karlsson and T. B. Subba. London: Kegan Paul.

————. 2018. "The Dalit Body: A Reading for the Anthropocene." In *The Empire of Disgust: Prejudice, Discrimination, and Policy in India and the US*, edited by Zoya Hasan, Aziz Z. Huq, Martha C. Nussbaum, and Vidhu Verma, 1–20. Oxford: Oxford University Press.

Chandra, Udhay. 2021. "Janu Sister-Supervisor of Migrant Construction Workers." In *Bombay Brokers*, edited by Lisa Bjorkman, 101–108. Durham, NC: Duke University Press.

Chatterjee, Partha. 2004. *The Politics of the Governed: Reflections on Popular Politics in Most of the World*. New York: Columbia University Press.

Chikovore, Jeremiah, Graham Hart, Moses Kumwenda, Geoffrey A. Chipungu, and Liz Corbett. 2015. "'For a Mere Cough, Men Must Just Chew Conjex, Gain Strength, and Continue Working': The Provider Construction and Tuberculosis Care-Seeking Implications in Blantyre, Malawi." *Global Health Action* 8 (1): 26292.

Choy, Timothy. 2011. *Ecologies of Comparison: An Ethnography of Endangerment in Hong Kong*. Durham, NC: Duke University Press.

————. 2012. "Air's Substantiations." In *Lively Capital*, edited by Kaushik Sunder Rajan. Durham, NC: Duke University Press.

Choy, Timothy, and Jerry C. Zee. 2015. "Condition-Suspension." *Cultural Anthropology* 30 (2): 210–223.

Ciotti, Manuela. 2010. *Retro-Modern India: Forging the Low-Caste Self*. New Delhi: Routledge.

Cody, Francis. 2013. *The Light of Knowledge: Literacy Activism and the Politics of Writing in South India*. Ithaca, NY: Cornell University Press.

Cohen, Ed. 2009. *A Body Worth Defending: Immunity, Biopolitics, and the Apotheosis of the Modern Body*. Ithaca, NY: Cornell University Press.

Cohen, Lawrence. 1998. *No Aging in India: Alzheimer's, the Bad Family, and Other Modern Things*. Berkeley: University of California Press.

———. 2007a. "Operability, Bioavailability, and Exception." In *Global Assemblages: Technology, Politics, and Ethics as Anthropological Problems*, edited by Aihwa Ong and Steven J. Collier, 79–90. Malden, MA: Blackwell.

———. 2007b. "Song for Pushkin." *Daedalus* 136 (2): 103–115.

Cohn, Bernard S. 1987. *An Anthropologist among the Historians and Other Essays*. Delhi: Oxford University Press.

———. 1996. *Colonialism and Its Forms of Knowledge: The British in India*. Princeton, NJ: Princeton University Press.

Comaroff, Jean. 1985. *Body of Power, Spirit of Resistance: The Culture and History of a South African people*. Chicago: University of Chicago Press.

Comaroff, Jean, and John Comaroff. 2003. "Transparent Fictions; Or, the Conspiracies of a Liberal Imagination: An Afterword." In *Transparency and Conspiracy: Ethnographies of Suspicion in the New World Order*, edited by Harry G. West and Todd Sanders, 287–300. Durham, NC: Duke University Press.

Condrau, Flurin. 2001. "'Who Is the Captain of All These Men of Death?': The Social Structure of a Tuberculosis Sanatorium in Postwar Germany." *Journal of Interdisciplinary History* 32 (2): 243–262.

Connor, Steven. 2010. *The Matter of Air: Science and the Art of the Ethereal*. London: Reaktion Books.

Copeman, Jacob. 2009. *Veins of Devotion: Blood Donation and Religious Experience in North India*. Studies in Medical Anthropology. New Brunswick, NJ: Rutgers University Press.

Craig, Gillian M., Louise M. Joly, and Alimuddin Zumla. 2014. "'Complex' but Coping: Experience of Symptoms of Tuberculosis and Health Care Seeking Behaviours—A Qualitative Interview Study of Urban Risk Groups, London, UK." *BMC Public Health* 14 (1): 1–9.

Craig, G. M., A. Daftary, N. Engel, S. O'Driscoll, and A. Ioannaki. 2017. "Tuberculosis Stigma as a Social Determinant of Health: A Systematic Mapping Review of Research in Low Incidence Countries." *International Journal of Infectious Diseases* 56: 90–100.

Crane, Johanna Tayloe. 2013. *Scrambling for Africa: AIDS, Expertise, and the Rise of American Global Health Science*. Ithaca, NY: Cornell University Press.

Creswell, Jacob, Andrew J. Codlin, Emmanuel Andre, Mark A. Micek, Ahmed Bedru, E. Jane Carter, Rajendra-Prasad Yadav, Andrei Mosneaga, Bishwa Rai, and Sayera Banu. 2014. "Results From Early Programmatic Implementation of Xpert MTB/RIF Testing in Nine Countries." *BMC Infectious Diseases* 14 (1): 1–12. http://www.biomedcentral.com/1471-2334/14/2.

Cunningham, Andrew, and Nicholas Jardine. 1990. *Romanticism and the Sciences*. Cambridge: Cambridge University Press.

Daftary, Amrita. 2012. "HIV and Tuberculosis: The Construction and Management of Double Stigma." *Social Science and Medicine* 74 (10): 1512–1519.

Daniel, E. Valentine. 1987. *Fluid Signs: Being a Person in the Tamil Way.* Berkeley: University of California Press.

Das, Veena. 1977. *Structure and Cognition: Aspects of Hindu Caste and Ritual.* Delhi: Oxford University Press.

———. 1995. *Critical Events: An Anthropological Perspective on Contemporary India.* Delhi: Oxford University Press.

———. 1996. "Language and Body: Transactions in the Construction of Pain." *Daedalus* 125 (1): 67–91.

———. 2007. *Life and Words: Violence and the Descent into the Ordinary.* Berkeley: University of California Press.

———. 2012. "Ordinary Ethics." In *A Companion to Moral Anthropology,* edited by Didier Fassin. Malden, MA: Wiley-Blackwell.

———. 2015. *Affliction: Health, Disease, Poverty.* New York: Fordham University Press.

Daston, Lorraine. 2016. "Cloud Physiognomy." *Representations* 135 (1): 45–71.

Derrida, Jacques. 1994. *Specters of Marx: The State of the Debt, the Work of Mourning, and the New International.* New York: Routledge.

———. 1998. *Of Grammatology.* Baltimore: Johns Hopkins University Press.

Derrida, Jacques, and Anne Dufourmantelle. 2000. *Of Hospitality.* Translated by Rachel Bowlby. Stanford, CA: Stanford University Press.

Deshmukh, R. D., D. J. Dhande, K. S. Sachdeva, A. N. Sreenivas, Ajay M. V. Kumar, and M. Parmar. 2018. "Social Support a Key Factor for Adherence to Multidrug-Resistant Tuberculosis Treatment." *Indian Journal of Tuberculosis* 65 (1): 41–47.

Desjarlais, Robert R. 2016. *Subject to Death: Life and Loss in a Buddhist World.* Chicago: University of Chicago Press.

Dharia, Namita. 2022. *The Industrial Ephemeral: Labor and Love in Indian Architecture and Construction.* Los Angeles: University of California Press.

Dirks, Nicholas B. 2001. *Castes of Mind: Colonialism and the Making of Modern India.* Princeton, NJ: Princeton University Press.

Ditiu, Lucica, and Blessina Kumar. 2012. "Tuberculosis Care: Why the Words We Use Matter." *International Journal of Tuberculosis and Lung Disease* 16 (6): 711–711.

Dixon, Justin, and Clare Chandler. 2019. "Opening Up 'Fever,' Closing Down Medicines." *Medicine Anthropology Theory* 6 (4): 53–79.

Donzelot, Jacques. 1979. *The Policing of Families.* New York: Pantheon Books.

Douglas, Mary. 1966. *Purity and Danger: An Analysis of Concepts of Pollution and Taboo.* London: Routledge.

D'souza, Desiree, Nerges F. Mistry, Tina S. Vira, Yatin Dholakia, Sven Hoffner, Geoffrey Pasvol, Mark Nicol, and Robert J. Wilkinson. 2009. "High Levels of Multidrug Resistant Tuberculosis in New and Treatment-Failure Patients from the Revised National Tuberculosis Control Programme in an Urban Metropolis (Mumbai) in Western India." *BMC Public Health* 9 (1): 1–9.

Dumont, Louis. 1974. *Homo Hierarchicus: The Caste System and Its Implications.* Chicago: University of Chicago Press.

Ecks, Stefan. 2014. *Eating Drugs: Psychopharmaceutical Pluralism in India*. New York: New York University Press.

Ecks, Stefan, and Ian Harper. 2013. "Public Private Mixes: The Market for Anti-Tuberculosis Drugs in India." In *When People Come First: Critical Studies in Global Health*, edited by João Biehl and Adriana Petryna, 252–275. Princeton, NJ: Princeton University Press.

Ehrlich, Rodney, Paula Akugizibwe, Nandi Siegfried, and David Rees. 2021. "The Association Between Silica Exposure, Silicosis and Tuberculosis: A Systematic Review and Meta-Analysis." *BMC Public Health* 21 (1): 1–18.

Engel, Nora. 2015. *Tuberculosis in India: A Case of Innovation and Control*. Delhi: Orient BlackSwan.

Engel, Nora, Gayatri Ganesh, Mamata Patil, Vijayashree Yellappa, Nitika Pant Pai, Caroline Vadnais, and Madhukar Pai. 2015. "Barriers to Point-of-Care Testing in India: Results from Qualitative Research across Different Settings, Users and Major Diseases." *PLoS One* 10 (8): e0135112.

Engelmann, Lukas, and Janina Kehr. 2015. "Double Trouble? Towards an Epistemology of Co-Infection." *Medicine Anthropology Theory* 2 (1): 1–31.

Epstein, Steven. 1998. *Impure Science: AIDS, Activism, and the Politics of Knowledge*. Berkeley: University of California Press.

Eriksen, Annelin, and Christine Jacobsen. 2019. "On Feminist Critique and How the Ontological Turn Is Queering Anthropology." In *Queering Knowledge: Analytics, Devices and Investments after Marilyn Strathern*, edited by Paul Boyce, E. J. Gonzalez-Polledo, and Silvia Posocco. London: Routledge.

Ernst, Waltraud. 2010. *Mad Tales from the Raj: Colonial Psychiatry in South Asia, 1800–58*. London: Anthem Press.

Fainzang, Sylvie. 1996. "Alcoholism, a Contagious Disease: A Contribution Towards an Anthropological Definition of Contagion." *Culture, Medicine and Psychiatry* 20 (4): 473–487.

———. 2015. *An Anthropology of Lying: Information in the Doctor-Patient Relationship*. Burlington, VT: Ashgate.

Farmer, Paul. 1997. "Social Scientists and the New Tuberculosis." *Social Science and Medicine* 44 (3): 347–358.

———. 1999. *Infections and Inequalities: The Modern Plagues*. Berkeley: University of California Press.

———. 2003. *Pathologies of Power: Health, Human Rights, and the New War on the Poor*. Berkeley: University of California Press.

Fassin, Didier. 2001. "The Biopolitics of Otherness: Undocumented Foreigners and Racial Discrimination in French Public Debate." *Anthropology Today* 17 (1): 3–7.

Favret-Saada, Jeanne. 1980. *Deadly Words: Witchcraft in the Bocage*. Cambridge: Cambridge University Press.

Fearnley, Lyle. 2020. *Virulent Zones: Animal Disease and Global Health at China's Pandemic Epicenter*. Durham, NC: Duke University Press.

Feldberg, Georgina. 1995. *Disease and Class: Tuberculosis and the Shaping of Modern North America*. New Brunswick, NJ: Rutgers University Press.

Filliozat, Jean. 1964. *The Classical Doctrine of Indian Medicine: Its Origins and Its Greek Parallels.* Translated by Dev Raj Chanana. Delhi: Munshiram Manoharlal.

Fischer, Michael 2003. *Emergent Forms of Life and the Anthropological Voice.* Durham, NC: Duke University Press.

Fortun, Kim, Mike Fortun, Erik Bigras, Tahereh Saheb, Brandon Costelloe-Kuehn, Jerome Crowder, Daniel Price, and Alison Kenner. 2014. "Experimental Ethnography Online: The Asthma Files." *Cultural Studies* 28 (4): 632–642.

Foucault, Michel. 1975. *The Birth of the Clinic: An Archaeology of Medical Perception.* New York: Vintage Books.

———. 1982. "The Subject and Power." *Critical Inquiry* 8 (4): 777–795.

———. 1990. *The History of Sexuality, Vol. 1: An Introduction* New York: Vintage Books.

———. 1991. *The Foucault Effect: Studies in Governmentality.* Edited by Graham Burchell, Colin Gordon, and Peter Miller. Chicago: University of Chicago Press.

———. 2009. *Security, Territory, Population: Lectures at the Collège de France 1977–1978.* Translated by Graham Burchell. London: Palgrave Macmillan.

———. 2010. *The Birth of Biopolitics: Lectures at the Collège de France 1978–1979.* Translated by Graham Burchell. Edited by Michel Senellart. New York: Picador.

Freitag, Sandria. 1985. "Collective Crime and Authority in North India Codification." In *Crime and Criminality in British India*, edited by Anand Yang. Tucson: University of Arizona Press.

———. 1991. "Crime in the Social Order of Colonial North India." *Modern Asian Studies* 25 (2): 227–261.

———. 1992. *Culture and Power in Banaras.* Los Angeles: University of California Press.

Fullwiley, Duana. 2011. *The Encultured Gene: Sickle Cell Health Politics and Biological Difference in West Africa.* Princeton, NJ: Princeton University Press.

Gandhi, Mohandas Karamchand. 1962. *Village Swaraj.* Ahmedabad: Navajivan Publishing.

Gandy, Matthew, and Alimuddin Zumla, eds. 2003. *The Return of the White Plague: Global Poverty and the New Tuberculosis.* New York: Verso.

Gangolli, Leena, Ravi Duggal, and Abhay Shukla. 2005. *Review of Healthcare in India.* Mumbai: Centre for Enquiry into Health and Allied Themes.

Garcia, Angela. 2010. *The Pastoral Clinic: Addiction and Dispossession along the Rio Grande.* Berkeley: University of California Press.

Gaudillière, Jean-Paul, Andrew McDowell, Claudia Lang, and Claire Beaudevin, eds. 2022. *Global Health for All: Knowledge, Politics, and Practices.* New Brunswick, NJ: Rutgers University Press.

Ghertner, D. Asher 2012. "Nuisance Talk and the Property of Property: Middle Class Discourse of a Slum-Free Delhi." *Antipode* 44 (4): 1161–1187.

———. 2021. "Postcolonial Atmospheres: Air's Coloniality and the Climate of Enclosure." *Annals of the American Association of Geographers* 111 (5): 1483–1502.

Ghosh, Avilasha. 2020. "India's Response to COVID-19 Pandemic: A Success Story?" *Medical Anthropology Quarterly.* https://medanthroquarterly.org/rapid-response/2020/06/indias-response-to-covid-19-pandemic-a-success-story/.

Glissant, Édouard. 2020. *Treatise on the Whole-World.* Translated by Celia Britton. Liverpool: Liverpool University Press.

Gold, Ann Grodzins. 1998. "Sin and Rain: Moral Ecology in Rural North India." In *Purifying the Earthly Body of God: Religion and Ecology in Hindu India*, edited by Lance E. Nelson, 165–196. New York: State University of New York Press.

———. 2009. "Tasteless Profits and Vexed Moralities: Assessment of the Present in Rural Rajasthan." *Journal of the Royal Anthropological Institute* 15 (2): 356–385.

Gold, Ann Grodzins, and Bhoju Ram Gujar. 2002. *In the Time of Trees and Sorrows: Nature, Power, and Memory in Rajasthan*. Durham, NC: Duke University Press.

Gooch, Pernille. 2006. "'We Are Van Gujjars.'" In *Indigeneity in India*, edited by Bengt Karlsson and T. B. Subba, 97–115. London: Routledge.

Good, Byron J. 1993. *Medicine, Rationality, and Experience: An Anthropological Perspective*. Cambridge: Cambridge University Press.

———. 2019. "Hauntology: Theorizing the Spectral in Psychological Anthropology." *Ethos* 47 (4): 411–426.

Good, Mary-Jo DelVecchio, Sandra Hyder, Sarah Pinto, and Byron Good, eds. 2008. *Postcolonial Disorders*. Berkeley: University of California Press.

Gordon, Avery. 1997. *Ghostly Matters: Haunting and the Sociological Imagination*. Minneapolis: University of Minnesota Press.

Gould, Harold. 1964. "A Jajmani System of North India: Its Structure, Magnitude, and Meaning." *Ethnology* 3 (1): 12–41.

Gradmann, Christoph. 2019. "Treatment on Trial: Tanzania's National Tuberculosis Program, the International Union against Tuberculosis and Lung Disease, and the Road to DOTS, 1977–1991." *Journal of the History of Medicine and Allied Sciences* 74 (3): 316–343.

Graeber, David. 2009. *Direct Action: An Ethnography*. Oakland, CA: AK Press.

Green, Nile. 2008. "Breathing in India, c. 1890." *Modern Asian Studies* 42 (2–3): 283–315.

Greenlees, Janet. 2019. *When the Air Became Important: A Social History of the New England and Lancashire Textile Industries*. New Brunswick, NJ: Rutgers University Press.

Gros, Frédéric. 2020. *Disobey! A Guide to Ethical Resistance*. Translated by David Fernbach. London: Verso.

Guha, Ranajit. 1997. *Dominance without Hegemony: History and Power in Colonial India*. Convergences. Cambridge, MA: Harvard University Press.

Gupta, Akhil. 1998. *Postcolonial Developments: Agriculture in the Making of Modern India*. Durham, NC: Duke University Press.

———. 2012. *Red Tape: Bureaucracy, Structural Violence, and Poverty in India*. Durham, NC: Duke University Press.

Gupta, Akhil, and Aradhana Sharma. 2006. "Globalization and Postcolonial States." *Current Anthropology* 47 (2): 277–307.

Gupta, Dipankar. 2005a. "Caste and Politics: Identity over System." *Annual Review of Anthropology* 21: 409–427.

———. 2005b. "Whither the Indian Village? Culture and Agriculture in 'Rural' India." *Review of Development and Change* 10 (1): 1–20.

Guru, Gopal. 2009. "Archaeology of Untouchability." *Economic and Political Weekly* 44 (37): 49–56.

Han, Clara. 2015. "Echoes of a Death: Violence, Endurance and the Experiences of Loss." In *Living and Dying in the Contemporary World*, edited by Veena Das and Clara Han, 493–509. Berkeley: University of California Press.

Hannig, Anita. 2017. *Beyond Surgery: Injury, Healing, and Religion at an Ethiopian Hospital*. Chicago: University of Chicago Press.

Haraway, Donna. 1991. *Simians, Cyborgs, and Women: The Reinvention of Nature*. New York: Routledge.

———. 2016. *Staying with the Trouble: Making Kin in the Chthulecene*. Durham, NC: Duke University Press.

Haraway, Donna, Noboru Ishikawa, Scott F. Gilbert, Kenneth Olwig, Anna L. Tsing, and Nils Bubandt. 2016. "Anthropologists Are Talking—About the Anthropocene." *Ethnos* 81 (3): 535–564.

Hardiman, David. 1987. *The Coming of the Devi: Adivasi Assertion in Western India*. London: Oxford University Press.

———. 2006. "Christian Therapy: Medical Missionaries and the Adivasis of Western India, 1880–1930." In *Healing Bodies, Saving Souls: Medical Missions in Asia and Africa*, edited by David Hardiman, 137–167. Amsterdam: Editions Rodopi B. V.

———. 2007. *Histories for the Subordinated*. London: Seagull Books.

Harlan, Lindsey. 2003. *The Goddesses' Henchmen: Gender in Indian Hero Worship*. Oxford: Oxford University Press.

Harper, Ian. 2006. "Anthropology, DOTS and Understanding Tuberculosis Control in Nepal." *Journal of Biosocial Science* 38 (1): 57–67.

———. 2014. *Development and Public Health in the Himalaya: Reflections on Healing in Contemporary Nepal*. London: Routledge.

Harper, Ian, and Nabin Rawal. 2015. "Living and Dying with Mycobacteria: Tuberculosis and the Regulation of Anti-Tuberculosis Drugs in Nepal." In *Living and Dying in the Contemporary World: A Compendium*, edited by Veena Das, 232–250. Berkeley: University of California Press.

Harris, Tina. 2021. "Air Pressure: Temporal Hierarchies in Nepali Aviation." *Cultural Anthropology* 37 (1): 83–109.

Hathaway, Michael J. 2013. *Environmental Winds: Making the Global in Southwest China*. Berkeley: University of California Press.

Helmreich, Stefan. 2009. *Alien Ocean: Anthropological Voyages in Microbial Seas*. Berkeley: University of California Press.

Herder, Johann Gottfried von. 2004. *Another Philosophy of History and Selected Political Writings*. Translated by Ioannis D. Evrigenis and Daniel Pellerin. Indianapolis, IN: Hackett.

Holdrege, Barbara A. 1998. "Body Connections: Hindu Discourses of the Body and the Study of Religion." *International Journal of Hindu Studies* 2 (3): 341–386.

Holley, Lonnie. 2018. "I'm a Suspect." Track on *Mith*. Jagjaguwar.

Hooja, Meenakshi. 2004. *Policies and Strategies for Tribal Development*. Delhi: Rawat Publications.

Howe, Cymene. 2015. "Life above Earth: An Introduction." *Cultural Anthropology* 30 (2): 203–209.

————. 2019. *Ecologics: Wind and Power in the Anthropocene*. Durham, NC: Duke University Press.

Hu, Tung-Hui. 2015. *A Prehistory of the Cloud*. Cambridge, MA: MIT Press.

Humphreys, Laura-Zoë. 2019. *Fidel between the Lines: Paranoia and Ambivalence in Late Socialist Cuban Cinema*. Durham, NC: Duke University Press.

Hunleth, Jean. 2017. *Children as Caregivers: The Global Fight against Tuberculosis and HIV in Zambia*. New Brunswick, NJ: Rutgers University Press.

Ingold, Tim. 2007. "Earth, Sky, Wind, and Weather." *Journal of the Royal Anthropological Institute* 13 (s1): S19–S38.

————. 2020. "On Breath and Breathing: A Concluding Comment." *Body and Society* 26 (2): 158–167.

International Union Against TB and Lung Disease. 2013. "44th Union World Conference on Lung Health, Paris, France, 2013." *International Journal of Tuberculosis and Lung Disease* 18 (11 S1): S1–S564.

Irigaray, Luce. 1999. *The Forgetting of Air in Martin Heidegger*. Translated by Mary Beth Mader. Austin: University of Texas Press.

Jaffrelot, Christophe. 2003. *India's Silent Revolution: The Rise of the Lower Castes in North India*. New York: Columbia University Press.

Jaggarajamma, K., G. Sudha, Vendachalam Chandrasekaran, Charles Nirupa, A. Thomas, Thottikkamath Santha, Malaisamy Muniyandi, and P. R. Narayanan. 2007. "Reasons for Non-compliance among Patients Treated under Revised National Tuberculosis Control Programme (RNTCP), Tiruvallur District, South India." *Indian Journal of Tuberculosis* 54 (3): 130–135.

Jasanoff, Sheila. 2007. *Designs on Nature: Science and Democracy in Europe and the United States*. Princeton, NJ: Princeton University Press.

Jobson, Cecil Ryan. 2020. "The Case for Letting Anthropology Burn: Sociocultural Anthropology in 2019." *American Anthropologist* 122 (2): 259–271.

Johnson, Andrew Alan. 2013. "Progress and Its Ruins: Ghosts, Migrants, and the Uncanny in Thailand." *Cultural Anthropology* 28 (2): 299–319.

Jouanna, Jacques. 2012. "Air, Miasma and Contagion in the Time of Hippocrates and the Survival of Miasmas in Post-Hippocratic Medicine (Rufus of Ephesus, Galen and Palladius)." In *Greek Medicine from Hippocrates to Galen*, edited by Jacques Jouanna. London: Brill.

Justice, Judith. 1986. *Policies, Plans and People: Culture and Health Development in Nepal*. Berkeley: University of California Press.

Kalidasa. 1868. *The Megha Dūta, or, Cloud Messenger*. Translated by Henri Aimé Ouvry. London: Williams and Norgate.

Kapoor, Sunil K., A. Venkat Raman, Kuldeep Singh Sachdeva, and Srinath Satyanarayana. 2012. "How Did the TB Patients Reach DOTS Services in Delhi? A Study of Patient Treatment Seeking Behavior." *PLoS One* (7) 8: e42458.

Karlsson, Bengt T., and Tanka Bahadur Subba. 2013. *Indigeneity in India*. London: Kegan Paul.

Kaufman, Sharon R. 2005. *And a Time to Die: How American Hospitals Shape the End of Life*. New York: Scribner.

Kehr, Janina. 2016. "The Precariousness of Public Health: On Tuberculosis Control in Contemporary France." *Medical Anthropology* 35 (5): 377–389.

———. 2018. "Colonial Hauntings: Migrant Care in a French Hospital." *Medical Anthropology* 37 (8): 659–673.

———. 2021. *Spectres de la Tuberculose: Une Maladie du Passé au Temps Présent*. Rennes: Presses Universitaires de Rennes.

Kenner, Alison. 2018. *Breathtaking: Asthma Care in a Time of Climate Change*. Minneapolis: University of Minnesota Press.

Keshavjee, Salmaan. 2014. *Blind Spot: How Neoliberalism Infiltrated Global Health*. Oakland: University of California Press.

Khare, R. S. 1996. "Dava, Daktar, and Dua: Anthropology of Practiced Medicine in India." *Social Science and Medicine* 43 (5): 837–848.

Khatri, G. R., and Thomas R. Frieden. 2002. "Rapid DOTS Expansion in India." *Bulletin of the World Health Organization* 80: 457–463.

Kirksey, Eben. 2015. *Emergent Ecologies*. Durham, NC: Duke University Press.

Kleinman, Arthur. 1998. "Experience and Its Moral Modes: Culture, Human Conditions, and Disorder." The Tanner Lectures on Human Values, Stanford University, April 13–16, 1998.

———. 2007. *What Really Matters: Living a Moral Life amidst Uncertainty and Danger*. New York: Oxford University Press.

———. 2019. *The Soul of Care: The Moral Education of a Husband and a Doctor*. New York: Viking.

Koch, Erin. 2008. "Beyond Suspicion." *American Ethnologist* 33 (1): 50–62.

———. 2011. "Local Microbiologies of Tuberculosis: Insights from the Republic of Georgia." *Medical Anthropology* 30 (1): 81–101.

———.2013. *Free Market Tuberculosis: Managing Epidemics in Post-Soviet Georgia*. Nashville, TN: Vanderbilt University Press.

Kondo, Dorinne K. 1990. *Crafting Selves: Power, Gender, and Discourses of Identity in a Japanese Workplace*. Chicago: University of Chicago Press.

Kumar, Pramod 1984. *Folk Icons and Rituals in Tribal Life*. New Delhi: Abhinav.

Kunnath, George J. 2017. *Rebels from the Mud Houses: Dalits and the Making of the Maoist Revolution in Bihar*. London: Routledge.

Kuriyama, Shigehisa. 1994. "The Imagination of Winds and the Development of the Chinese Conception of the Body." In *Body, Subject and Power in China*, edited by Angela Zito and Tani E. Barlow. Chicago: University of Chicago Press.

———. 1999. *The Expressiveness of the Body and the Divergence of Greek and Chinese Medicine*. New York: Zone Books.

Lachenal, Guillaume, Céline Lefevre, and Vinh-Kim Nguyen. 2014. *La Médecine du Tri: Histoire, Éthique, Anthropologie*. Paris: Presses Universitaires de France.

Laidlaw, James. 2005. "A Life Worth Leaving: Fasting to Death as Telos of a Jain Religious Life." *Economy and Society* 34 (2): 178–199.

Lamb, Sarah. 2000. *White Saris and Sweet Mangoes: Aging, Gender, and Body in North India*. Berkeley: University of California Press.

Lambert, Helen. 1992. "The Cultural Logic of Indian Medicine: Prognosis and Etiology in Rajasthani Popular Therapeutics." *Social Science and Medicine* 34 (10): 1069–1076.

————. 1997. "Illness, Inauspiciousness and Modes of Health in Rajasthan." *Contributions to Indian Sociology* 31 (2): 253–271.

————. 2017. "Plural Traditions? Folk Therapeutics and 'English' Medicine in Rajasthan." In *Western Medicine as Contested Knowledge*, edited by Andrew Cunningham and Bridie Andrews, 191–211. Manchester, UK: Manchester University Press.

Lamoreaux, Janelle. 2016. "What If the Environment Is a Person? Lineages of Epigenetic Science in a Toxic China." *Cultural Anthropology* 31 (2): 188–214.

Landecker, Hannah. 2016. "Antibiotic Resistance and the Biology of History." *Body and Society* 22 (4): 19–52.

Langford, Jean. 2002. *Fluent Bodies: Ayurvedic Remedies for Postcolonial Imbalance.* Durham, NC: Duke University Press.

————. 2013. *Consoling Ghosts: Stories of Medicine and Mourning from Southeast Asians in Exile.* Minneapolis: University of Minnesota Press.

Laszczkowski, Mateusz, and Madeline Reeves, eds. 2018. *Affective States: Entanglements, Suspensions, Suspicions.* New York: Berghahn.

Latour, Bruno. 1987. *Science in Action: How to Follow Scientists and Engineers through Society.* Cambridge, MA: Harvard University Press.

————. 1988. *The Pasteurization of France.* Translated by John Law. Cambridge, MA: Harvard University Press.

Lee, Joel. 2017. "Odor and Order: How Caste Is Inscribed in Space and Sensoria." *Comparative Studies of South Asia, Africa and the Middle East* 37 (3): 470–490.

————. 2021a. *Deceptive Majority: Dalits, Hinduism, and Underground Religion.* Cambridge: Cambridge University Press.

————. 2021b. "Disgust and Untouchability: Towards an Affective Theory of Caste." *South Asian History and Culture* 12 (2–3): 310–327.

Livingston, Julie. 2012. *Improvising Medicine: An African Oncology Ward in an Emerging Cancer Epidemic.* Durham, NC: Duke University Press.

Lock, Margaret M. 2002. *Twice Dead: Organ Transplants and the Reinvention of Death.* Berkeley: University of California Press.

Lock, Margaret M., and Vinh-Kim Nguyen. 2018. *An Anthropology of Biomedicine.* 2nd ed. Hoboken, NJ: Wiley-Blackwell.

Lowe, Celia. 2010. "Viral Clouds: Becoming H5N1 in Indonesia." *Cultural Anthropology* 25 (4): 625–649.

MacDonald, Helen, and Ian Harper, eds. 2019. *Understanding Tuberculosis and Its Control: Anthropological and Ethnographic Approaches.* New York: Routledge.

Mahmood, Saba. 2011. *Politics of Piety: The Islamic Revival and the Feminist Subject.* Princeton, NJ: Princeton University Press.

Malkki, Liisa. 1992. "National Geographic: The Rooting of Peoples and the Territorialization of National Identity among Scholars and Refugees." *Cultural Anthropology* 7 (1): 24–44.

Mani, Chandra Mauli. 2008. *Memorable Characters from the Ramayana and the Mahabharata.* Delhi: Northern Book Centre.

Marder, Michael. 2016. *Dust.* New York: Bloomsbury Academic.

Marriott, McKim. 1955. *Village India: Studies in the Little Community.* Chicago: University of Chicago Press.

Marriott, McKim, and Ronald Inden. 1977. "Toward an Ethnosociology of South Asian Caste Systems." In *The New Wind: Changing Identities in South Asia*, edited by Kenneth David, 227–239. The Hague: Mouton.

Martin, Emily. 1987. *The Woman in the Body: A Cultural Analysis of Reproduction*. Boston: Beacon Press.

Marx, Karl. 1853. "The British Rule in India." *New-York Daily Tribune*, June 25, 1853.

———. 1971. *The Grundrisse*. New York: Harper and Row.

Marx, Karl, and Friedrich Engels. 1998. *The German Ideology: Including Theses on Feuerbach and Introduction to* The Critique of Political Economy. Amherst, MA: Prometheus.

Masquelier, Adeline. 2002. "Road Mythographies: Space, Mobility, and the Historical Imagination in Postcolonial Niger." *American Ethnologist* 29 (4): 829–856.

———. 2005. *Dirt, Undress, and Difference: Critical Perspectives on the Body's Surface*. Indianapolis: Indiana University Press.

Mathew, George. 2000. *Status of Panchayat Raj in the States and Union Territories of India*. Delhi: Concept Publishing.

Mattingly, Cheryl. 1998. *Healing Dramas and Clinical Plots: The Narrative Structure of Experience*. Cambridge: Cambridge University Press.

Mauss, Marcel. (1935) 2006. "Techniques of the Body." In *Techniques, Technology and Civilization*, edited by Nathan Schlanger, 77–96. New York: Berghahn.

Mazzarella, William. 2006. "Internet X-Ray: E-governance, Transparency, and the Politics of Immediation in India." *Public Culture* 18 (3): 473–505.

McCormack, Derek P. 2018. *Atmospheric Things on the Allure of Elemental Envelopment*. Durham, NC: Duke University Press.

McDowell, Andrew. 2012. "Echoing Silence: Backwardness, Governmentality and Voice in Contemporary India." *Journal of Asian and African Studies* 47 (4): 348–362.

———. 2017. "Mohit's Pharmakon: Symptom, Rotational Bodies, and Pharmaceuticals in Rural Rajasthan." *Medical Anthropology Quarterly* 31 (3): 332–348.

McDowell, Andrew, and Madhukar Pai. 2016. "Alternative Medicine: An Ethnographic Study of How Practitioners of Indian Medical Systems Manage TB in Mumbai." *Transactions of The Royal Society of Tropical Medicine and Hygiene* 110 (3): 192–198.

McGoey, Linsey. 2015. *No Such Thing as a Free Gift: The Gates Foundation and the Price of Philanthropy*. London: Verso.

———. 2021. "Philanthrocapitalism and the Separation of Powers." *Annual Review of Law and Social Science* 17: 391–409.

McGregor, R. S., ed. 1993. *The Oxford Hindi-English Dictionary*. Oxford: Oxford University Press.

McKay, Ramah. 2018. *Medicine in the Meantime: The Work of Care in Mozambique*. Durham, NC: Duke University Press.

McMillen, Christian W. 2015. *Discovering Tuberculosis: A Global History, 1900 to the Present*. New Haven, CT: Yale University Press.

Mead, Margaret. 1963. *Sex and Temperament in Three Primitive Societies*. New York: William Morrow.

Meghwal, Kusum. 2019. *Rajasthan Ke Mulnivasi, Sheshit Sangharsh aur Itihas*. Delhi: Samyak Prakashan.

Meinert, Lotte, and Jens Seeberg, eds. 2022. *Configuring Contagion: Ethnographies of Biosocial Epidemics.* New York: Berghahn.

Meiu, George Paul. 2016. "Belonging in Ethno-Erotic Economies: Adultery, Alterity, and Ritual in Postcolonial Kenya." *American Ethnologist* 43 (2): 215–229.

Mines, Diane P. 2005. *Fierce Gods: Inequality, Ritual, and the Politics of Dignity in a South Indian Village.* Bloomington: Indiana University Press.

Mistry, Nerges, Monica Tolani, and David Osrin. 2012. "Drug-Resistant Tuberculosis in Mumbai, India: An Agenda for Operations Research." *Operations Research for Health Care* 1 (2–3): 45–53.

Mody, Perveez. 2020. "Care and Resistance." *Anthropology and Humanism* 45 (2): 194–201.

Moffat, Michael. 1979. *An Untouchable Community in South India: Structure and Consensus.* Princeton, NJ: Princeton University Press.

Mol, Annemarie. 2003. *The Body Multiple: Ontology in Medical Practice.* Durham, NC: Duke University Press.

———. 2008. *The Logic of Care: Health and the Problem of Patient Choice.* London: Routledge.

Mol, Annemarie, Ingunn Moser, and Jeannette Pols, eds. 2010. *Care in Practice: On Tinkering in Clinics, Homes and Farms.* Bielefeld, Germany: Transcript Verlag.

Moodie, Megan. 2015. *We Were Adivasis: Aspiration in an Indian Scheduled Tribe.* Chicago: University of Chicago Press.

Munro, Salla A., Simon A. Lewin, Helen J. Smith, Mark E. Engel, Atle Fretheim, and Jimmy Volmink. 2007. "Patient Adherence to Tuberculosis Treatment: A Systematic Review of Qualitative Research." *PLoS Medicine* 4 (7): e238.

Murhekar, Manoj V., et al. 2021. "Seroprevalence of IgG Antibodies against SARS-CoV-2 among the General Population and Healthcare Workers in India, June–July 2021: A Population-Based Cross-sectional Study." *PLOS Medicine* 18 (12): e1003877.

Murphy, Michelle. 2006. *Sick Building Syndrome and the Problem of Uncertainty.* Durham, NC: Duke University Press.

Murray, Christopher, Karel Styblo, and Annik Rouillon. 1990. "Tuberculosis in Developing Countries: Burden, Intervention, and Cost." *Bulletin of the International Union Against Tuberculosis and Lung Disease* 65 (1): 6–24.

Nading, Alexander M. 2014. *Mosquito Trails: Ecology, Health, and the Politics of Entanglement.* Oakland: University of California Press.

———. 2017. "Local Biologies, Leaky Things, and the Chemical Infrastructure of Global Health." *Medical Anthropology* 2 (36): 141–156.

Nancy, Jean-Luc. 2002. "L'Intrus." *CR: The New Centennial Review* 2 (3): 1–14.

Nathavitharana, Ruvandhi R., Ananja van der Westhuizen, Helene-Mari van der Westhuizen, Hridesh Mishra, Annalean Sampson, Jack Meintjes, Edward Nardell, Andrew McDowell, and Grant Theron. 2021. "'If I've Got Latent TB, I Would Like to Get Rid of It': Derivation of the CARD (Constraints, Actions, Risks, and Desires) Framework Informed by South African Healthcare Worker Perspectives on Latent Tuberculosis Treatment." *PLoS One* 16 (8): e0254211.

Nathavitharana, Ruvandhi, Hridesh Mishra, Amanda Sullivan, Shelly Hurwitz, Philip Lederer, Jack Meintjes, Edward Nardell, and Grant Theron. 2022. "Predicting Airborne Infection Risk: Association between Personal Ambient Carbon Dioxide Level

Monitoring and Incidence of Tuberculosis Infection in South African Health Workers." *Clinical Infectious Disease* 75 (8): 1297–1306.

Nguyen, Vinh-Kim. 2010. *The Republic of Therapy: Triage and Sovereignty in West Africa's Time of AIDS.* Durham, NC: Duke University Press.

Nichter, Mark. 1994. "Illness Semantics and International Health: The Weak Lungs/ TB Complex in the Philippines." *Social Science and Medicine* 38 (5): 649–663.

Nietzsche, Friedrich. 1974. *The Gay Science: With a Prelude in Rhymes and an Appendix of Song.* Translated by Walter Kaufmann. New York: Vintage Books.

Niewöhner, Jörg, and Margaret Lock. 2018. "Situating Local Biologies: Anthropological Perspectives on Environment/Human Entanglements." *BioSocieties* 13: 681–697.

Ogden, Jessica, Walt Gill, and Louisiana Lush. 2003. "The Politics of 'Branding' in Policy Transfer: The Case of DOTS for Tuberculosis Control." *Social Science and Medicine* 57 (1): 179–188.

Ong, Aihwa. 1987. *Spirits of Resistance and Capitalist Discipline: Factory Women in Malaysia.* Albany: State University of New York Press.

Ortner, Sherry. 2016. "Dark Anthropology and Its Others: Theory since the Eighties." *HAU: Journal of Ethnographic Theory* 6 (1): 47–73.

Packard, Randall M. 1989. *White Plague, Black Labor: Tuberculosis and the Political Economy of Health and Disease in South Africa.* Berkeley: University of California Press.

Pai, Nitika Pant, and Madhukar Pai. 2012. "Point-of-care Diagnostics for HIV and Tuberculosis: Landscape, Pipeline, and Unmet Needs." *Discovery Medicine* 13 (68): 35–45.

Pandian, Anand. 2009. *Crooked Stalks: Cultivating Virtue in South India.* Durham, NC: Duke University Press.

Pandolfo, Stefania. 2018. *Knot of the Soul: Madness, Psychoanalysis, Islam.* Chicago: University of Chicago Press.

Parikka, Jussi. 2015. *A Geology of Media.* Minneapolis: University of Minnesota Press.

Parry, Jonathan P. 1994. *Death in Banaras.* Cambridge: Cambridge University Press.

Paxson, Heather. 2008. "Post-Pasteurian Cultures: The Microbiopolitics of Raw-Milk Cheese in the United States." *Cultural Anthropology* 23 (1): 15–47.

Peterson, Kristin. 2014. *Speculative Markets: Drug Circuits and Derivative Life in Nigeria.* Durham, NC: Duke University Press.

Peterson, Marina. 2021. *Atmospheric Noise: The Indefinite Urbanism of Los Angeles.* Durham, NC: Duke University Press.

Petryna, Adriana. 2002. *Life Exposed: Biological Citizens after Chernobyl.* Princeton, NJ: Princeton University Press.

Petryna, Adriana, Andrew Lakoff, and Arthur Kleinman. 2006. *Global Pharmaceuticals: Ethics, Markets, Practices.* Durham, NC: Duke University Press.

Piliavsky, Anastasia. 2021. *Nobody's People: Hierarchy as Hope in a Society of Thieves.* Stanford, CA: Stanford University Press.

Pinto, Sarah. 2004. "Development without Institutions: Ersatz Medicine and the Politics of Everyday Life in Rural North India." *Cultural Anthropology* 19 (3): 337–364.

———. 2008. *Where There Is No Midwife: Birth and Loss in Rural India.* New York: Berghahn.

———. 2011. "Rational Love, Relational Medicine: Psychiatry and the Accumulation of Precarious Kinship." *Culture, Medicine and Psychiatry* 35: 376–395.

———. 2020. *The Doctor and Mrs. A.: Ethics and Counter-Ethics in an Indian Dream Analysis*. New York: Fordham University Press.

Porter, John D., and Jessica Ogden. 1997. "Ethics of Directly Observed Therapy for the Control of Infectious Diseases." *Bulletin de l'Institut Pasteur* 95 (3): 117–127.

Povinelli, Elizabeth A. 2016. *Geontologies: A Requiem to Late Liberalism*. Durham, NC: Duke University Press.

Prasad, Srirupa. 2015. *Cultural Politics of Hygiene in India, 1890–1940: Contagions of Feeling*. New York: Palgrave Macmillan.

Prasse-Freeman, Elliott. 2022. "Resistance/Refusal: Politics of Manoeuvre under Diffuse Regimes of Governmentality." *Anthropological Theory* 22 (1): 102–127.

Rabinow, Paul. 1996. *Essays on the Anthropology of Reason*. Princeton, NJ: Princeton University Press.

———. 2002. *French DNA: Trouble in Purgatory*. Chicago: University of Chicago Press.

Radhakrishna, Meena. 2001. *Dishonoured by History: "Criminal Tribes" and British Colonial Policy*. New Delhi: Orient Longman.

Raheja, Gloria Goodwin. 1988. *The Poison in the Gift: Ritual, Prestation, and the Dominant Caste in a North Indian Village*. Chicago: University of Chicago Press.

Rahimi, Sadeq. 2021. *The Hauntology of Everyday Life*. London: Palgrave Macmillan.

Raizada, Neeraj, K. S. Sachdeva, Achuthan Sreenivas, Bhavin Vadera, R. S. Gupta, Malik Parmar, Shubhangi Kulsange, Ameet Babre, Rahul Thakur, and Christen Gray. 2014. "Feasibility of Decentralised Deployment of Xpert MTB/RIF Test at Lower Level of Health System in India." *PLoS One* 9 (2): e89301. https://doi.org/10.1371/journal.pone.0089301.

Ramanujan, Attipat Krishnaswami. 1989. "Is There an Indian Way of Thinking? An Informal Essay." *Contributions to Indian Sociology* 23 (1): 41–58.

Ramberg, Lucinda. 2014. *Given to the Goddess: South Indian Devadasis and the Sexuality of Religion*. Durham, NC: Duke University Press.

———. 2016. "Backward Futures and Pasts Forward: Queer Time, Sexual Politics, and Dalit Religiosity in South India." *GLQ: A Journal of Lesbian and Gay Studies* 22 (2): 223–248.

Rangarajan, Mahesh, and K. Sivaramakrishnan. 2014. *Shifting Ground: People, Animals, and Mobility in India's Environmental History*. New Delhi: Oxford University Press.

Rao, Anupama. 2009. *The Caste Question: Dalits and the Politics of Modern India*. Berkeley: University of California Press.

Rao, Shanta Rameshwar. 1968. *The Mahabharata*. Delhi: Orient Longman.

Rao, Ursula. 2018. "Biometric Bodies, or How to Make Electronic Fingerprinting Work in India." *Body and Society* 24 (3): 68–94.

———. 2019. "Population Meets Database: Aligning Personal, Documentary and Digital Identity in Aadhaar-Enabled India." *South Asia: Journal of South Asian Studies* 42 (3): 537–553.

Rawat, Ramnarayan S. 2011. *Reconsidering Untouchability: Chamars and Dalit History in North India*. Bloomington: Indiana University Press.

RNTCP (Revised National Tuberculosis Control Program). 2012. *Guidelines on Programmatic Management of Drug Resistant TB (PMDT) in India*. Delhi: Ministry of Health and Family Welfare.

————. 2013. *TB India 2013: Revised National TB Control Programme Annual Status Report*, edited by Directorate General of Health Services. New Delhi: Government of India.

Roche, David. 2000. "The 'Ḍhāk,' Devi Amba's Hourglass Drum in Tribal Southern Rajasthan, India." *Asian Music* 32 (1): 59–99.

Rose, Nikolas S. 2007. *Politics of Life Itself: Biomedicine, Power, and Subjectivity in the Twenty-First Century*. Princeton, NJ: Princeton University Press.

Rosin, R. Thomas. 2000. "Wind, Traffic, and Dust: The Recycling of Wastes." *Contributions to Indian Sociology* 34 (3): 361–408.

Rothman, Sheila M. 1995. *Living in the Shadow of Death: Tuberculosis and the Social Experience of Illness in American History*. Baltimore: Johns Hopkins University Press.

Rubel, Arthur J., and Linda C. Garro. 1992. "Social and Cultural Factors in the Successful Control of Tuberculosis." *Public Health Reports* 107 (6): 626–636.

Ruddock, Anna. 2021. *Special Treatment: Student Doctors at the All India Institute of Medical Sciences*. Stanford, CA: Stanford University Press.

Saria, Vaibhav. 2021. *Hijras, Lovers, Brothers: Surviving Sex and Poverty in Rural India*. New York: Fordham University Press.

Sarin, Rohit, and L. B. S. Dey. 1995. "Indian National Tuberculosis Programme: Revised Strategy." *Indian Journal of Tuberculosis* 42: 95–100.

Sarkar, Tanika. 1992. "The Hindu Wife and the Hindu Nation: Domesticity and Nationalism in Nineteenth Century Bengal." *Studies in History* 8 (2): 213–235.

Sarukkai, Sundar. 2009. "Phenomenology of Untouchability." *Economic and Political Weekly* 44 (37): 39–48.

Satyanarayana, Srinath, Sreenivas Achutan Nair, Sarabjit Singh Chadha, Roopa Shivashankar, Geetanjali Sharma, Subhash Yadav, Subrat Mohanty, Vishnuvardhan Kamineni, Nevin Charles Wilson, and Anthony David Harries. 2011. "From Where Are Tuberculosis Patients Accessing Treatment in India? Results from a Cross-Sectional Community Based Survey of 30 Districts." *PloS One* 6 (9): e24160.

Scheduled Areas and Tribes Commission. 1961. *Report of the Scheduled Areas and Scheduled Tribes Commission 1960–1961*. Delhi: Manager of Publications.

Scott, James C. 1985. *Weapons of the Weak: Everyday Forms of Peasant Resistance*. New Haven, CT: Yale University Press.

Scott, Michael W. 2016. "To Be Makiran Is to See Like Mr Parrot: The Anthropology of Wonder in Solomon Islands." *Journal of the Royal Anthropological Institute* 22 (3): 474–495.

Seale-Feldman, Aidan. 2019. "Relational Affliction: Reconceptualizing 'Mass Hysteria.'" *Ethos* 47 (3): 307–325.

Seeberg, Jens. 2013. "The Death of Shankar: Social Exclusion and Tuberculosis in a Poor Neighbourhood in Bhubaneswar, Odisha." In *Navigating Social Exclusion and Inclusion in Contemporary India and Beyond: Structures, Agents, Practices*, edited by Uwe Skoda, Kenneth Bo Nielsen, and Marianne Qvortrup Fibiger, 207–226. New York: Anthem Press.

————. 2014. "The Event of DOTS and the Transformation of the Tuberculosis Syndemic in India." *Cambridge Journal of Anthropology* 32 (1): 95–113.

————. 2020. "Fear of Drug-Resistant Tuberculosis as Social Contagion." *Ethnos* 85 (4): 665–678.

seth, katyayni. 2018. "Asking Questions: Interviews and Expertise in Global Health Research." *Medicine Anthropology Theory* 5 (5): 53–70.

————. 2022. "Artifacts of Care: The Collection of Medical Records by Families in North India." *Culture, Medicine, and Psychiatry*: 47 (1): 176–194.

Sethi, Aman. 2011. *A Free Man*. Noida: Random House India.

Shah, Esha. 2012. "'A Life Wasted Making Dust': Affective Histories of Dearth, Death, Debt, and Farmers' Suicides in India." *Journal of Peasant Studies* 39 (5): 1159–1179.

Shange, Savannah. 2019. "Black Girl Ordinary: Flesh, Carcerality, and the Refusal of Ethnography." *Transforming Anthropology* 27 (1): 3–21.

Shapiro, Nicholas. 2015. "Attuning to the Chemosphere: Domestic Formaldehyde, Bodily Reasoning, and the Chemical Sublime." *Cultural Anthropology* 30 (3): 368–393.

Sharma, Aradhana. 2008. *Logics of Empowerment: Development, Gender, and Governance in Neoliberal India*. Minneapolis: University of Minnesota Press.

Shewade, Hemant Deepak, Vivek Gupta, Srinath Satyanarayana, Prabhat Pandey, U. N. Bajpai, Jaya Prasad Tripathy, Soundappan Kathirvel, Sripriya Pandurangan, Subrat Mohanty, and Vaibhav Haribhau Ghule. 2019. "Patient Characteristics, Health Seeking and Delays among New Sputum Smear Positive TB Patients Identified through Active Case Finding When Compared to Passive Case Finding in India." *PloS One* 14 (3): e0213345.

Singh, Bhrigupati. 2012. "The Headless Horseman of Central India: Sovereignty at Varying Thresholds of Life." *Cultural Anthropology* 27 (2): 383–407.

————. 2015. *Poverty and the Quest for Life: Spiritual and Material Striving in Rural India*. Chicago: University of Chicago Press.

Sisodia, R. S., D. F. Wares, S. Sahu, L. S. Chauhan, and M. Zignol. 2006. "Source of Retreatment Cases under the Revised National TB Control Programme in Rajasthan, India, 2003." *International Journal of Tuberculosis and Lung Disease* 10 (12): 1373–1379.

Sivaramakrishnan, K. 2015. "Ethics of Nature in Indian Environmental History." *Modern Asian Studies* 49 (4): 1261–1310.

Sloterdijk, Peter. 2011. *Spheres. Volume 1, Bubbles: Microspherology*. Pasadena, CA: Semiotext(e).

Snodgrass, Jeffrey G. 2001. "Beware of Charitable Souls: Contagion, Roguish Ghosts and the Poison(s) of Hindu Alms." *Journal of the Royal Anthropological Institute* 7 (4): 687–703.

————. 2006. *Casting Kings: Bards and Indian Modernity*. Oxford: Oxford University Press.

Solomon, Harris. 2016. *Metabolic Living: Food, Fat and the Absorption of Illness in India*. Durham, NC: Duke University Press.

————. 2021. "Living on Borrowed Breath: Respiratory Distress, Social Breathing, and the Vital Movement of Ventilators." *Medical Anthropology Quarterly* 35 (1): 102–119.

————. 2022. *Lifelines: The Traffic of Trauma*. Durham, NC: Duke University Press.

Sommerland, N., E. Wouters, E. M. H. Mitchell, M. Ngicho, L. Redwood, C. Masquillier, R. Van Hoorn, S. Van Den Hof, and A. Van Rie. 2017. "Evidence-Based Interventions to Reduce Tuberculosis Stigma: A Systematic Review." *International Journal of Tuberculosis and Lung Disease* 21 (11): S81–S86.

Sontag, Susan. 1990. *Illness as Metaphor and AIDS and Its Metaphors*. New York: Doubleday.

Srinivas, Mysore Narasimhachar. 1952. *Religion and Society among the Coorgs of South India*. Oxford, UK: Clarendon Press.

———. 1959. "The Dominant Caste in Rampura." *American Anthropologist* 61 (1): 1–16.

———. 1976. *The Remembered Village*. Berkeley: University of California Press.

Srinivas, M. S., and A. M. Shah. 1960. "The Myth of Self-Sufficiency of the Indian Village." *Economic and Political Weekly* 12 (37): 1375–1378.

Stevenson, Lisa. 2014. *Life Beside Itself: Imagining Care in the Canadian Arctic*. Oakland: University of California Press.

Stewart, Kathleen. 2007. *Ordinary Affects*. Durham, NC: Duke University Press.

———. 2011. "Atmospheric Attunements." *Environment and Planning D: Society and Space* 29 (3): 445–453.

Stoler, Ann Laura. 2013. "'The Rot Remains': From Ruins to Ruination." In *Imperial Debris: On Ruins and Ruination*. Durham, NC: Duke University Press.

Stonington, Scott. 2022. "Ontological Collateral: The Entanglement of 'Cancer Pain' and 'Chronic Non-Cancer Pain' in Thailand." *Cultural Anthropology* 37 (1): 99–124.

Strathern, Marilyn. 2005. *Kinship, Law and the Unexpected: Relatives Are Always a Surprise*. New York: Cambridge University Press.

———. 2020. *Relations: An Anthropological Account*. Durham, NC: Duke University Press.

Street, Alice. 2014. *Biomedicine in an Unstable Place: Infrastructure and Personhood in a Papua New Guinean Hospital*. Experimental Futures: Technological Lives, Scientific Arts, Anthropological Voices. Durham, NC: Duke University Press.

———. 2018. "Ghostly Ethics." *Medical Anthropology* 37 (8): 703–707.

Subbaraman, Ramnath, Ruvandhi R. Nathavitharana, Srinath Satyanarayana, Madhukar Pai, Beena E. Thomas, Vineet K. Chadha, Kiran Rade, Soumya Swaminathan, and Kenneth H. Mayer. 2016. "The Tuberculosis Cascade of Care in India's Public Sector: A Systematic Review and Meta-analysis." *PLoS Medicine* 13 (10): e1002149.

Subramaniam, Banu. 2020. *Holy Science: The Biopolitics of Hindu Nationalism*. Seattle: University of Washington Press.

Sue, Kimberly. 2019. *Getting Wrecked: Women, Incarceration, and the American Opioid Crisis*. Oakland: University of California Press.

Sundar, Nandini. 1997. *Subalterns and Sovereigns: An Anthropological History of Bastar, 1854–1996*. Delhi: Oxford University Press.

———. 2002. "'Indigenise, Nationalise and Spiritualise': An Agenda for Education." *International Social Science Journal* 54 (173): 373–383.

Sunder Rajan, Kaushik. 2006. *Biocapital: The Construction of Postgenomic Life*. Durham, NC: Duke University Press.

Taneja, Anand Vivek. 2012. "Saintly Visions: Other Histories and History's Others in the Medieval Ruins of Delhi." *Indian Economic and Social History Review* 49 (4): 557–590.

———. 2017. *Jinnealogy: Time, Islam, and Ecological Thought in the Medieval Ruins of Delhi*. Stanford, CA: Stanford University Press.

Tarlo, Emma. 2001. *Unsettling Memories: Narratives of the Emergency in Delhi*. Berkeley: University of California Press.

Teltumbde, Anand. 2017. *Dalits: Past, Present and Future*. London: Routledge.

Thomas, Beena E., Ramnath Subbaraman, Senthil Sellappan, Chandra Suresh, J. Lavanya, Savari Lincy, Agnes Lawrence Raja, B. Javeed, S. Kokila, and S. Arumugam. 2018. "Pretreatment Loss to Follow-Up of Tuberculosis Patients in Chennai, India: A Cohort Study with Implications for Health Systems Strengthening." *BMC Infectious Diseases* 18 (1): 1–11.

Thomas, Deborah A. 2019. *Political Life in the Wake of the Plantation: Sovereignty, Witnessing, Repair*. Durham, NC: Duke University Press.

Thompson, E. P. 1964. *The Making of the English Working Class*. New York: Pantheon Books.

Throop, C. Jason. 2010. *Suffering and Sentiment: Exploring the Vicissitudes of Experience and Pain in Yap*. Berkeley: University of California Press.

Ticktin, Miriam. 2011. *Casualties of Care: Immigration and the Politics of Humanitarianism in France*. Berkeley: University of California Press.

Trawick, Margaret. 2017. *Death, Beauty, Struggle: Untouchable Women Create the World*. Philadelphia: University of Pennsylvania Press.

Trnka, Susanna. 2021. "Be Kind: Negotiating Ethical Proximities in Aotearoa/New Zealand during COVID-19." *Cultural Anthropology* 63 (3): 368–380.

Trnka, Susanna, and Catherine Trundle. 2017. *Competing Responsibilities: The Politics and Ethics of Contemporary Life*. Durham, NC: Duke University Press.

Tronto, Joan 1993. *Moral Boundaries: A Political Argument for an Ethic of Care*. New York: Routledge.

Tsing, Anna Lowenhaupt. 2015. *The Mushroom at the End of the World: On the Possibility of Life in Capitalist Ruins*. Princeton, NJ: Princeton University Press.

Tsing, Anna Lowenhaupt, Andrew S. Mathews, and Nils Bubandt. 2019. "Patchy Anthropocene: Landscape Structure, Multispecies History, and the Retooling of Anthropology: An Introduction to Supplement 20." *Current Anthropology* 60 (S20): S186–S197.

Tuberculosis Chemotherapy Center. 1959. "A Concurrent Comparison of Home and Sanatorium Treatment of Pulmonary Tuberculosis in South India." *Bulletin of the World Health Organization* 21 (1): 51–144.

Tulasidas. 2018. *The Epic of Ram, Volume 3*. Translated by Philip Lutgendorf. Cambridge, MA: Harvard University Press.

Ulysse, Gina Athena. 2016. "Seven Keywords for This Rasanblaj." *Anthropology Now* 8 (3): 122–125.

Unnithan-Kumar, Maya. 1997. *Identity, Gender, and Poverty: New Perspectives on Caste and Tribe in Rajasthan*. Providence, RI: Berghahn.

Urban, Hugh B. 2003. *Tantra: Sex, Secrecy, Politics, and Power in the Study of Religions.* Berkeley: University of California Press.

——. 2009. *The Power of Tantra: Religion, Sexuality and the Politics of South Asian Studies.* London: Bloomsbury Publishing.

Vaidya, Anand P. 2022. "New Villages for Old: Collective Action and Conditional Futures after India's Forest Rights Act." *PoLAR Political and Legal Anthropology Review* 45 (1): 42–55.

Valmiki, Omaprakash. 2003. *Joothan.* New York: Columbia University Press.

Van Hollen, Cecilia. 2013. *Birth in the Age of AIDS.* Stanford, CA: Stanford University Press.

Van Hollen, Cecilia Coale. 2018. "Handle with Care: Rethinking the Rights versus Culture Dichotomy in Cancer Disclosure in India." *Medical Anthropology Quarterly* 32 (1): 59–84.

Venkat, Bharat Jayram. 2016. "Cures." *Public Culture* 28 (3): 475–497.

——. 2021. *At the Limits of Cure.* Durham, NC: Duke University Press.

Vine, Michael. 2019. "Beyond Touch: Cultivating Caring Atmospheres in Arid America." *Journal for the Anthropology of North America* 22 (1): 22–34.

Weiss, Margot. 2020. "Intimate Encounters: Queer Entanglements in Ethnographic Fieldwork." *Anthropological Quarterly* 93 (1): 1355–1386.

WHO (World Health Organization). 2011a. *Policy Statement: Automated Real-Time Nucleic Acid Amplification Technology for Rapid and Simultaneous Detection of Tuberculosis and Rifampicin Resistance: Xpert MTB/RIF System.* Geneva, Switzerland: World Health Organization.

——. 2011b. *Rapid Implementation of the Xpert MTB/RIF Diagnostic Test: Technical and Operational "How-to" Practical Considerations.* Geneva, Switzerland: World Health Organization.

——. 2014. *Standards for TB Care in India.* Delhi: WHO.

——. 2022. Global Tuberculosis Report 2022. Edited by Global Tuberculosis Programme. Geneva, Switzerland: World Health Organization. https://www.who.int/teams/global-tuberculosis-programme/tb-reports/global-tuberculosis-report-2022.

Wiser, William Henricks. 1988. *The Hindu Jajmani System: A Socio-economic System Interrelating Members of a Hindu Village Community in Services.* New Delhi: Munshiram Manoharlal Publishers.

Wiser, William Henricks, Charlotte Viall Wiser, and Susan Snow Wadley. 2000. *Behind Mud Walls: Seventy-Five Years in a North Indian Village.* Berkeley: University of California Press.

Witmarsh, Ian. 2011. *Biomedical Ambiguity: Race, Asthma, and the Contested Meaning of Genetic Research in the Caribbean.* Ithaca, NY: Cornell University Press.

Wolford, Wendy. 2021. "The Plantationocene: A Lusotropical Contribution to the Theory." *Annals of the American Association of Geographers* 111 (6): 1622–1639.

World Bank. 1993. *World Development Report 1993: Investing in Health, Volume 1.* Washington, DC: World Bank.

Yates-Doerr, Emily. 2020. "Antihero Care: On Fieldwork and Anthropology." *Anthropology and Humanism* 45 (2): 233–244.

Zachariah, R., A. D. Harries, S. Srinath, S. Ram, K. Viney, E. Singogo, P. Lal, A. Mendoza-Ticona, A. Sreenivas, N. W. Aung, B. N. Sharath, H. Kanyerere, N. van Soelen, N. Kirui, E. Ali, S. G. Hinderaker, K. Bissell, D. A. Enarson, and M. E. Edginton. 2012. "Language in Tuberculosis Services: Can We Change to Patient-Centered Terminology and Stop the Paradigm of Blaming the Patients?" *International Journal of Tuberculosis and Lung Disease* 16 (6): 714–717.

Zee, Jerry C. 2021. *Continent in Dust: Experiments in a Chinese Weather System.* Oakland: University of California Press.

INDEX

Adivasi, 2, 111
affect, 11, 12, 17, 54, 78-79, 94, 114, 174, 196, 213n16, 215n43
affection, 105, 167, 216n14
affective atmosphere 24, 89, 175, 186
affliction, 48, 97, 177, 204n62. *See also* TB (tuberculosis)
afterlife, 25, 169–88. *See also* death; ghosts
Agee, James, 1
agriculture, 4–5. *See also* extractive economies; poppy fieldwork
air, 24, 77–99, 213n16. *See also under* atmosphere; wind
alcohol, 135, 181, 213n6
Allocco, Amy, 173, 222n29
Amba Mata, 177
Ambawati community, 2–6; atmospheres of, 10–12, 23; COVID-19 in, 189–93; health services in, 209n1; as research location, 20, 21–23
annadata, 160, 220n31
anonymous care, 66–67
anthropology and atmospheric entanglements, 195–200, 213n13
antibiotic treatment, 7, 43, 56–57, 59, 63–72, 103, 119, 120, 149–50, 152, 154. *See also* drug resistance; multiple-drug-resistant tuberculosis (MDR-TB)
Appadurai, Arjun, 40
atmospheres, 23, 98–99. *See also* air
atmospheric care, 17–18, 36
atmospheric entanglements, 2–6, 10–14, 16, 78, 187–88, 191–200
atmospheric places and selves, 94–96
atmospheric turn, 10, 12, 198, 203n37

At the Limits of Cure (Venkat), 189
Aulino, Felicity, 205n72
author's positionality, 20, 215n35

backwardness, 60, 64, 101, 109
Bahujan Samaj Party, 52
Barad, Karen, 14
Bellamy, Carla, 49
Bengali, as term, 220n22
Bhairav, 46-47
Bhajan, Kabiri, 169
Bharatiya Janata Party (BJP; Indian People's Party), 202n14
bhopa, 177, 180
bidis, 27–28
bioavailability, 204n49, 208n33
biomorality, 13–14, 132, 138, 179, 196, 204n49, 207n17, 208n35
biopolitics, 16, 57, 64, 66, 101–2, 168, 174, 205n67, 210n21
bios, 175, 178, 179, 180
biosociality, 7, 24, 125–32, 145, 193, 201n8
Black anthropologists and scholars, 210n14
BPL (Below Poverty Line) cards, 107, 112–13, 117, 217n21, 217n34
breath, 14–15, 23–24, 26–48, 207n17
breath control, 48–51
British colonial government, 60
broken breath, 186
burning the dust, 212n58

casted air, 92–94
caste system, 5–6, 16, 94, 214n17, 215n37
Chabrol, Fanny, 54–55

249

strength-breath. See *dam*
Styblo, Karel, 57–58
subjectivity, 9–10, 15
Subramaniam, Banu, 166
subsidized government aid, 4–5
suffering and breath, 15
Suresh, 26, 42-43, 52-53, 59, 66-67, 90,
  156-157,
surveillance, 59–60
suspicion, 52, 53, 66

takhat, 207n14
tantra, 43–47, 94, 138, 208n42
TB (tuberculosis), 2–4, 6–10; afterlife
  and, 25, 169–88; air and, 24, 77–99,
  213n16; breath and, 14–15, 23–24,
  26–48; clouds and, 12, 13, 123–45,
  218n18; diagnosis techniques of,
  73–74, 107–8; dust and, 24, 52–76;
  forests, 24–25, 146–68; medicine box
  of, 53, 59, 61, 65; mud and, 24, 100–
  122; penal logics and language of,
  211n28; Sontag on, 218n11; statistics
  of, 6; treatment options of, 3, 26–27.
  See also *names of specific patients*
TB medicine box, 53, 59, 61, 65. *See also*
  TB (tuberculosis)
tendu leaves, 27–28

theft, 163–65
Trawick, Margaret, 55, 186
Treatise on the Whole-World (Glissant), 146
Trnka, Susanna, 191

unqualification, as concept, 220n19
Urban, Hugh, 44
urinary tract infections, 214n27

Valmiki, Omprakash, 94
vayara, 86–89, 215n29
vayro naakno, 87, 88
Venkat, Bharat, 9, 167, 189
Vine, Michael, 17, 36, 77–78

Wagri language, xiii–xiv, 206n7
water, 215n45
wind, 1, 11, 78, 96, 98, 201n3, 213n14,
  215n28. *See also* air
World Bank, 58, 102
World Health Organization (WHO),
  73–74, 211n29

Xpert MTB/Rif machine, 73–74, 75
X-ray, 108, 110, 113–21, 182, 218n39, 220n28

Zee, Jerry, 11, 209n4
zoē, 170-171, 179-180

*Protestant Textuality and the Tamil Modern: Political Oratory
and the Social Imaginary in South Asia*
Bernard Bate, Edited by E. Annamalai, Francis Cody, Malarvizhi
Jayanth, and Constantine V. Nakassis (2021)

*Special Treatment: Student Doctors at the All
India Institute of Medical Sciences*
Anna Ruddock (2021)

From Raj to Republic: Sovereignty, Violence, and Democracy in India
Sunil Purushotham (2021)

The Greater India Experiment: Hindutva Becoming and the Northeast
Arkotong Longkumer (2020)

Nobody's People: Hierarchy as Hope in a Society of Thieves
Anastasia Piliavsky (2020)

*Brand New Nation: Capitalist Dreams and Nationalist
Designs in Twenty-First-Century India*
Ravinder Kaur (2020)

Partisan Aesthetics: Modern Art and India's Long Decolonization
Sanjukta Sunderason (2020)

Dying to Serve: the Pakistan Army
Maria Rashid (2020)

In the Name of the Nation: India and Its Northeast
Sanjib Baruah (2020)

Faithful Fighters: Identity and Power in the British Indian Army
Kate Imy (2019)

For a complete listing of titles in this series, visit the
Stanford University Press website, www.sup.org.

Printed and bound by CPI Group (UK) Ltd, Croydon, CR0 4YY

23/04/2025

14660937-0005